Family Hunger

Breathe Life Into Your Family History

By Todd W. Neel, BA, MSW, LCSW
Edited by Rev. Jeni St. Claire, BA
Published by Family Hunger, PLLC

Family Hunger, PLLC

ISBN-13: 978-1-7313-0356-1

Published by Family Hunger, PLLC.

Mention of specific companies, organizations, or authorities in this book does not imply endorsement by or for them. While I use ancestry.com where I post my family tree, it is only one of the resources where I do genealogy research. I know there are other very fine online genealogy resources available also. Ancestry.com lists "Living Person" rather than their names so as to not violate people's privacy.

Permission is likely to be given to you to copy and share this information. My philosophy is generosity, but please contact me if you are to make copies of this. I ask that you give credit to the authors and researchers who have done their hard work (myself and others included). Brief quotations may be used for reviews or references without permission. Contact information is provided below.

Todd William Neel, MSW, LCSW
twneel@gmail.com
familyhunger.com
Family Hunger, PLLC

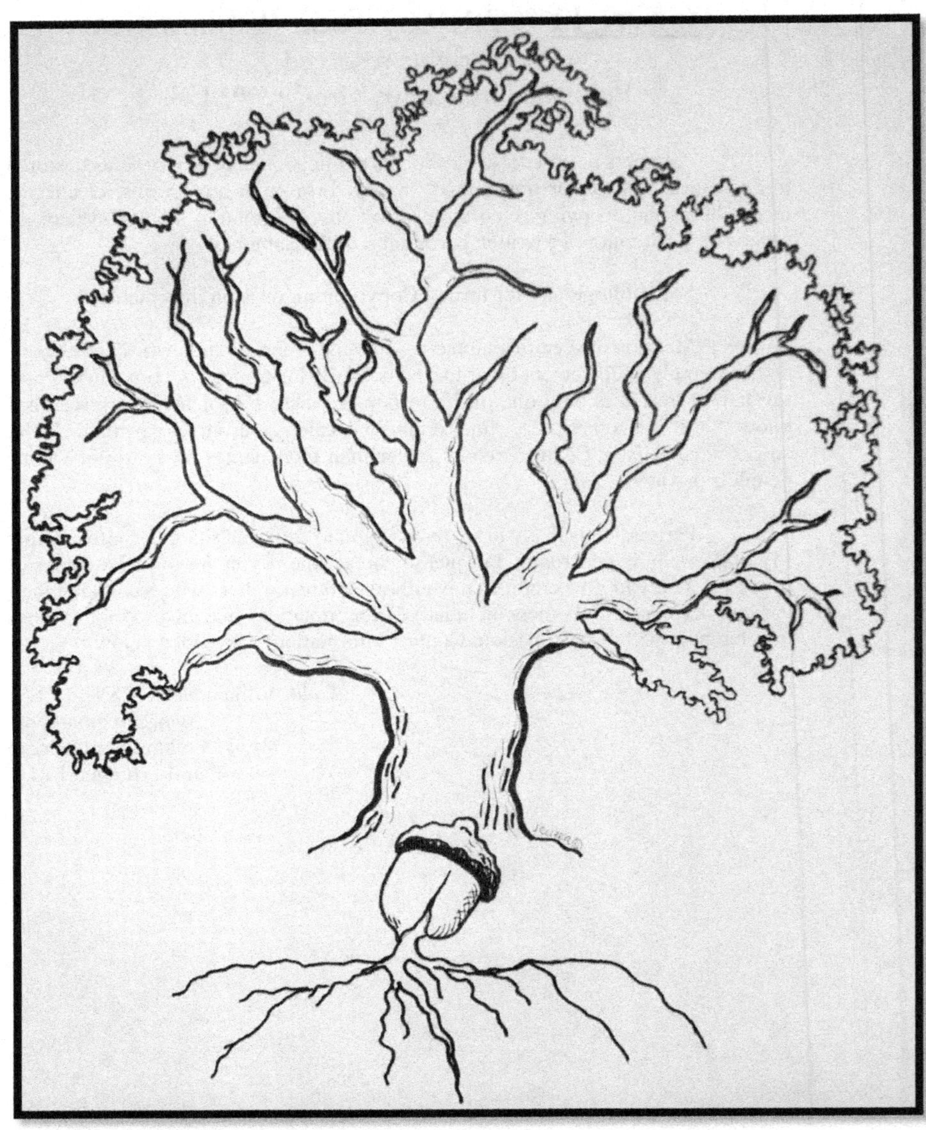

TABLE OF CONTENTS - BRIEF

TABLE OF CONTENTS - EXPANDED

Chapter 1
Prologue

This book is a social worker's point of view about genealogy. However, I'm not like every social worker. And I am not like every recovering alcoholic/addict. I am unique. So are you. (Isn't that a cliché?) I want to be sure I'm not terminally unique.

This is a work of creative non-fiction. I try to be as accurate about the facts as much as possible by verifying the sources, but some of that is impossible due to the historical nature of genealogy work and the lack of clear records. Therefore there are errors and inconsistencies in the data. My apologies for that. I try to cite my resources with a good bibliography to back my professional perspective.

What is creative about this is that it's my point of view. This is my subjective opinion about the history of my family, my take on other families, and what happened to ours. Other members of my family have their own points of view about our history. I want to be respectful of that.

Subjective points of view will be different, and may by their nature be seen as an error unless we are open- minded.

Can we agree to disagree sometimes? Rumi said something like '*Out beyond right and wrong there is a field. I'll meet you there.*'

I wrote previous home-published editions of these books (like Family Hunger - A Neel and McCool Family History and … A Carson Family History) for my family members and for those who were searching to see if we were related, which include names of living persons. This edition, Family Hunger – Breathe Life Into Your Family History, is written for public consumption with respect for the privacy of living family members. Names of living persons are left out here unless I have permission. At times this makes for awkwardness because I must use initials or a pseudonym.

This book's purpose is to motivate you to search for and create your own family history. This is not intended to be a "how to" book or a guidebook to genealogy tools and resources, as there are already plenty of those out there. I've got a closet full of them!

Instead, I want to entice you to sit down at the Dinner-Table-of-Life, calling to you by wafting pleasant aromas from the other room, to provide an attractive visual presentation on your plate, and to excite you to recognize and to feed your own "family hunger." *I am hoping to inspire you to honor the feast that is your family!* I hope my story will be an encouragement for you to search out your ancestors, to talk to your living relatives, and leave morsels for your descendants and other relatives to find by recording your own story!

Be in relationship with your family members. Get to know them and help them record their life stories. Tell and record your life story.

Did you get that part about "talk to your living relatives"? *While this is about dead people, it is also very much about living people!*

I want this to be a journey of discovery for you, the reader, to be a catalyst for you to find yourself through your relationships with others, and to realize not only where you came from, but to find what we each leave behind.

As this seems to be a time when reading and writing is somewhat a lost art, I want this to make you hungry for more of both.

Some have noticed that being with family has fallen into distaste, and believe that the move away from sitting down regularly with family at the dinner table is related to the failure of the fabric that holds our society together. I want to show you how being in relationship and sharing family stories can help connect and preserve our identity as individuals and as family members, and also to restore the fabric of our community, culture, and society as a whole.

We are individuals in the context of our families and

our communities! Each of us is a thread in the tapestry of our families' quilts. *We can do together what I cannot do alone!*

Family Feast

What senses would flood your family feast? Mine fills the senses with the smell of fresh, home-made breads and other delicious foods just out of the oven, and the sights and sounds like a traditional Thanksgiving dinner gathering. There is a symphony of conversation, so much that I can't keep track of it all and I want to capture all of it! Can you hear the clinking of the silverware and the family's best china plates and glasses as they are being set out? The kitchen is so crowded I can hardly get through there. What kinds of pies were brought for dessert? Can I sneak some tastes of the warm food from the counter as it just came out of the oven and stovetop? The matriarch shouts: "Get your hands off!" When we sit down together, I see there are leftover stains on Grandma's tablecloth from food and drink from past meals shared, *stains from Life* on the tablecloth and on our family books as we open them and tell stories and connect more deeply with each other by doing so. This would be nothing by myself. This is so rich with my family! Richer because the recipes and the stories come from a variety of individuals.

I wrote most of the stories in this book, but other family members wrote some. Just by living our lives we are writing epic sagas! Maybe you can think about these stories like recipes, an invitation for you to gather and write and preserve your own recipes in your own family cookbook, or family history book.

My wife's cookbooks that she loves and uses often are filthy from stains of the ingredients from her delicious meals that she prepares and nurtures our family with. Family stories are like that, as the ones you love are not always pristine.

We do have some favorite stories, as we have some favorite meals, but we enjoy variety also. I hope my stories nurture you, and are examples of the kinds of stories or recipes you could write for your own family.

This work causes me to want to ask more questions

about my family history, wishing I still had those relatives around who are no longer at the table so I could ask them more questions (parents, grandparents, aunts and uncles, cousins, my missing brother, etc.). It causes me to be grateful for the family that I have access to, and to want to work to preserve those connections I have.

"Dis-ease" can mean "not at ease".

However, I won't preserve them at any cost as some family dynamics cause me to be "sick" with "dis-ease" (or to be "not at ease").

Are you at ease with your family?

Healthy and/or Unhealthy?

Being comfortable or at ease, and the other end of the spectrum, that of being uncomfortable or *dis-eased*, is a dynamic balancing act. These feelings *may* be indicators of what is healthy or unhealthy, what is good or not. Sometimes the sweetness can fool us, just as the bitterness of some sour stories can deceive us. They are not mutually exclusive.

It's not always good <u>or</u> bad, but sometimes good <u>and</u> bad.

We may, or may not, be willing and able to *tolerate* being uncomfortable for a while in order to have relationships with some of our relatives (like during holidays or other special gatherings). Maybe we're not willing or able to go anywhere near some members of our families (just like we may not be willing to try certain foods). Being uncomfortable for a while can offer us opportunities to heal and grow, if needed. Willingness is the first step! Being able is next.

As stated above, "healthy" and "unhealthy" is not always clearly black or white. Learning skills to recognize, express, and appreciate the various shades of grey and other countless emotions, like the infinite colors in the rainbow, is a valuable life lesson. Certain aspects of relationships can be both healthy and unhealthy at the same time. *Ambivalence* can be very useful. Learning to tolerate the bitterness of grapefruit might help us to gain the benefits of such a sourness. Dealing with the stress of an old conflict might be difficult at the time, but doing so may help clean out old hurts or other unfinished business in relationships.

By sharing this I hope to inspire you to reach into and climb the branches of your own family tree. Do you want to climb into yours, or would you rather avoid it altogether? Whatever choice you make, make a conscious choice. *Eyes wide open.*

<u>Inspiration</u> means "to breathe life into".

When reading this book, if you are inspired with thoughts of your own story, or stories about other family members, or you want to make contact with a relative before it's too late, then *put this book down and take advantage of your inspiration.*

Write down your own thoughts, a paragraph, a chapter, or write your own book! Or make an audio or video recording. Develop a style of organizing your records so you can find it again, and so others can find it after you are gone if that is your intention.

Maybe you just want to write for yourself with plans to never share that with others. There is great value in this also.

And if you develop a style of writing that invites readers to continue reading your stuff, that helps! Smell good! Do what you can to be attractive! Clean up if you need to!

This process of writing life stories can refer to cleaning up any old unfinished business in relationships if you have some: Do you have amends you need to make to someone else? Are you holding onto resentments because you feel someone owes you amends?

Impression?

There is a saying that goes: "*Impression without expression can lead to depression.*" I'm a firm believer that if life has impressed you, you need to express it somehow for your own mental and emotional health. Depression can take many forms, and there are many other ailments besides depression if we don't clean out emotional infections. My life has certainly impressed me. I'm expressing some of it here. If we don't let it out, it can come squirting out sideways, misdirected and inflicting harm where it wasn't intended. Of course, we don't want to puke on others in doing so. We need to be respectful of the boundaries of privacy and good taste. We need to examine whether revenge is our intention, as that is not in our best interest.

Adoption and Foster Care

Part of my own strong feelings about families are about children and foster care, which is related to my own family-of-origin story. My oldest brother was adopted into our family. I discovered emotions and questions about my family-of-origin that led me towards my chosen professional field of social work. I have found some answers in this profession as well as more questions. After having worked in my job as a social worker for more than twenty-seven years in "child welfare" (child protection, mental health, addictions, juvenile justice, counseling, group and family therapy), I have been involved with many families where parents have had children removed from their care. I also worked with foster care alumni who are graduates and survivors of the foster care system. I want to acknowledge with compassion and deep respect the pain that these human beings have experienced after having had a family member taken away from them by a system such as the state and/or county government and placed in foster care, in guardianship, or adopted out. Some of you may also have this deep family hunger (or some deep unidentified stuff, like abandonment) that reverberates with similar emotions.

Dream

My dream is that this Family Hunger book causes you to move beyond the tipping point of passive, mild curiosity or unspoken questions about your relatives and ancestors whose shoulders you stand upon, and to actively recognize that you are an ancestor of your actual or potential descendants. We all are standing on the cusp of history, past, present, and future!

Your creative ideas and actions can also be your descendants!

This also means you have descendants of your creative ideas, values, and actions even if you never have children! *We do not live in isolation!*

We inspire and make impressions upon others, even if we are not aware of it (or don't want to). That person across the street may be watching us as we take care of our yard. Or the person who picks up the piece of trash that we dropped may be inspired by our garbage! *Be conscious, be intentional, and be respectful in your search and your mission. Be mindful! Leave something honorable behind, and be deliberately curious!*

My ***themes throughout this book*** *are*:

- Write your own *life story*.
- Seek out and *be in relationship* before it's too late.
- Recognize and acknowledge and honor your *chosen family* (your friends which also may be your family members that you like to be with).
- Gather others' life stories, and *encourage them to write or record* and share theirs *before it is too late!*
- *Be conscious* that there may be some family members that you do not want an active relationship with and that is okay – *some relationships are better from afar.*

- Recognize that your thoughts, words, and most importantly, *your actions are also your offspring, even if you don't have children.*

- *We can do together what I cannot do alone!*

The clock is ticking … do it! (Or, don't do it, but make a conscious, deliberate choice.)

I hope you find my "family hunger" to be interesting, entertaining, and/or appetizing, causing you to want more. *Breathe life into your own family tree as you watch me breathe life into and out of my family tree, here. We can change history!*

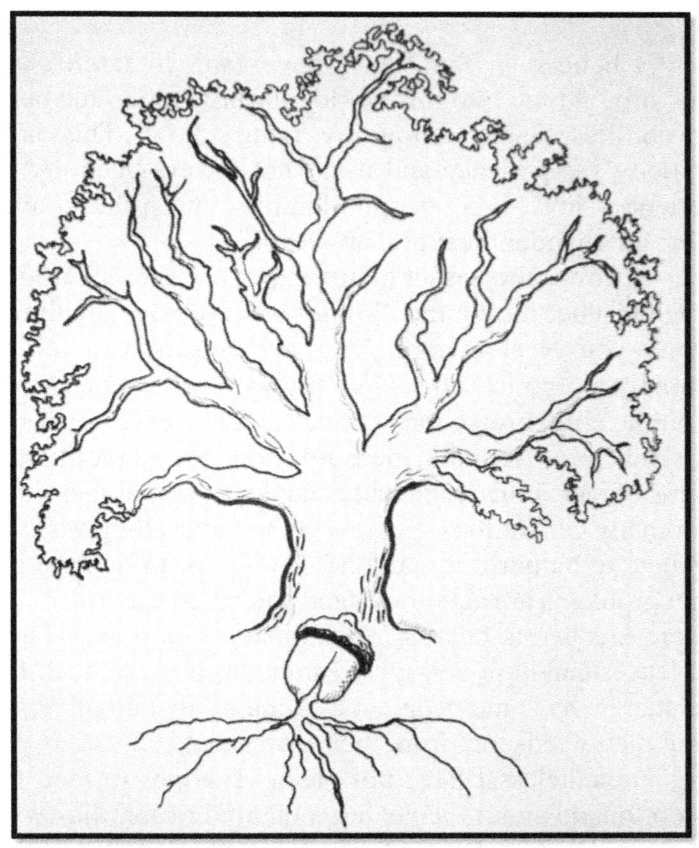

Chapter 2
Introduction

Quantum physics tells us that linear time is an illusion.
The truth, instead of time being linear and logical,
is that the past, the present, and the future
can cross paths.
When we read about, study, write about,
and create family history,
we can make those paths cross.
Genealogy and family history work can prove this.

I believe in families. I have faith in families. My family brought me into this world, nurtured me to the best of their abilities, and I enjoy my family now. This is not everybody's experience and it has not always been my own experience. For some people families mean hurt, abuse, neglect, or abandonment at many levels.

My own unpleasant family experiences range from my adopted brother telling me "I don't want to have anything to do with you Neel children," to my cousin who told me essentially to "go to hell …," to my work as a social worker in a public child protection service agency where you see the really bad ones. (Actually, there are really no bad families, just patterns of bad choices and bad behaviors – sometimes that go on for many generations. Some seem to have a long way to go to change to be nurturing and life-giving, or to be functional so that problems are acknowledged and taken care of. As long as there are hearts beating, though, there is hope.) Family experiences can hurt, and these same families can heal. But I understand why some people may want to give up all hope of getting their needs met from their own families.

Nonetheless I have not given up hope! In fact, I am very optimistic about the healing potential of families. I love my family that I live with. I miss my extended family that I don't live with. I grieve my family that has passed on. And I embrace *my chosen family*, my friends and spiritual brothers and sisters, and even some of my co-workers that I interact with regularly.

I have seen the healing power of families from a professional point of view where old patterns can be changed, past injuries can be taken responsibility for, justice can be found, and the recovery process can begin. New generations become healthier and can be less damaging to the next generation.

I have experienced my own family-of-origin heal from where things had seemed pretty hopeless, to where we have moved to stages of healing, and we now seek one another out and regularly gather together again. We are re-establishing a new "normal," re-creating new traditions of family gatherings.

I recognize my own needs for human interaction that are met by my family (including my chosen family) for the most part. I recognize that not everyone has the same social needs that I have.

NOTE To the Redundancy Police: I have been accused of stating the same thing over-and-over. I use this as a strategy and style to get my point across. I will use occasional boxes of text like this to emphasize some important issues, which is redundant. These also offer little nuggets to taste if you want to flip ahead to see what interests you.

The *Introduction* from here on covers a breadth of topics briefly, which can be skimmed and may be re-visited more in-depth later in this book or with further research on your own.

Motivation, Intention, Needs, Wants

My journey writing this book has literally brought me to tears with anticipation and excitement of discovery of my living and deceased relatives and ancestors, and those emotions are sometimes confusing to me. I was not clear on what I needed or wanted when I started this journey. While my motivations haven't always been clear, *my feelings told me this is important*. Motivations are related to intentions. I write about more on this in *Chapter 18 - The Role of Emotions*.

Motivations are related to intentions. Emotions are wisdom that can move us on the way.

See the title of this book? I ask you: What are you hungry for that made you pick up and read this book? Do you recognize what you are longing for? What nutrition do you need? What do you want?

It is important to know that there is a difference between "wants" and "needs." What we *need* are basics like food, water, housing, stability, belonging, security, etc. - things we need for our *survival*. What we *want* is metaphorically like frosting on the Cake of Life that we can survive without but which makes our lives richer - things like the desire for creativity, beauty, peace, balance, connection, purpose, and deep meaning. *Wants are things that help us to thrive, beyond mere survival*. Maybe some of what we want are just distractions (or maybe even addictions), but we may need those for respite or rest sometimes (like "mindless" entertainment), but if they cross into addictions they may be killing us.

People who are struggling for *survival* may not be able to notice and seek out things that help them *thrive*.

Stable relationships are much more valuable over the span of our lifetime than just winning the lottery once!

Is family a basic need for you? Family may not be a basic need, but *family is a vitally important resource*, one of the ways we get our basic needs met (especially when we are young). Family is a means to the ends. Have you learned not to kill the goose that laid the golden egg? The "goose" may be actual people, like our parents, but most importantly it is a metaphor for relationships we have where we get our "mother's milk." It is the *stream* that brings us physical and emotional nutrition. It should be a constant throughout our lifetime, not just in the first few years of our lives. Have you learned that access to the resources that allow us to fulfill our basic daily needs should be constant or at least regular, and doesn't happen just once?

Family is the learning ground where we learn skills to fulfill our needs out in the world after we have left home. *We take our concept of "home" with us!* That is where we learn our model of relationships that we seek out and re-create outside of our family's home.

Speaking for myself, I have my basic needs met, AND I *want* the full course meal! I want to taste that rich dessert! I want to *survive* and I want to *thrive* in the richness of life! And my family (blood, legal, and chosen) can help me do that.

But, some say that life isn't worth living if we don't get what we want. (Can you consider this when you look in the eyes of homeless people in our communities?)

Home and the Dinner Table

Where is your "home," the source of what you really need and want? What does "home" mean to you? Expand on the idea of "home" to include these questions:

- What did your dinner table at home look like when you were a child?

- What does your dinner table look like now?

- Do you sit down together as a family tradition, giving you all a chance "be in relationship" on a regular basis that you can count on most evenings, giving you all a chance to talk about how your day went or what your hopes and dreams are?

- Or are you isolated with your dinner plate on your lap and the television on or cruising the Internet on your smartphone?

Maybe you're gagging on my attempts to link family genealogy work to eating, but I am trying to speak of "home" as the source of the emotional food we need, as well as the source of our basic physical, material needs. This emotional food is the desire to know that we are OK, to know that we are loved and have a place where we belong. It is to know who we are and where we come from, and to be connected with our sources. For some, this also means to know where we are going to, including questions about what we leave behind.

"Home" is the source of emotional food we need to be the best that we can be.

At a deeper level, we need to know that *we have a purpose that gives meaning* to our lives, and *to know that someone is there for us so we can be there for someone else*. Experts on attachment believe that without healthy emotional attachment to at least one secure adult when we are children that we will shrivel up and die. Some people call this "marasmus", usually used as a nutritional term, but it can also be used as an attachment and bonding term. This was discovered during the World Wars when infant orphans were institutionalized with minimal affection, and only their basic physical needs were met on a strict schedule.

Unfortunately, it is true that for some people a caregiver who is the source of secure attachment, the source of that emotional food that is especially necessary at the early stages of life, is not found at home. But they might be found outside of the home. Or sometimes not at all.

A Book and a Meal

Reading a book can be like eating a very fine meal. You can inhale it without an appreciation for the writer's (and the cook's) effort in creating it, the recipes and where they came from, the source of the main ingredients and subtle spices (including the farmers and their families), how long it took to prepare and cook all the different parts, the table setting and the presentation, etc. There are the physical aspects to a book (and a meal), but what about the emotional aspects? (These eating metaphors apply to both eating and reading.)

This reference to food may be a gender and a cultural issue, depending on your upbringing, as some women may get more into this about food more than some men do. There are family cultural differences as well about the value of food.

A reader could speed read a book from cover-to-cover, reading it in a week or less and claim they got it (and there really are some readers who can read like that). But I like to consume a good book like a good meal, slowly tasting one bite at a time, cleansing the palate with the chosen beverage between bites, remembering dessert is still coming (asking "I wonder how this is going to come out?"). I enjoy the company by talking about it while deepening relationships by sharing and listening to other's opinions about it. I like having some time between servings for digestion, going for a walk before dessert. Oh, and the leftovers are sometimes better than the actual meal and the leftovers of the actual book.

I like to read books that I really love slowly, considering the concepts and reflecting on them, making notes and coming up with more questions, knowing that what I read can change my life. I like reading the really deep books over and over, like the classics or poetry. Can discovering and feeding your intellectual hunger and emotional curiosity sustain you or even extend your life? I'd like to think the answer is "yes."

What is your reading style? Cover-to-cover, front to back, every scrap consumed and cleaning your plate like your mother taught you? Or maybe flipping through, tasting only the servings that get your attention, skipping the distasteful parts? Do you like pictures to break up the text? Is presentation and appearance very important to you? Maybe you like reading the ending first, checking to see what is for dessert?

I broke up this book knowing that very few people read cover-to-cover anymore, unless it's a novel. I put many sub-headings for sections throughout each chapter, and I even included "word bubbles" if you just want to flip through and take one nibble at a time.

Maybe you could use this book like a cookbook. Go ahead and get messy with it! I give you permission to go ahead and dog-ear the corners of the pages and write notes in the white spaces. Spill some coffee or tea on it! I would be honored, not offended, if you mark up my book!

Don't forget that the culture of families, their flavors, their uniqueness, and their intimacy is expressed so clearly in their meals they share together. *Inclusion* is felt strongly in the kitchen as well as belonging together at the dinner table! Do you have some favorite family recipes that you want to share?

But most of all, as I've said elsewhere, if you are inspired to write your own story, put this book down and start writing your own!

Fried Rice

I learned this recipe from my mother, and I make it for my wife and children. It's a family favorite. It's not healthy, but it's good for the soul! It's a comfort food!

Start with the rice. My mother used Uncle Ben's Converted White Rice. I like to use Jasmine or Basmati rice. If you want to try to be a little more healthy, you can use brown rice. I like to make an amount so the dish can have enough for leftovers the next day, as it usually tastes better the second time you cook it. For a family of four, I put in our rice cooker 2 cups of rice with 2 and ¼ cup water for one night's meal, or 4 cups of rice and 4 and ½ cups of water for leftovers. My mother did not have a rice cooker. How did she live without that wonderful kitchen device?

While the rice is cooking, I take the package of bacon out of the freezer for dicing up. I like the bacon frozen because I find it's easier to cut up this way, but your fingers will get real cold! Of course, good quality bacon is nice, but it's the grease from the fat that makes this dish so tasty.

Vitamin G! (G = grease!)

If I'm going to make enough fried rice for two nights of meals, I use our two cast iron fry pans for the quantity for two meals.

Start frying the bacon while you dice up an onion. My mother used a yellow onion, but I like to use a large red onion. I find the red onion makes more of a sweetness to the dish. I put the onion in the large fry pan(s) just before the bacon starts to get just short of crispy. You want the onions to be done as the bacon is thoroughly crispy, but sometimes some burned bacon is not offensive to the family. Too much burned bacon is, of course, too much.

Drain or spoon off some of the bacon grease but not all of it, as you don't want to forget that the secret ingredient to happy souls for this dish is Vitamin G!

Just as the white fat of the bacon and the onions are sizzling hot in the bacon grease, add the rice, with enough grease left to keep the rice from sticking to the bottom of the pan as it cooks, stirring frequently as it gradually crisps up over a fairly hot burner (but not too hot and not left alone too long to burn it, of course). You'll have to experiment with this. If you don't want that much grease, maybe you can find an alternative way to keep the rice from sticking to the bottom of the pan, but this is how I do it.

Fry the rice, bacon, and onions, frequently stirring to keep it from sticking to the bottom while beginning to make the rice slightly crispy. Add soy sauce to make the rice brown like fried rice is supposed to be! (My wife prefers low sodium soy sauce, but I like real soy sauce because of the saltiness. Like I said, this is not a healthy dish!)

My Mom used to turn down the heat to low at this stage and fry the rice over a simmering low heat for a long time, slowly making the rice crispy. Thinking back in my memory, this cooking over low heat was when Mom and Dad were toasting in the living room to their daily "Happy Hour," which was their traditional drinks of whiskey on the rocks for Dad, and a Martini for Mom. (Martinis are made with gin and vermouth, and I got drunk and had my first blackout in my alcoholic career when I was age 12 on gin I stole from my parents' liquor cabinet.) This stage of cooking the fried rice was also when I would sneak into the kitchen as a child and taste the rice as it was cooking, learning about my preferences for the various textures at different stages of cooking. It was also when I would get impatient and learn to deny my feelings as a child in my family – and also to begin to learn that it's not all about "me" and my hunger. It's not like I was starving to death or anything.

I can hear Mom shout, "Todd! Is that you in the kitchen eating the rice? I can hear you! Knock it off!"

Then this last stage of making fried rice like my Mom did went like this: Just before the rice is done to your liking (and as I said mine is just slightly crispy), you push the fried rice back to the outer edges of the frying pan, with the center open for scrambling eggs in the middle. Melt butter in the open center of the fry pan first, then drop in the eggs sometimes with salt and pepper. I like to put about six eggs into each of the two pans. Keep the integrity of the eggs mostly to themselves by scrambling them in the center until they get firm, although you can't help but get some rice mixed in with the rice from the outside. I like bite-size chunks of scrambled eggs mixed into the dish, not egg-coated rice where you can't see the scrambled eggs anymore.

Mix it all together, and enjoy! My family still loves it!

Vegetables are optional, but don't ruin it.

This may be a dysfunctional family dish. It's comfortable and familiar, but it may be killing us by clogging up our veins. Is it a problem we don't talk about?

Vision

A saying goes "*Thoughts in mind produce likeness in kind.*" Nothing begins without a vision. The chair you are now sitting in began with someone's vision. By reading or listening to my words you are fulfilling my vision. My vision is influenced by the one in the movie "Antwone Fischer" where the main character finds his long-lost family, and they welcomed him to feast at their table (I think it's a great movie, and I highly recommend it). I have an image of my family being whole and complete and welcoming to all, including guests. What is your vision, your dream?

Toot Your Horn - Beyond Dead People!

Some people think this is a book mostly about dead people, and a little bit about the living people looking for the dead ones. But it's actually about the living!

Not everyone has an appetite for this. Are you one of them? It takes living people with this craving to find the dead ones, and it takes living people to leave footprints ... or fingerprints ... or even smaller traces like DNA. What kind of prints will we leave behind?

I write and share these words with mixed feelings, as it may appear I am trying to "toot my own horn," inflating my own ego (a potentially dangerous thing for some people), or trying to extend my own life into immortality in the printed word. But by sharing these words my hope is that you are moved to get up and do what needs to be done and to toot your own horn, and toot your family's horn.

I remember sitting around the kitchen table with my Dad listening to Garrison Keillor on public radio. He tells us about the fictitious Powdermilk Biscuits on the Prairie Home Companion radio show which "gives us the strength to get up and do what needs to be done." It does take strength and backbone to break the old family rules of "Don't talk." It takes respect to not hurt other people while doing so.

Inspiration and Perceptions

I was inspired to do this genealogy work by others. Most of this research has already been done before me. I am just re-gathering it, re-organizing it, and reflecting my own perceptions, my own experience, strengths, and hopes which come from the seeds of original creativity. This is the Big

Bang still expanding!

I hope my viewpoint will be fresh enough to your eyes, your heart, and your mind that it will appear original, or better yet to inspire you to create your own fresh, unique, original family story.

Be reassured others have been here before you, and you can stand on their shoulders. Others are standing on your shoulders, believe it or not (whether you have children or not). A continuing theme throughout this book: even if you don't have biological children, your words, deeds, footprints, echoes, etc. are your offspring!

As stated in the preface, I like this interpretation of "inspire," which is: "to breathe life into." Are you inspired?

Legacy and Impact on Others

What do I want my sons, my family and friends to know about me and what difference will it make? What is the purpose of all this? As I make statements like this, I suggest that you turn the question around to ask yourself: What do you want your family and friends to know about you? What do you want left of you after you turn to dust?

I am as conscious and awake as I am able to be at this time, but I have limited awareness of my own behaviors and words and their ramifications. I do have blind spots, but I try to be sensitive about my impact upon others. I desire to be "awake" but I do "sleep" with my eyes open sometimes. At times some people thought I was disrespectful because of my blind spots, and this is not the way I want to be. I desire to be responsible for my own behaviors, thoughts, and feelings, and I desire relationships with others who want to be responsible for their own behaviors, thoughts, and feelings. If I have stepped on your toes, I apologize. Please let me know. Consider the question: Do you have any blind spots?

I want to do no harm, and I want to leave the world a better place than I found it. ("*Ahimsa*" is the Hindu, Buddhist, and Jain philosophy of non-violence, and of revering all life and refraining from harm to any living thing.)

My children's sense of who they are and how they

interact with the world is affected by what I show them on a daily basis by my words and my actions. And at this time of life, I am acutely aware of when I have lost my patience, and how my sons have been impressed by me when they lose their patience now and cuss "like a sailor" like I do! (It is not fit-for-print here of what comes out of my mouth when I hit my thumb with a hammer, or when I have frustrations over even lesser events.) This is not a trait that I am proud of!

It's interesting that I am a *son of a sailor* (my dad was a Captain in the Navy), and my wife is the granddaughter of a minister. It's not like my dad cussed like a blue-collar factory worker, but when he let it out, his swearing came out in such a way was to implant that skill deeply into my own nervous system. And, living with my wife is the perfect place for me to work on that issue as she has deeply seated sensitivities to certain four-letter words.

As psychologists tell us, the foundations of my children's sense of security, attachment, appetite for relationships and the ability to have them, and their personalities are already laid down (especially since they are in their mid-20's now). There is not a lot I can do to change their character or personality now. But as long as our hearts are still beating, we are still breathing, and we are all still developing, I have hope that seeds of passion for their family hunger may take root any day now.

What legacy will we leave behind?

The Audience, Inspired by Dick Case

In the year 2002 I sat down with my friend, Dick, and we discussed the "audience" I intend these books to be written for. In the future, it's clear my intended audience is my children and their children, and their children's children, if we are all so lucky. Dick suggested I contemplate what I want my sons to know, and I considered writing "Dear Nathan …" and "Dear Joshua …" chapters. I still intend to do that someday, but I haven't done it yet. I need some motivator, some "tipping point" that will cause me to act on this. What "*2-by-4 therapy*" will happen to get me to act on this? ("2-by-4 therapy" is that crisis that occurs that smacks us between the eyes to get us up to do what needs to be done! Sometimes it's a 4-by-8 or an even a bigger stick to get us to act!)

I intended to write to each of my sons on the day they were born, but alas, too many distractions, and now it's too late for that snapshot in time. The intense memories of those sweetest moments of their birth are lost. Forgotten are so many details since those peak experiences. (Where is that shirt that I wore on that day of their birth?) ***Hint/Suggestion***: If you have a newborn child or grandchild, or if you have a new birth coming up in your family soon, it is suggested that you write to them now.

Rest in peace, Dick. Thanks for this inspiration!

Hey, on a rousing note, I recently found an old journal buried in a drawer that had an entry in my own handwriting of the intimate details in the hospital of the day my son, Josh, was born, and it was very sweet to read that again! Do you have such treasures?

Presently, *my audience is you*, the reader (after my first audience, me - write for yourself, first, and edit later for your readers). You are a member of that group of handsome and beautiful persons who have this "family hunger," this appetite for our family roots and who feel a connection with where we come from. I hope you feel responsibility for what kinds of footprints we leave behind.

This is for those who are living – no, better yet it is for those who *feel* their aliveness, and who have evolved enough in our own development and consciousness to appreciate the connections we have with all of our relations, past, present, and future.

My own sons may not appreciate these words at this time the way I hope they will in the future. I hope they find these words of mine someday, and that they write their own stories. I offered them copies of my <u>Family Hunger</u> books in the past, and they responded with something like "No, thanks, Dad, if we have questions about that, we know where to find you." Well, good luck with that, buddy! My memories are slipping away more and more every year. I'll keep my seatbelt fastened when I get on the highway tonight, and hope that car in the oncoming lane doesn't have a driver who is drinking tonight! (Support MADD – Mothers Against Drunk Driving!)

Each breath is precious! Don't take it for granted!

Developmentally Acquired Taste

This family hunger is an acquired taste. It may be a developmental phase of life which can be nurtured (or squashed) by family and cultural experiences. It may have been there from the very beginning that I just didn't recognize until later in my life. Do you recognize this in you?

Developmentally, my sons may not have this "family hunger" yet as I do, but I know I am whetting their appetites and planting seeds as they watch me do this work. Over the years they looked over my shoulder as I typed these words on my computers, several of which I have worn out. They have repeatedly gone over and looked at the large family tree tacked on the wall of our basement, stained with coffee and scribbled on with handwritten notes. This genogram has since had pieces torn; it has fallen apart, been taken down, and is rolled up in the corner now, gathering dust and cobwebs.

Relationship Bias

Because of my experiences and training as a social worker, I feel our relationships are everything and are all important! Without relationship and family and friends to share with, what else do you have? We're left with just "stuff," things, and loneliness! There is a saying that "*No man is an island*," and another that says "*We can do together what I cannot do alone*." We are "herd animals" necessary for own survival. I believe that we literally can't live without other humans, but some of us seem to need less of these social resources for our nutrients than others. Some of us choose to have less involved social connections. Some of us choose to live more in isolation than others and to be "off the grid." Some of us don't have the social skills to stay connected with the relationships that we might be hungry for.

But for those of us who recognize that we are "herd animals" and desire social connections, what should we call this thing we hunger for? This is the *Stream of Life* that brings us vital nutrients. This river and our relationships are the spiciness and sweetness of life!

Some of us just don't have time to nurture all of the relationships that feed us. There are plenty of distractions in our current times that interfere with social connections with family and friends. Some say this is the "age of isolation," but this is nothing new. Isolation is just done in different ways now.

Blow Up Your TV!

Hint/Suggestion: I recommend that you turn off your TV now if it's on. I believe electronic stimulation consumes so much of our time that we don't get to know our family or friends or neighbors anymore the way we used to. Television, video games, computers, the internet, e-mail, Facebook, texting, Twittering, etc. are all a "double-edged sword," allowing us to get connected with others in ways that were never previously possible. But, these miracles also keep us from being connected in intimate, face-to-face ways if we spend too much time on these devices and accessing these services. I am guilty of this, too. I utilize these devices and services myself and I have tremendously benefited as well. But, if you don't get rid of your TV or internet connection, then I suggest you *notice* how much time you spend in these activities, try to reduce your time on these devices, and spend more time with family and friends! *There is a lot of power in just noticing*. Notice that you are reading this book! Notice the pattern of how you spend your time, watch if you spend more time with your own thoughts and feelings, and you might notice your appetite for connection in relationships changing.

Karl Marx said something about "religion is the opiate of the people," which many people remember as meaning "opiate of the masses." I think *addiction to screen time* is a very fitting description of our culture these days, with some parallels to religion like this.

Genealogical Societies and Groups

As I previously stated, I was inspired to gather this genealogy information by my family, parents, friends, teachers in college, and social work trainings. In the past years, I have also attended some great genealogy trainings held locally with local and nationally known presenters. I thank the Kootenai County Genealogy Society in Hayden and Coeur d'Alene, Idaho (that meets regularly at the Hayden Library), and the Eastern Washington Genealogy Society in Spokane, Washington for these.

I encourage you to find a "genealogy playmate" who will listen to your questions, support your progress, make suggestions to you, help you in your search, and to provide mutual encouragement for each other.

Ending of Introduction

And because reading as a lost art seems to be enhanced by photos and graphics, I am including a family photo here. There will be a limited number of family photos and stories in this book for public consumption, but if you write your own family book I encourage you to put lots of photos in yours.

Here is an undated photograph of a McCool family gathering which may have been taken about 1907 or 1908, the year of the birth of the infant in this photograph.

I found a copy of this picture on the wall of Gary McCool's home. (See *Chapter 23 -McCools Are Cool – or Compost, Ashes, and Lagoons*.) My paternal grandmother, Estella Augusta McCool, is standing in the back row, second from the right. Top left is Emmett McCool, who is married to Cora (Colling) McCool sitting in front of him. In back second from left is Harry Derrick, who is married to Lydia (McCool) Derrick, sitting in front of him. In back third from left is Paul McCool (or "uncle Cooley"). In front of "uncle Cooley" is Margie Hedges (the infant in the little stroller), and the little girl standing in front just to the left of the baby is Fay McCool

Malleck. The man sitting and holding the baby is William Andrew McCool, my great-grandfather. Above him in the back, third from right is Gladys (McCool) Donnely, the only red head we found for a while from past generations. (I have red hair, and so does my sister.) Again, in the back row second from right is my paternal grandmother, Estella Augusta "Stella" (McCool) Neel, who I remember fondly. In front of my grandmother is Sarah (Garber) McCool, my great-grandmother. (William and Sarah McCool here would be my great-grandparents, my father's maternal grandparents - see "*Memories of Stella McCool Neel"* in *Chapter 8 - The Neels & The McCools - Not The Hatfields & The McCoys* that my grandmother wrote when she was in her 90's. The man on the upper right is Clark Hedges, who is married to Minette "Nette" (McCool) Hedges, sitting on the far right in front of him. Sitting on the lower right is Jessie (McCool) Malleck, who married the brother of Fay McCool's husband. As I look at this photograph, I look for physical traits that are like mine and the relatives I know, and I think about who in this photo had to exist in order for me to physically be here today, to be able to think these thoughts, and who had to exist and had influential interactions with one another in their relationships to pass on this "family hunger." Did they have family hunger? Did they like one another? Did they want to be here for this photo?

Chapter 3
Why "Family Hunger"?

First, a poem …

With Passion
(Translation of Rumi by Daniel Ladinsky)

With
passion pray. With
passion work. With passion make love.
With passion eat and drink and dance and play.
Why look like a dead fish
in this ocean
of
God?

(From the Penguin Publication, *Love Poems From God: Twelve Sacred Voices of the East and West* by Daniel Ladinsky, copyright 2002, and used with permission)

I do have a passion for families. Some may say I'm on a search for dead fish. Genealogy is more than that. It's also about living people who have passions and beating hearts.

This chapter suggests why I named this book for public consumption, Family Hunger – Breathe Life Into Your Family History. I have written a series of other books which I printed on my home computer for family consumption, books with the names of both dead and living relatives like Family Hunger – A Neel & McCool Family History.

I have a passion or hunger for genealogy and writing, and I also have fear of and respect for the living.

Fear and Respect

Out of respect for my living family members, both those I actively love and those I fear, I will not put their names in public print unless I have their permission. They should not be reading about themselves unless I specifically have their consent, or unless they have come back from the dead.

I sometimes use a pseudonym as I did for my adopted brother who is infamous for some people because of his legal and criminal record. There is much information about him available to the public through the Internet and legal Court records because of his criminal convictions, if you know his proper name and date of birth. I use an alias for his name as I didn't know if he was alive as of early August 2018, and because I do have reasons to fear him. I had been out of touch and unable to locate him for about 15 years, as of the time of this writing. I was assuming he was dead because the last time I heard from him he said he had cancer and didn't want to take the medical treatments. In late August 2018 I discovered he is still alive, as I found out that for a sibling, the Social Security Administration will provide me with information about the date and location of his death if he had passed away. While I was filling out Form # 3288 to access this information at my local Social Security office, the staff behind the thick glass looked at their computer screen and told me "he's still ticking."

There is a difference between what is legally right, and what is ethically correct. Because of our history with our adopted brother and his lifetime pattern of behaviors which have profoundly affected us, I feel my anger and a protective duty to warn his victims and the public to guard yourself from him. I acknowledge that I may not be seeing clearly because of this history. Because it appears that he may be alive, I will show enough respect to not name him, and I celebrate that he is keeping himself out of jail. I don't want to make his life any more difficult for him that it already has been.

There are brief chapters on our adopted brother later in this book that does not include his whole story. One is about our mother's words (*Chapter 5 - A Mother's Story*), and another on him in my words (*Chapter 6 - A Brother's Story*) later in this book. These chapters were longer in early August 2018 as I had therapeutically written them for myself under the assumption that he was dead. Since I have found out he is alive, these chapters are much shorter now, and if you want to see more complete information on him, you will have to wait for my next book, titled Chasing Headstones, if the grim reaper has a plan to allow this.

My intention is not to print "dirt" or to gossip, getting attention for myself at the expense of others. My purpose is to honor those who have come before us and those who come after us. This is to illustrate the best of our families and also show those who have offered us challenges and to demonstrate how we may have handled it. Some call these later people the "worst of us," but there is a saying that goes "when life gives you lemons, make lemonade."

Gossip is to get attention for ourselves at the expense of someone else.

To use the word "challenges" is an understatement for victims of my adopted brother's crimes. Lemonade may not be an option for some.

I understand some of my stories may trigger uncomfortable memories or symptoms for some people, especially for those who may have PTSD (Post Traumatic Stress Disorder) or traumatic histories. I encourage you to respect yourself and to skip through some parts of this book if it triggers or bothers you. If you are willing to feel these uncomfortable responses from your body, there may be lessons or wisdom that your emotions are pointing to, areas of healing that you may need to work on if you are ready. Get help if you need it.

Doing our own personal family work can help us to put up healthier boundaries. We don't have to take responsibility for the behaviors and attitudes of our relatives or ancestors. To be healthy, we shouldn't take *responsibility for* anyone else except ourselves unless we're the parent of a minor aged child or the guardian of someone. We can learn skills to have *responsibility to* others, but not for them (to be able to respond to them, but not for them). We may be able to learn skills to protect ourselves better and to offer hope to others from our own challenging experiences.

If we understand others, we may not have to "stand under" them anymore.

Resentment is anger held onto. Anger can protect us. There can be wisdom in fear. Sometimes a tiger and his behaviors remain just like other wild tigers with sharp teeth and claws, and it is healthy to continue to fear them. Forgiveness is to give up all hope of a different past. It is possible that we have some control over a different future.

Breathe Life into Your Family History

History is not dead. Past history is just resting, and it comes alive in our minds when we look at it, feel it, smell it! We make history with our living deeds. If it isn't documented, it didn't happen. (Well, sort of.) Future history is being written right now. Live a life you can be proud of. Be alive! Be constructive! Make a difference!

We can leave some morsels of emotional nutrition and insights for those who come after us who have this same family hunger, those that wonder who we were that came before them, and those who care about what kind of world they leave behind.

Appreciation

I appreciate my ancestors on whose shoulders I stand. I love my family members who hold me up when I need it. I hope that I am there for you if you need me.

As some of my living family members know, there have been times, sometimes long periods of time, when I have missed them and our gatherings and our traditions. I honor and respect whatever space we needed at the time, and I'm glad that's behind us. A cousin of mine said "life is too short ..." to get caught up in any bitterness that keeps us apart. Let us celebrate the time we have together!

Hunger?

Some people ask why I like Family Hunger in my title. Some ask me if we lived in poverty as a child. No, my family did not live in financial poverty. We always had enough to eat. I remember being warm, having more than adequate shelter, and mostly able to wear the clothes I wanted. Our basic needs were met by our parents' commitment to us. We grew up in a middle-class family in America. Our father served as an officer in the U.S. Navy and retired as a Captain when I was ten years old. His active-duty and retirement income always seemed to meet our physical needs. Sometimes our mother worked, but I'm not sure this was a financial need for the family as she also volunteered for many activities outside the home. Maybe, though, we lived in "emotional poverty" that left me hungry for … something, but what was that? What is this itch that I need to scratch? What is it that I am hungry for?

What is emotional poverty?

What is this itch I need to scratch?

I felt this hunger, this emotional poverty, as I learned the language of psychology and social work. I didn't feel good about myself growing up but I didn't always recognize it, and I didn't know what to do with it. I acted out some of it by drinking alcohol (sometimes lots of it), and using and abusing other drugs which led me down a path towards my personal recovery, and the tools to help me be clean and sober. Through this I learned about families as "people factories," (Peoplemaking, Virginia Satir, 1972), and about different kinds of families. People factories are like industrial factories – some more successful than others.

Looking back on my childhood, I identify my family-of-origin as a "dysfunctional family." (See section later in this chapter on *Dysfunctional vs. Functional Families*.) This relates to the "emotional poverty" that I mentioned above.

I want to acknowledge *the functional elements* of my family as well. My parents did the best they could with what they had, despite many stressors that I am grateful I do not have.

I believe my parents were invested in looking good to the community we lived in, which sometimes meant that we kept secrets. Sometimes we put up a "front." We lied by omission. Some refer to this as healthy boundaries for privacy, and others say these stories are the family's business and nobody else's.

But when information is kept a *secret* so tightly that it becomes toxic and burdensome, it is unhealthy. I have needed to *tell my story*, at the right times and in the right places to the right audiences, to clear emotional and psychological poisons out of my system, and to be able *to make sense* of what happened to us. I want to not puke on others by doing so, either to the audience I am telling my story to, or to puke on the persons the story is about.

In my training and practice as a social worker, I learned about and have taught others about Claudia Black's dysfunctional family rules of "Don't talk; Don't trust; Don't feel," and the recovering rules of "Do talk; Do trust; Do feel" (from It Will Never Happen to Me! by Claudia Black, 1981). When I began to work my own recovery process, and as I continue with it, I occasionally bump into other people who don't agree with me. At times I still get very strong push-back messages of "Don't talk" about certain issues, with comments like "They don't need to know about that!" from my immediate family. I have respected some of these family member's wishes, but I can't help but feel instead that I am being "edited" and not allowed to tell my truth.

"Don't talk" is about the famous "elephant in the room"

Basic Needs

First, before you do your own genealogy and family-of-origin work, are your basic needs met? If this work causes you to neglect what you need for survival, you may need to look at that and re-examine what your priorities are.

When I spend times of intensely diving into my

genealogy and personal family work, I do neglect some regular daily activities, like reading the newspaper or responding to e-mails. I'm not neglecting to eat, though, and it hasn't caused me to be homeless, yet.

I do sometimes wonder if this work has caused me to feel alienated from some family members.

While some people may be living lives of desperation and scrambling for survival, they may be unclear about their motives and the battles they are fighting. When people are preoccupied with their struggles for survival, they may not have anything left for reading, writing, education, research, or even re-writing their family story creating the possibilities of a different future. But sometimes without insight or reflection, we may be repeating unhealthy family history unknowingly, wrestling with ghosts from our past, interfering with rising to our highest potential. We need a balanced diet, and we may need to "chew our cud" like a cow until we're ready to fully digest our food and to make sense of what we have been fed.

If I am alienated from some family members, I need to ask: Are they what I need, or what I want? They are a resource to help me get my needs and wants met, but my extended family is not responsible for my basic daily living needs, especially at this elder time of my life. I am individuated, but I need them to put me in, or on the ground in the end (i.e. burial or cremation). I would like that if they did.

Family Systems

As a social worker, I was trained to think about families as systems. While in graduate school working towards my MSW degree (Masters in Social Work) at Eastern Washington University, I interned with Agency Field Instructor John Brennan (RIP, John). He told me if I wanted to do family therapy, then I needed to "*think, eat, and breathe families*." My desire to learn about family systems and to work with families meant that I needed to take John's words to heart. So, *I do "think, eat, and breathe families!"*

When I meet with an individual (professionally or otherwise), I often think about who they have "with" them, and their family connections and relationships that got them here. I sometimes imagine strings of light from them to their families in the past to the present moment, who they came from and who they are going home to be with tonight. I wonder who else they have in the room with us!

I might ask them what kind of family-of-origin they grew up in. I wonder about who their role models are that affect what they think is normal. I might try to guess and ask how many siblings they had and what birth order they were in. I ask questions like: Did their parents remain married or did they get divorced? What were their grandparents like, and what multi-generational patterns of strengths and unresolved issues might be affecting them? Pictures flood my mind, and I start drawing a genogram (a family tree) in my head or on paper. Are they from a blended family? Was there was an adoption into or out of their family, and if so what were the circumstances? Sometimes my own ghosts enter the room as I think about my own adopted brother.

I wonder about alienation, connection, disconnection, and about secure and insecure attachment strategies. I wonder what traumas and secrets they have.

I see family dysfunction and community dysfunction like Sherlock Holmes sees clues to a crime. I sometimes see pathology when it isn't there, and I have to remind myself to be "strengths-based." What was healthy about the family they came from? I look for characteristics of resiliency, and I am impressed by their survival skills.

I wonder and *may cautiously inquire* about what trauma they have experienced, as this *might* trigger undesirable symptoms if I ask too early or without understanding and compassion. What losses and unresolved grief do they have? I try to place myself in their shoes in coming to appreciate what they have endured, as we all have baggage.

I consider what "family" means for them, as sometimes they see the friend who is putting with them up on their couch or in their extra bedroom as their "brother" or "auntie" when there is no biological or legal relationship (what we might call "fictive kin" or "chosen family").

I am curious if I am perceived by them as part of the problem or part of the solution when I ask them questions in a probing manner as an outside visitor to their family.

I remember the guiding principle of "Do no harm" from the medical and other helping professions as I interact with them.

I look for the "*spiritual child*," that "us" or the Being that was created in the synergy and the bond of our relationships that are bigger than the sum of the parts. This is not a religious concept – this is a teaching lesson that can be used to clarify if we are nurturing, neglecting, or abusing our relationship, our "spiritual child" that was conceived or birthed the moment we met. I see the potential for their future new family they might create and see the preciousness of future generations, those not born yet. (This future new family is for future relationships, and not just potential real children.)

Sometimes I think about the dinosaurs who are now extinct, and the indigenous people that used to walk this earth and the traces they left behind on cave walls that we find, and I wonder *what traces we will leave behind*, including clues to our own tribal or social behaviors.

What happens when our eyelids (and other body parts) turn to dust? What's left?

And yes, sometimes I do this wondering all in my head at the coffee shop or standing in the check-out line at the grocery store where it's none of my business!

Professional Perspective

SNORE FACTOR WARNING: This section may put you to sleep, or it may really excite you, depending on your point of view (p.o.v.). Feel free to skip over it if you wish.

Aspects of families that I was trained to consider are the following:

- stages of development (both the individuals' and the family's development)
- attachment and bonding issues
- trauma and resiliency

- subsystems and their function and their flexibility (i.e. the parental executive subsystem, the children/sibling subsystems, the extended family, coalitions, etc.)
- gender and sexuality (heterosexual, asexual, or LGBTQ+ issues)
- disability issues, diagnosed and undiagnosed ("disability means ability not found")
- guilt and shame issues
- boundaries (enmeshed, clear, or disengaged), and I often ask the question "Where do I end, and where do you begin?" for myself or out loud as instruction for the person(s) I am meeting with
- power and influence (control issues)
- alignments (affiliation, over-involvement, emotional incest, conflicts, detouring, etc.)
- triangles (pursuing, distancing, cliques, ganging up on another, or alienating and gossiping)
- communication styles (computer style, distracter style, placator style, blamer, leveler, etc.)
- addiction and mental health issues
- cultural issues
- family rules/ myths/ ideals/ secrets
- therapeutic strategies such as joining/ planning/ challenging/ reframing/ enactment/ etc.
- focusing, intensity, etc., etc.

I worked for decades in CPS, and casework in the field with this difficult population nearly killed me. It practically saved my life by transitioning to the role of an Agency Field Instructor for social work students working on their BSW and MSW degrees who were doing their internships with our agency. I have many fond memories of these experiences, and for my students and for nostalgic purposes I will summarize the topics on my "white board" on the wall of my office that I used as a cheat sheet as I looked over my students' shoulders:

- IPT (Intern Placement Tracking)
- ITP (Integrating Theory with Practice)

    - I notice (retrieving facts, data)
    - I feel (reflection)
    - I wonder (link to professional knowledge and theory)
    - I will (response as a professional)
        - What? So what? Now what?
- Theories
    - Narrative therapy
    - Behavioral therapy
    - Medical model
    - Addictions model
    - Systems theory
    - Developmental theory
    - Social Learning theory
        - P.I.E. – person in environment
    - Attachment theory
    - Trauma informed practice
    - TBRI (Trust Based Relational Intervention)
    - Freudian theory (superego, ego, id), including psychological defense mechanisms
        - TA (Transactional Analysis – Parent, Adult, Child)
- Perspective
- Approaches
- JoHari Window
- Boundaries continuum
- Diversity and cultural sensitivity
- MAPS (measurable, attainable, positive, specific goals)
- IL (Independent Living) Domains
    - Education
    - Supportive relationships and community connections
    - Daily living and self-care skills
    - Physical and mental health
    - Employment and money management
    - Cultural and personal identity formation
    - Housing /legal /transportation /etc.

These concepts are complicated, and they have provided much insight and relief from the confusion not only with the families I work with as a professional, but confusion about my own family-of-origin. I learned these concepts from graduate courses in my MSW program, at subsequent workshops I have taken, in supervision and therapy I have received, and on-the-job experience where "the rubber meets the road".

I do a lot of reading, and these are some of my ***favorite books*** on this topic:

- Families and Family Therapy by Salvador Minuchin
- Peoplemaking by Virginia Satir
- It Will Never Happen to Me by Claudia Black
- On Becoming A Person by Carl Rogers
- Parenting From The Inside Out by Daniel Siegel and Mary Hartzell
- The Changing Family Life Cycle and The Expanded Family Life Cycle edited by Betty Carter and Monica McGoldrick
- Handbook on Attachment, Theory, Research, and Clinical Applications, edited Jude Cassidy and Phillip Shaver
- The Boy Who Was Raised As A Dog by Bruce Perry and Maia Szalavitz
- Bradshaw On: The Family by John Bradshaw

Do you have any suggested books that you love that you think I should read? Or any books or messages that you want your family or friends to read? Or do you have a book inside you that you want your descendants to read?

I make reference to these professional aspects of my view of families for you, the reader, to be aware of, to see the bias I have towards family systems, recognizing them, honoring them, and to make recommendations for your own further reading. My trainings and experiences as a social worker have an effect on my genealogy and family history lenses.

The seeds of this professional perspective were

planted before my graduate school education while I worked on my Bachelors' degree in Psychology that I eventually earned from the University of Montana in 1980 (see *Chapter 12 - Who am I? And how did I get Here? Psychology and Genealogy* that I wrote in 1979 at twenty-three years of age).

Seeds of my personal point-of-view about families sprouted at our dinner table as a child, and before that in my mother's womb, affected by her mother's womb, etc.

Don't talk, Don't trust, Don't feel

Claudia Black wrote about dysfunctional family rules of "Don't talk, Don't trust, Don't feel" as survival skills, which I saw occurring in my family-of-origin. A great portion of the "Don't …" rules in my family related to the behaviors of my older, adopted brother and my family's coping strategies, including my parents' authoritative ways. We continue using the "Don't talk/ trust/ feel" rules when we get close to stresses of pain, embarrassment, shame, (or other reasons) about sensitive issues.

To remedy dysfunction, we must try to live by the alternative functional family rules of "Do talk, Do trust, and Do feel," which is sometimes like swimming upstream all alone when the rest of the family doesn't agree. I think sometimes my own family members perceive my "Do talk" style as me having a big mouth and violating their privacy, which is a very good point, well taken. (Well, sometimes not so well taken.)

The answer is: Do talk, Do trust, Do Feel!

A clear reference to the "Don't talk" rule is the alcoholic family that doesn't talk about the *elephant in the living room*. You've heard of that one, haven't you?

Another aspect of the "Don't talk" rule to consider may be that this behavior of avoidance is to ponder Elisabeth Kubler-Ross's *stages of grief* (denial, anger, bargaining, depression, acceptance), especially the stage of denial. (See Elisabeth Kubler-Ross, Death, The Final Stage of Growth, 1975.) It's possible that a family is just stuck in this stage of grief, not able to let go of what is not to be anymore. There are "*big deaths*" when someone actually dies, and there are "*little deaths*" about aspects of life where our bodies and physical lives continue but some aspect that we hoped for and dreamed of are not to be anymore. We can deeply grieve loses like a separation and divorce, loss of intimacy or former closeness in a relationship that used to be there, or loss of traditions like holidays together just like somebody we loved has died. The "Don't talk" rule can serve a functional purpose for a while until under examination we decide to move on, or a spontaneous event may help us change. (I was introduced to the concept of the grief process by Kubler-Ross when I was a volunteer for Hospice, and also during my psychology and social work courses. If this concept is of interest to you, I encourage to do further research and/or processing on your own or with help.)

Narrative Therapy and other schools of thought say that if we *"tell our story," then our story doesn't have to "tell us*." If we don't work through our issues, they can come squirting out sideways. Whether it be with a friend or a partner, through physical activity with consciousness about our motivation, with an individual therapist, in group therapy, in self-help support groups, in journaling, in writing groups, or by writing a book (and there are risks in all of those), expressing ourselves can help us clear out unresolved issues, like busting lose a blood clot before it causes a stroke.

Unconscious acting out of our unresolved issues can be destructive. (This is called "puking our process.")

In my recovery and in what I thought was doing the right thing, I have offered words of advice to my siblings to "Do talk" and to be honest with one another, and I fear this has backfired on at least one occasion. I take ownership and apologize and wish to make amends with my family about this. I want us to be closer together, not further apart. I need to watch my boundaries and stay on my side of the street.

An aspect of *the "Don't trust" rule* to consider is that we can lose trust in a relationship in a heartbeat, and due to psychological defense mechanisms we may not be consciously aware of it. As human beings with the ability for learning (about trust, for example), we are capable of changing our minds and healing when we learn new concepts. This can help us to process our "stuff," to get past our unresolved, unconscious issues, and move them to a level of consciousness where we can make active choices, rather than just reacting from our old styles. With this in mind, consider the following:

Think about the concept of *Trust Savings Accounts* in relationships. Trust is not a fixed, black & white issue. We make deposits and withdrawals all the time. We can dip into the red without our conscious awareness. If you can be open to think about trust as an ever-changing dynamic issue, then you can think about *transactions in relationships* (behaviors, words, and deeds) that make deposits and withdrawals in our Trust Savings Account with another person continually. The balance is always going up and down. And we both have access to the account as co-signers. In some Trust Savings Accounts, there may be power differences like in a parent-child relationship or an employer, or when one partner may be more outspoken than the other.

An example of where such a transaction can occur unconsciously and instantaneously may be where we have a first impression upon meeting someone, or we may or may not like someone and we dismiss the process of how we came to this conclusion. We just stick with our gut, not being clear how we came to this. It's best if we can be conscious about all the cogs and wheels turning around in our minds that led us here.

Can I trust you? Can I trust myself?

Another issue regarding trust is this: I might be clear in my own thinking about whether or not I trust you, and why. But also, *can I trust myself to handle whatever you say or do?* Can I take full responsibility for my own feelings, thoughts, and behaviors? What a concept! I don't have to be a Victim! I can take full responsibility for myself!

Regarding *the "Don't feel" rule*, it is my perspective that *my family taught us that some feelings were okay, and some feelings were not.* Anger, for instance, was not an okay emotion to have or to express (*like gasoline stored in open containers in the living room*), so we were told that if we couldn't say anything nice, then we were told "Go to your room!" until we could "behave ourselves." I have since learned that you can do great things with anger (and with gasoline), if you don't store it in open containers inside the house, and if you let it out very carefully. You need to keep it stored safely in a closed container, and with it, at the right time you can run powerful engines and build great things! Some people in my family have their own leftover issues with anger (including myself), and I still have to be very careful with messages like "Hey, don't do that because the house could catch on fire!" (When I raise my voice because I think there is an urgent situation or I need to be heard I sometimes get accused of being abusive.)

One result of living by the "Don't feel" rule is being one of the "walking dead." We have our five senses and our emotions for our survival. Without full access to them, we can place ourselves in dangerous situations.

I have a lot more to say about emotions. Please see *Chapter 18 - The Role of Emotions* later in this book.

Guilt vs. Shame

Of particular interest to me is the topic of guilt and shame, which I learned about by listening to John Bradshaw (1933 - 2016). He is available on many sources like tapes, videos, PBS television programs, and books, (one of which is Bradshaw On: The Family – A Revolutionary Way of Self-Discovery, 1988).

Bradshaw talked of guilt being about feeling bad about our behavior, and shame about feeling bad about ourselves. Guilt is about when we do something wrong, like breaking something or hurting someone's feelings, and there is a way back by taking responsibility for it and making it right, like apologizing and paying for the damage. Shame is about feeling like a bad person who did something wrong, who has always done bad things, so why try to get better because a shame-based person is going to do it wrong again because we are a screw-up, a bad person. It's hopeless! A shame-based person may do shame-cover-ups by drinking, drug usage, blaming, running, ducking, dodging, getting locked up in prison, getting tattoos that say "Loser!" and never taking care of the problem by taking responsibility for it and fixing it. Some may even have a mental health diagnosis of a personality disorder. Some groups may even want to call these people "evil." Do you know anyone like that?

Sometimes I feel shame, like a bad person, when I talk about my family. It sometimes feels like I am breaking the "Don't talk" rule, and therefore I feel like the "black sheep," and I'm not included in family events or communications because of this. What's the solution? Talk! Ask questions like: Am I offending you? Am I stepping on your toes? What did I do? How can I make it right?

From a healthier mental health point of view, I believe there is no such thing as a "bad person." In recovery groups we learn about the disease concept, and we talk about being good persons trying to get well not bad people trying to get good. However, it seems there are some people in the world who keep doing bad things, and they seem like bad people. Are some hopeless? What do you believe about this concept?

Bystander or Upstander?

Some terms I have recently heard were "*bystander*" and "*upstander*." It's pretty clear that to be a bystander is to be a witness, but not necessarily one who speaks up and states clearly what they see. An upstander is one who stands up and says "Hey! Do you see what I see? Do you see what's going on?" This can happen when the family or the community culture has the rule of "Don't talk." In such cultures an upstander may be one who is unpopular (for a while anyway) because they are

Are you an "upstander"? Will you stand up and do the right thing, or will you just be a bystander?

stating something like "Hey, do you see that the King is not wearing any clothes?"

Suggestion/Hint: If you become aware that you are changing your own pattern of behaviors by talking, for instance, about family issues that were previously avoided, and you notice that other family members are not talking to you anymore the way they used to, you might make note of that and make a conscious decision about your own integrity, boundaries, etc., and maybe ask them: Is what I'm talking about leaving you feel uncomfortable? (See other sections on passiveness, assertiveness, aggressiveness, passive-aggressiveness, and non-violent communication elsewhere in this book and in other sources.)

I need to own my part in contributing to my family's dysfunction. I am a recovering alcoholic/addict. (See *Chapter 16 - My Alcoholism – A Family Deal.*) I have created stress in my family-of-origin, and I have outright lied (like when my mother asked me if I smoked pot). When our mother was dying of cancer and she had marijuana for medicinal reasons, I stole some of her drugs for my own use - this was one of the tipping points that contributed towards my getting clean and sober. In my addiction I have not always behaved responsibly and with integrity, and in my recovery I have also made mistakes.

Dysfunctional vs. Functional Families

I want to comment on my labeling of my family as "dysfunctional." Functional and dysfunctional families both have problems. Functional families acknowledge and resolve the problems and meet their family members' needs, as best they can. Dysfunctional families have problems that don't get resolved in a healthy way because issues are denied, and family members' needs are not as well-met. In dysfunctional families, survival can be questionable. In functional families, members have a better chance of survival, and they often thrive when their needs are met so that they have the opportunity to rise to their greatest potential. Sometimes in dysfunctional families, seeds of great accomplishments may be planted, also.

Whether a family is "functional" or "dysfunctional" is not clearly black and white. Most any family has traits of being both. With awareness of what these traits are, we can make conscious decisions about whether we are contributing by asking "Am I part of the problem?" or "Am I part of the solution?" We make choices like "Do talk" or "Don't talk" right now, and hundreds of times per day, whether we are conscious of it or not. The pattern of these choices make up our character.

If we do choose to talk about what's on our minds, we can make choices about other conditions, like doing it with respect to another person's rights and privacy, or not, and the forum in which we express ourselves.

For some, stating "I am from a dysfunctional family" is a badge of honor. For others, it is a statement of shame.

Family Roles

Claudia Black wrote about roles that family members take on in dysfunctional families. She writes about *healthy or functional families* here: "Many times, there are clearly defined roles within the family. It is typical for adults in the family to divide, or share the roles of being the breadwinner and the administrator - the one who makes the decisions within the home. Children raised in homes where open communication is practiced and consistency of lifestyles is the norm usually have the ability to adopt a variety of roles, dependent on the situation. These children learn how to be responsible, how to organize, to develop realistic goals, to play, laugh, and enjoy themselves. They learn a sense of flexibility and spontaneity. They are usually taught how to be sensitive to the feelings of others, and are willing to be helpful to others. These children learn a sense of autonomy and also how to belong to a group" (from It Will Never Happen to Me by Claudia Black, p. 6, 1981). If you grew up in a healthy family like this, great!

In a dysfunctional family, *survival roles* can be a problem when we put on a mask and not be our real selves.

These survival roles can help to cope with a chaotic family where there is inconsistency and unpredictability, to try to establish stability that is lacking, and/or to try to make sense to what is going on around them. This can make it easier and less painful, even when such family members may not recognize the pain because it is just what is "normal" for their family. Such family members may believe that all families are like this.

Or we may feel "*scripted*" to fulfill someone else's agenda for us, and we never really learn who we are without our masks. Claudia Black uses the terms "The Responsible One," "The Acting Out Child," "The Adjuster," and "The Placator" roles. Other professionals in the field use such terms as the "Family Hero," "Scapegoat," "Family Pet," or "Lost Child." I recognize some aspects of each of these survival roles in members of my family.

The problem with learning a role to help us survive in a dysfunctional situation (in our families or other settings in the community like our work environments), is that we don't learn to be true to ourselves. It's a foreign concept. Instead, always asking "What do you want me to be?" can be a skill that helps us survive, but some say they feel they have lost their childhood when this happens. (This is a trait of co-dependency that I will talk more about later.)

There's a story I remember from a workshop I attended about Children of Alcoholics from the books about Tom Sawyer and Huckleberry Finn written by Mark Twain. (When I have re-told this story in my professional work I was told "You got it wrong! That's not how the book goes!") From the workshop, I remember that Huckleberry Finn's father was the town drunk, and he was physically abusive towards Huck. If the dad came home drunk and Huck would be honest and say "Don't hit me, Dad! It scares me when you come home like that!," then it was more likely his father would hit him. So, Huck learned to put on a mask and be what his father wanted him to be. To be the Placator or Lost Child would help Huck keep from getting hurt so much.

Part of a survivor role I learned for myself was to be a Placator or Lost Child where I learned how to be a people pleaser, to be passive, and to deny my own feelings. I am learning how to undo this lesson as it's not always in my best interests to remain this old way.

Adopted Brother

As stated elsewhere, I grew up in a family that was dysfunctional because of my family's reactions to my older adoptive brother's behaviors. There was probably family dysfunction before this brother arrived. The questions occur: Which came first, the chicken or the egg? Did this brother's behaviors cause us to be dysfunctional? Did my parents' attempts to cope with my brother's challenging behaviors leave some of our needs unmet? Or was he the "symptom bearer" and did we cause him to be our Scapegoat to distract from our dysfunctional multi-generation patterns? The truth is probably a combination of all of these explanations. This brother was adopted at a very young age (when he was between 3 and 6 months old). We don't know what genetic issues he inherited from his mother or father or grandparents, or what issues in the womb he may have experienced, like possible substance abuse by the birth mother, or other neurological or chemical assaults on the fetus. What about the emotions of the biological mother about him before he was born? What was the moment of conception like? Was there love?

There may have been traumas he experienced at that very young age after birth and before he was placed with my parents. There may have been attachment and bonding issues he may have experienced with his biological parents.

And, as the oldest child, my parents were "cutting their teeth" and learning new parenting skills with their first child.

My family's developmental issues are such that my adopted brother was the first and oldest child of my parents after they were initially not able to conceive a pregnancy. Were there issues about sexuality between my parents? (Some of these things we just don't want to think about, but they are a reality in our heritage.)

This older brother told me he felt different than the rest

of our sibling group, and he felt like he was treated differently. It was obvious that he looked different because of genetics. He told me he felt our parents were abusive towards him, and he thought that our parents were alcoholics/addicts, while I don't see it that way. I do see that his hyperactive behavior invited corporal punishment that was "normal" for my parents' generation, which my brother perceived as their abuse of him. There are many confusing and confounding factors, some of which will never be clear. Many of these led me to my chosen profession as a social worker.

Does your family have an adoption story?

Compassion

I do have much compassion for my parents, for their generation, and all of the hardships that they and our ancestors went through so that I may experience the comfort and riches of my current life (and I don't mean financial riches). My father was born in 1914, at the time of World War I. He and his family lived through many diseases including flu epidemics. (Did you know that the flu epidemic of 1918 killed more people than were killed in World War I?) My mother was born in 1921, and both of my parents and their families lived through the economic Great Depression of the 1930's. My father was in the U.S. Navy, stationed in Hawaii at the bombing of Pearl Harbor in December 1941. They lived through many hardships and didn't have the luxury as we do of talking about feelings and analyzing what their parents "did to them" and be bitter and blaming about it, and being stuck as a Victim. I hope I do not come across as being bitter about my family. My parents did the best they could with what they had. The context of my parents' lives was much harsher than I experienced. I am so very grateful for what they gave me. I know that I am standing on their shoulders, and I wouldn't be here without them.

I am compassionate about my adopted brother, my birth siblings, and my parents. I do not live within my adopted brother's skin, and I don't share his biology or nervous system. While I had my own struggles with feelings of not belonging and low self-esteem at times, at least I did look more like I belonged in my family, whereas he did not look like the rest of our family. Very likely he struggled with feelings of belonging.

Troubled vs. Nurturing Families

If you don't like the terms "dysfunctional" and "functional" to describe families, Virginia Satir in Peoplemaking (1972) uses the terms "troubled families" and "untroubled or nurturing families." She *thinks of families as "people factories"* where the adults are supposed to be the "*people makers*." In this model she watches traits of self-worth, communication, rules, and how family members connect with the outside society. In troubled families, she noticed that: self-worth was low; communication was indirect, vague, and dishonest; rules were rigid, inhuman, and non-negotiable; and the linking or connection with society was fearful, placating, and blaming. In untroubled or nurturing families, she saw that self-worth was high; communication was direct, clear, specific, and honest; rules were flexible, human, appropriate, and subject to change; and the connection with society outside the family was open and hopeful. *If you consider yourself as coming from a functional, nurturing, and untroubled family, consider yourself lucky and blessed!*

Assertiveness and Non-Violent Communication

Communication styles range from passiveness to assertiveness to aggressiveness. *Passiveness* means that my rights are not as important as your rights, and I will not stand up for myself. (I am not okay, and you are okay.) *Assertiveness* means that I recognize and respect your rights, and I also recognize and respect my rights, and I will do the best I can to stand up for myself, and allow space for you to stand up for yourself. When I claim "my space" I need to not violate your space. (I am okay, and you are okay. This is the healthiest posture.) *Aggressiveness* means my rights are more important than your rights, and I will stand up for myself and

I don't care to listen to what you want or need. (I am okay, and you are not okay.) Another style of communication might be called *passive-aggressiveness*, which means I am putting my wants and needs above yours in a passive way, like putting a tack on your seat or talking about you behind your back. Gossip is passive-aggressive, especially if it involves "character assassination." Passive-aggressiveness might be like "I can't take this anymore, and now I'm going to get even!" behind someone's back rather than going directly to the person. A gross and graphic way of looking at passive-aggressiveness is like a puppy dog licking your face while pissing on your leg! (Thomas Harris, I'm OK, You're OK, 1969)

An assertive statement model (a.k.a. an "I statement"):
When you ___(describe the other person's behavior)______,
I feel _(describe how the other person's behavior affects you),
because __(describe why their behavior affects you this way),
and I would like __(describe what you want or need)_______,
or else __(you could describe your bottom line – optional)___.

Non-violent communication means standing up for myself (and you standing up for yourself) in such a way as we have a relationship where we each to try to express our feelings and needs, and encourage each other to express what we each feel and need. This school-of-thought teaches that most conflicts between individuals or groups arise from miscommunication about our human needs, due to coercive or manipulative language or behavior that aims to induce fear, guilt, shame, etc. (All behavior is communication.) These "violent" modes of communication, when used during a conflict, divert the attention of the participants away from clarifying our needs, feelings, perceptions, and our requests, thus perpetuating the conflict.

A Non-Violent Communication (a.k.a. Compassionate Communication) model:

1. Observation – What are my thoughts about this

situation (in twenty-five words or less).

2. Feeling – What are my feelings or emotions about this situation? How do I know what I am feeling (through sensations in the body)? What does it feel like when my needs are being met, and what does it feel like when my needs are not being met?
3. What do I need? (Refer to Maslow's hierarchy of needs.) Different than what I want - Wants vs. Needs.
4. Make a request to have my needs met. (Request vs. Demands.) Don't make a request if you aren't prepared for a "no" response from the other party. Be prepared that they may say something like "It's your problem, not mine."

A couple of other comments about non-violent/ compassionate communication:

- Choice/control – We can't force another person to use compassionate communication. I can only choose to use it myself. We don't want to attack another person with our own boundary setting.
- Anger – We, or the other person, may react from anger, which is often a cover-up for fear. Getting in touch with it and taking responsibility for our part in it is healthy.

It's a whole lot more complicated than this, but assertiveness and non-violent communication are *a cornerstone of my identity*, who I am and who I want to be. I want to encourage others, family members, friends, and whole communities, to learn how to stand up for each of ourselves and what we believe in, and to work on relationships so that we recognize and respect what other people believe in. I'm not perfect at this, and I still do not always live up to this ideal. But, to try is good politics! (from NVC: A Language of Life, 3rd Edition by Dr. Marshall B. Rosenberg, © 2015, www.nonviolentcommunication.com.)

Bitter or Grateful?

Am I bitter, blaming, and resentful for the family I was raised in? No. It was the perfect family to bring me to where I am today, and I have peace, most of the time. (Although, I am still grieving, and there are times that my emotions come up that surprise me when I discover my own "unfinished business.") Again, I am grateful for what my parents gave me. I know they did the best they could with what they had, and I hope they are peaceful wherever they are.

I am not a perfect parent, and I wonder what my children think about their parents (my wife and me), and about our family. I wonder, sometimes, if there are seeds of bitterness and resentment, and if they will need therapy someday. I wonder what they will write about me. I hope they write about me!

The following was given to me by an old girlfriend, hand copied from a book, as we were breaking up years ago:

> *"**Sooner or later a person begins to notice** that everything that happens to him is perfect, relates directly to who he is, had to happen, was meant to happen, plays its little role in fulfilling his destiny.*
>
> *"When he encounters difficulty, it no longer occurs to him to complain— he has learned to expect nothing, has learned that loss and frustration are a part of life, and come at their proper time—instead he asks himself, why is this happening? ...by which he means, what can I learn from this, how will it strengthen me, make me more aware? He lets himself be strengthened, lets himself grow, just as he lets himself relax and enjoy (and grow) when life is gentle to him.*
>
> *"Strengthened by this simple notion, simple awareness, that life is perfect, that all things come at the proper moment and that he is always the perfect person for the situation he finds himself in, a person begins to feel more and more in tune with his inner nature, begins to find it easier and easier to do what he knows is right. All chance events appear to him to be intended; all intentional actions he clearly perceives as part of the workings of Chance. Anxiety seldom troubles him; he knows his death will come at its proper moment; he knows his actions are right and therefore whatever comes to pass as a result of them will be what is meant to happen. When he does feel anxiety, he realizes it is because of that thing he's been*

meaning to do but hasn't done, some unfulfilled relationship he's been aware of, but ...He perceives the anxiety as a message that he'll have to stop hesitating if he wants to stay high ...He knows that he is out of tune because he's let himself get out of tune; and because he knows he can, he begins to take action. He enjoys his high life; does not enjoy anxiety; so he stops hesitating and does what he has to do.

"He does not live in a state of bliss, though perhaps he feels himself moving toward one— or toward something, he doesn't know what it is but it is the way he has to go, the journey towards it is the only life he enjoys. It is hard; it is exciting; it is satisfying, lonely, joyous, frustrating, puzzling, enlightening, real; it is his life, that's all. He accepts it.

*"**Sooner or later a person begins to notice**..."*

From "<u>Das Energi</u>" by Paul Williams (1973)

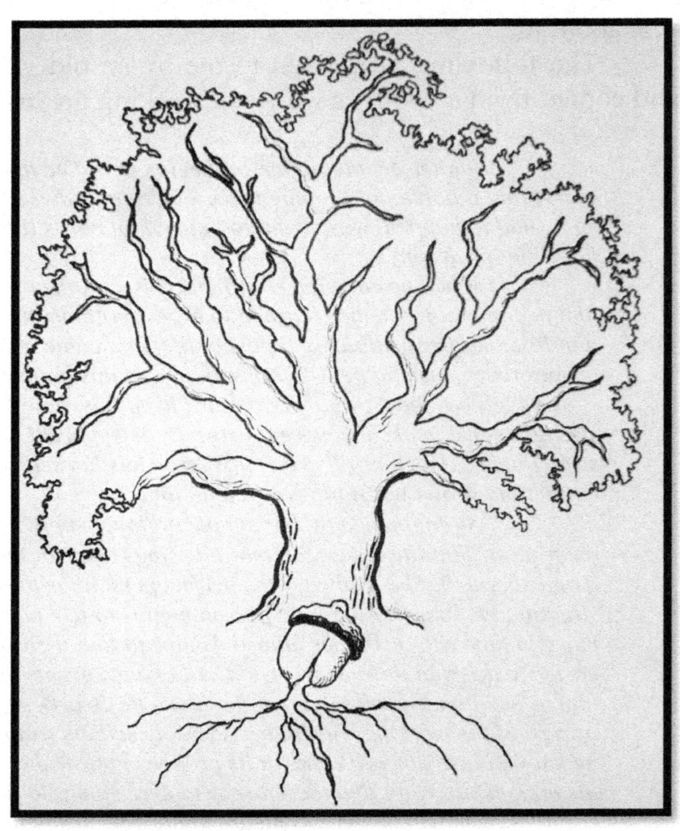

Chapter 4
Gravestones and Markers

What kinds of markers do we leave behind after we are physically gone? When I first wrote this chapter at age fifty-eight (in 2014), I was not ready to think about what I wanted to be written on my headstone, but this book is something to leave behind that I can be proud of – a marker of my life to be remembered by if someone stumbles over it.

Have you thought about what you want to be left behind? What will be your legacy?

Both of my parents wanted to be cremated and have their ashes scattered. While Mom wanted a ceremony after her death (and she had a grand one!), Dad did not want any kind of services. Funeral services create memories for those who attend.

Now, neither of my parents have gravestone markers left behind for us to go and visit. Their ashes are scattered on the mountain behind their house in Alberton, Montana. The only evidence is what I carved in a tree at the top of the cliff overlooking their home where we scattered Dad's ashes to the winds.

I know the human mind is not an accurate recorder of history. While the human heart helps to remember, it is tainted by emotions of ghosts from our past, both positive and negative. The human brain is not always accurate or permanent either, different from the mind.

What's written on a headstone can be very short, if there is such a marker. They talk about the "dash" between the date of birth and date of death is what really matters.

What's written on paper might preserve echoes of our time here a little longer than the human brain, heart or mind, especially if our words get published, or if someone finds our journals. We might leave traces of our fingerprints or footprints on the path of our lives we leave behind (i.e. like the journal that says "… and then in 1966 we moved to Missoula, Montana … and in 1976 we moved into the house in the woods in Alberton, which was Mom and Dad's castle on the hill …").

What about pixels on a computer screen, or bits and bytes on a hard drive, or information on our web site or our Facebook page? How long will those last?

And will anyone care? Will anyone notice any evidence of our existence? Can anyone find those records if they're looking for evidence of us? Are we searchable in Google's database?

Will anyone read this book? If they find this book, will they skip this chapter?

And, *do we WANT to be found*? Were we that important?

Here's a marker, a brief record of my mom, Alice Dewey (Johnson) Neel (4/14/1921 – 9/4/1980): I know my mother did a lot of important things in her life. If she hadn't been here, I wouldn't be here! She had a lot of energy, had a great sense of humor, and she was very entertaining. She was in the Navy where she met my dad. She was a foster mom and an adoptive mom. She gave birth to three children and raised four. She was the wife of a Navy Captain, my Dad. She was a church organist and choir director. She sang in church and in community choirs and chorales, and she was recorded and put on a vinyl record in Pensacola, Florida (singing Handel's "Messiah," of which we have a copy). She volunteered for the Red Cross and transcribed braille for the blind. She worked as a bank teller at the First National Bank in Missoula, Montana. But what did she leave behind for others to remember her by? Did anyone ask her to tell her story and did it get recorded? How do we remember her?

As her son, I'm almost embarrassed that I'm having trouble writing more about her here - *this is an example of the problem of not writing down important family members' stories*.

She has been gone now for about thirty-eight years (as of this update in 2018). This makes me hungry - I need to do more research … (My cousin, Marinell Reeves, is researching the Johnson family line – which is my mother's maiden name and lineage.) Are you a Johnson? Well, if you are, then "Howdy, Cousin!"

My father did leave more tangible evidence of his time here – he left trunks full of documents from his career in the Navy, magazine articles he wrote and read, letters to Admirals in the Navy, and also letters from his first wife, Beth, that we are still going through. (What happened to the letters he wrote to Beth?) Too much to write about here in this short chapter. There is a chapter about him later in this book. See *Chapter 10 – John William Neel – My Dad* if you want to read more about him.

Some random thoughts of mine about echoes of what we leave behind:

- The lives we lead, the differences we made …
- Behaviors, choices, actions, and the results of those decisions and actions …
- Things we lost and were forgotten, only to be found by others …
- Memories that other people have of us, especially how we touched their hearts …
- Words we have written down and might remain behind … (Was there something you wrote that you wanted to make sure nobody found? This might be the time to find and destroy it if that was your intention.)
- Pictures we have taken or were taken of us …
- The art we have created …
- How we affected others …
- Lessons we taught, morals, ethics, honesty, integrity
- Children … grandchildren … or not …

I do, at this time, want to be cremated, and have my ashes scattered on Dominion Peak, on the Montana-Idaho state line near Lookout Pass, a few miles off Interstate 90. At this time I do not want a marker left on top of that lonely mountain, just my scattered ashes (I might change my mind later). I feel my heart is in Montana, and my ass is in Idaho – sorry for the bad word, Nathan and Josh or anyone else that might be offended by my Sailor word. Please read the short *Chapter 9 - Sojourn into Montana – home of my heart* later in this book about this.

Stories about people's lives are a kind of a marker left behind. The stories might get passed along verbally, and if so they might be distorted or forgotten eventually. Written family stories might last longer, and I have included some of my family stories in this book and other family books.

This chapter and my book are incomplete, as I hope my life is yet incomplete. I have faith that I have tomorrow to continue this work (and next month and next year, I hope, but I know a traffic accident or other unforeseen event could happen any day for any of us). Consider this an undeveloped photograph. Don't dip me in lacquer yet …

In family versions of my Family Hunger books, for this chapter I include pictures of headstones and stories about particular family members. Since this version is for public consumption, these may not interest you so I leave them out.

Chapter 5
A Mother's Story

"Bob" is the adopted son of my parents, my oldest brother. I use an alias for his name as I recently found that he is still living, and I may know where he is located. We've been out of touch for the last fifteen years as he said he didn't want anything to do with us. The last time we communicated, he said he had cancer but didn't want to take the treatments.

This story is my own and about our mother's story, not his.

This is a chapter where a living person, Bob, could be named without his permission, but I don't want to do that for various reasons: 1) my credibility - I said elsewhere in this book that I wouldn't name living persons without their permission; 2) for legal reasons; 3) for ethical reasons; and 4) out of my own fear.

I fear this brother. I have a healthy respect for and fear of sharks and bears. I try to keep my body parts away from their jaws or claws! Sharks and bears may bite out of their own hunger or fear or for other complicated reasons, and so may human beings.

I want to do no harm. Bob's story is his own to tell. I don't want to make his life worse for him. Yet I feel a loyalty to his victims. I had contact with the victim of his crime from 1977, and she sent me transcripts of his legal trial. I feel a duty to warn, but again, I want to do no harm.

Bob has violated the rights of many people. I have deep compassion for my brother's victims. If you, the reader, are one of his victims I am sorry that he has harmed you. I am sorry that a person with our family name has hurt you. I am working my boundaries by saying that I cannot take responsibility for his behaviors.

It is certainly not my intention to do any further harm by sharing this story, or even by alluding to this story. I will not tell his full story here because he is still alive as far as we know. The clock is ticking.

If you are triggered by reading this, take care of yourself.

Self-Care

There are various ways I take care of myself if I am overwhelmed or uncomfortable. I listen to my body, and if it's too much, I turn away. I suggest you stop reading this if you are uncomfortable. It may be helpful to examine why we are uncomfortable and address it through self-reflection, write in a journal, go for a walk or run, lift weights, hit a punching bag, go to counseling, etc. Sometimes I take care of myself by turning on the TV and eating junk food, and while this may provide respite, it doesn't address the cause of the discomfort. I can ask "Why is this happening, again? Is this a pattern? Can I connect the dots?"

Another way I take care of myself is "working my boundaries," by asking "Where do I end, and where do you begin?"

Back to the story …

Now, back to the story about my mother's story: This is not meant in any way to make excuses for my brother and his choices or to defend him in any way. This is intended to try to help understand why he did the things he did and to understand the impact he has had on other people, including the greater community as well as our immediate family. As stated elsewhere, *to "understand" does not mean we have to "stand under" the power of someone else's issues anymore!* We do not have to accept someone puking their process on us! That would not be good for us, and it would not be good for them to allow this! I have some compassion for this brother, but the scales are not balanced. While it appears he has not left a good mark on the world, *I don't think I would be the person I am today if he hadn't been in our family, flaming much passion and curiosity for me and leaving me wondering*

"What happened to us? How did we get here?"

I have mentioned that he is infamous to some people because of his legal records, some of which are public information. I had a girlfriend at one time who told me that when she attended law school that they studied my brother's case in class, which is embarrassing for me. Again, working my boundaries here.

Prior to late August 2018, I was prepared to share in this book about twenty pages of my mother's owns words about what it was like for her to be the adoptive mother of a troubled son because we assumed he was dead. These words are precious to me as there is so little I have left of my mother since she died in 1980 at the young age of fifty-nine. Her words are invaluable to me because they tell so much about why we are the way we are as a family.

I love you, Mom.

I hope to publicly share her words when and if Bob passes away before I do in my next planned book, Chasing Headstones. (Do you get the irony of that title? I'm chasing his headstone. Or maybe he is chasing mine as he would like to bury this story.)

I'm sorry so much is missing for you as the reader here – there is much context to our family history that is not expressed here, and many lessons. I believe some of our current family dynamics, i.e. communication skills, emotional affect, coping mechanisms like denial, projection, blaming, etc. from the old ways still show themselves at times.

Our mother's story appears to have been written between 1970 and 1977, and covers the period of time between 1960 and 1977 when he was arrested for one of his crimes in Missoula, Montana.

For more on this, please read my next *Chapter 6 – A Brother's Story.*

Chapter 6
A Brother's Story

I shared this chapter with my men's group in 2016. One man's reaction to the story was something like "There are many things I did in my childhood that I wouldn't ever want to be told." Because of this, I had thoughts about changing this chapter, leaving some parts out and keeping them secret. Do I want to send negative vibes out to the universe? (No.) If I have unresolved issues, what is the price I pay for not working them out? ("Stuff" can come squirting out sideways.) Is my writing about my brother one of my ways to sort out what happened to me, and what happened to us as a family? (The answer is a resounding: Yes!) Writing is a way to express myself, to clean emotional and psychological toxins out of my system, and especially to make sense of what happened so there is not a repeat of negative history.

But publicly sharing what we write is a critical decision.

There are other ways to clean out emotional toxins, like private journal writing, ghost letters, therapy, support groups, etc.

Keeping childhood memories private is one thing. Keeping secrets for a convicted felon is different. Does "Bob" have a right to his privacy?

I feel anger at my adopted brother, "Bob." I feel stupid about myself for letting him get so close to my wife and children as I allowed him into our home and to sit down for dinner with us after he was released from prison.

I have had communication with the victim his crime that he was convicted of in 1977. She provided me with a copy of the transcript of his trial in which she testified. I told her I would like to post his story after he dies, but not before his death without his permission for ethical reasons and because of my own fear of his retribution. I want to do no harm. She responded that she would like to make public the crimes of "Bob" because "no good can come from denial."

I am torn about this disclosure. She said according to the trial transcript, Bob had previously committed the same crime in California and returned to Montana to avoid prosecution. Therefore, he is considered a violent repeat offender. There is other public information about other crimes for which he was convicted, also.

Writing and sharing stories with a broader audience, like in this book, has a more substantial impact to consider as well. It can be a lesson for others, which is part of my intention with this book.

I'm aware that I am a role model to readers who might find themselves in similar situations struggling with doing the right thing. "Don't talk" is not the right thing to do if you want to live in recovery with integrity. That's exactly what I did at times to cope, and I've stuffed my story about my adopted brother away for years.

"Don't talk" is a survival skill in some situations. Disclosure needs to be balanced with consideration about the further harm that might come from talking or writing about an event. There is a risk with talking and also with keeping secrets. There needs to be discernment and discretion, which means finding the right time and place to disclose. It is good to be as fully conscious as we can be, and to make fully informed choices. Getting help from others is an excellent way to figure out what is the right thing to do if you have the time and the resources, but the situation may not allow that in a crisis.

Because of the public nature of legal records, it might be legally correct to disclose Bob's crimes. But because he is still alive, in the field of genealogy and social work it is not ethically correct to reveal his story.

I'm putting my story about Bob away, not making the details public until after it is confirmed that he has passed away. He has no children, so concern about his legacy and how it affects them is not an issue.

The race is on. Who is going to die first, him or me?

As stated above, Bob's story is his own to tell, but our

story is our own. I'm sharing some aspects of how living with this person affected my family and me, and I'm trying to be careful working my boundaries here.

We can re-write our histories, not changing the facts but changing the way we look at what happened to us. We might try to distort the facts, and while that is not healthy it may help us to survive! It's normal and natural in some circumstances to distort. Human beings are poor historians. We can change how our experiences affect us, and if used correctly we can grow by processing it, squeezing all the lessons and wisdom out of the story. We can use this to be less of a Victim or victim of others' actions and move towards being safer and taking more responsibility for our own lives, including all of our own behaviors, thoughts, and emotions.

Being a victim (small "v") means it could happen to anyone, and we are the innocent recipients of a negative event. Being a Victim (large "V") means we played a part in setting ourselves up to be at the receiving end of getting hurt. When we recognize this, we can consciously make a choice: I see I placed myself in harm's way, I'm tired of getting run over or being a doormat for other people wiping their shoes on me, so I am going to stop placing myself at risk! (I do not want to imply that I am blaming the victim when I am writing about Victim. No matter how provocatively someone may dress or behave does not give another person the right to violate them!)

Wisdom can come from this – to dive deep and integrate our histories into our identities in a productive way, to be the best person we can be with everything we were gifted with. As I re-write and edit this story again, I consider that maybe we are all in "draft form" for as long as our hearts are beating … we are all still growing if we are willing. I am changing the way my history affects me.

When I visited my brother inside the prison in 1981, I witnessed an event that was a crime, but it was not reported. At this time I will not share it in this book. From modern terminology, I was "triggered" by the experience. See *Chapter 7 - Attachment, Bonding, and Trauma* later in this book, as well as *Chapter 18 -The Role of Emotions*.

I consulted with several people before coming to a

decision about how to share this story. An additional factor is that it has been thirty-seven years since that significant incident happened with my brother in prison, and it has been about fifteen years since I last heard from him when he shared he had cancer, and that he didn't want to take the treatments.

To not be entirely "awake" or to be fully conscious with all of our senses and talents that were gifted to us is to be one of the "walking dead" or to be "sleepwalking," which I prefer not to be in most circumstances. However, sometimes I do prefer to sleep through some situations in life, so pass the popcorn and hand me the remote control! Choices! I know that's a bold statement, maybe a little over-dramatic (to sleepwalk by flaking out with the TV), but I use it to make a point. "Talk," or "Don't talk"? Consciousness or unconsciousness? What will it be for you? (Do you have a story inside you that needs to get out? What will you do with it?)

There are still lots of people in the world who live by the "Don't talk" rule, every day. Some people are just very private about their personal issues. Some live by this rule and call it "street code." Some think this is normal and don't make conscious decisions about what they share. It's just ordinary for them. Some must live this way for their very survival.

Expression or Depression

As stated elsewhere, there is a saying in my field of social work that goes: "Impression without expression leads to depression." I was impressed by my brother way before I visited him in prison in 1981 with all the experiences we had as children and into young adulthood. I was certainly impressed by this prison experience with him. It was a traumatic experience for me, one I don't wish to re-live, and I have ghosts from the past because of this. I try to keep them in their place so they don't come squirting out sideways. I do try to find the right time and place to express it for my own health, and to get the lessons I need from it.

The Rev. Dr. Jane Simmons talks about "Pain not transformed is pain transmitted," which exactly means that our issues may come squirting out sideways if we don't take care of our unresolved stuff. She also talks about our choices to try to ignore our shadow side, but that some random life events may trigger us like "paper cuts" if ghosts from the past pop up. Our projections can help us if we're open to them. We may have filters or lens where we interpret the world around us as "Life is unsafe," or "I am not worthy, there is something wrong with me." With awareness and conscious choices, we could see the world through the lens of: "Why is this happening to me, again? Isn't this interesting … this reminds me of that time when … but that was then, and this is now." How about a lens of: *"I am an ever-expanding conscious intelligence. Wow, what an amazing universe! Look at all that blood!"*

Why do our buttons get pushed? Why do seemingly random events take us to places that we don't want to go? Human relationships are where the rubber meets the road. People can be a mirror of ourselves, reminding us of our own stuff with our projections. The Rev. Dr. Jane enlightened me of HSD (Human Sleep Disorder), or "sleep apnea of the soul" in her talk and book "You Can't Sleep Through Your Awakening." I highly recommend this book.

This prison experience with my brother, Bob, was a significant stressor in my life. I did revert to some of my old ways of coping to get through it. It does affect who I am today, some thirty-seven years later.

As I made a reference about a "vague childhood memory" with my brother, history is not always clear, especially with our organic hard drives. Sometimes we are swinging at "ghosts from our pasts" without recognition of what our conflict is about.

The definition of "complex trauma" is repeated exposure to stressful events, without resolution, without productive expression. It affects our development. It changes who we are and can interfere with achieving our full potential. My lifetime of traumatic experiences has affected my personality development. (I relate to the words "… changed the very fiber of my being" from the 7/3/2018 issue of The Spokesman-Review about an interview of a woman who had been the recipient of long-term threats by Jarrod Ramos, who allegedly massacred five employees at the Capitol Gazette newsroom in Annapolis, Maryland). I have experienced depression sometimes, and my addictions were an attempt to cope with my uncomfortable feelings and unresolved issues. My recovery from addiction is a huge part of my identity now. I am a grateful recovering alcoholic/addict. I try my best to make these experiences for the good!

Compassion

As stated above, I have made contact with the victim of Bob's crime that he was convicted of and imprisoned for, and we have exchanged communications through e-mails. These were very powerful contacts for me, but we have since lost touch with each other. I often wonder how she fares. Can more healing be done here? Yes, but I cannot force it. I must be respectful. I do have deep, heartfelt compassion for her. I recall some of our last communications included "How will we know when he is dead?"

I have seen Bob since he was released from prison, out of compassion for him, and out of being blind-sided by him as he dropped in on my hometown unannounced. As I said elsewhere, I do feel compassion for him, but this does not mean I support him or justify or defend any harm he has caused other people. I do not feel sorry for him. I do not feel safe with him. We should not let our guard down.

I know how important it is to have connection and attachment to our own parents and biological family, and what a struggle that can be even when we do have access to them. Our families are supposed to be a secure base from which to launch (but for some people their families are an insecure base). We sometimes need them as a life raft in the waters of life way into adulthood and even into our elder years. As an adopted person as in this brother's case, he didn't have access to his biological family so how could he get answers to essential questions like his own and his birth family's medical and mental health history, about belonging and worthiness, or about why they let him go. (See comments about my "Dream" about him in the next section.)

There is a term in the field of social work: Compassion Fatigue. That's pretty self-explanatory. It is possible to care about something and about others too much and for too long. I need to back off in my caring about this for a while.

Will I have compassion or fear if I ever hear from this brother again? That is yet to be seen. (Bob, are you still out there?)

Dream

I have a recurring dream about my brother, Bob, that goes something like this: He is a wild animal with his leg caught in a trap, so desperate to escape that he tries to chew off his own limbs to obtain his freedom. It is a bloody mess! It is a nightmare that I still awaken in sweat from!

In our awaking life, I wonder if he found answers about his birth family and about where he came from, that he may not need to be so destructive. I interpret my dream to be about his unanswered questions to be his trap. (I am aware that these may be more about my questions than about his questions. This is my story, not his story.)

I've heard stories about and met many people who have been adopted, and I've been involved in the lives of many adoptees in my job as a social worker. For some, when they found their birth family, they profoundly changed as a person. Most of the time for the better, but not always.

Adoption and Identity

A video called "The Other One" highlighted Bob Weir of the Grateful Dead musical group. He'd been adopted, but the band became his family. Still, his unknown history had left a hole, and he felt that something was missing, so he hired a private investigator to find his birth parents. He did find his mother and many siblings, as well as his father. After he met up with his dad, he commented "We sat and began to like each other … we didn't have to … there was no onus (no obligation or duty) …."

It's frosting on the cake if we can get the message from those we care about that they like us just the way we are!

It's important to know from where we came. That is who we are! That is part of our identity!

Siblings

On the wall of one of my co-worker's office hangs a poster that says "*Sibling relationships outlast marriages, survive the death of parents, resurface after quarrels that would sink any friendship. They flourish in a thousand incarnations of closeness and distance, warmth, loyalty and distrust*" (from Erica E. Goode). I do feel this is a truth with my birth sister and my birth brother. Yet this relationship with our adopted brother, Bob, does not seem to carry this quality. Whether he is physically alive or not, he lives in my memories, and he affected my development.

Conclusion

I can't change the facts of my history. If I feel violated, how can I get out from under that? I've heard it said from a wise man: "Forgiveness is giving up all hope of a different past." I can deny or distort some of my stories, but that can be destructive. If I don't take care of my stuff, my stuff will take care of me. I can change the way I look at events from my past.

Forgiveness is giving up all hope of a different past.

Chapter 7
Attachment, Bonding, and Trauma

John Bowlby, one of the founders of Attachment Theory (A Secure Base: Parent-Child Attachment and Healthy Human Development, 1988) stated that human beings are wired for connection and the need for connection continues from cradle to grave.

Like the foundation of a house being built, attachment and bonding are the building blocks for later stages of our children's development and their ability to trust the world. Children grow up to be adults, and the attachment strategies they have developed affect how well they will function in many areas, including their personal psychology, interpersonal relationships, and what kind of parent or caregiver they become.

A function of attachment and bonding is for the physical survival of the child, to keep them close to their caregiver for safety, nutrition, and their basic needs being met. Caregivers can be a mom, and/or a dad (preferably both), extended family members, child care providers, neighbors, or even institutions like schools or the foster care system. For the infant to develop trust, the caregivers need to be attentive and fulfill the child's needs. Some people just call it love.

Good attachment can be achieved when the child's needs for comfort and protection are met unconditionally. Conditions like good manners that help us be "civilized" come later. Some parents I talk with, mostly fathers, are concerned that if they pick up their crying baby it will spoil them. Spoiling comes from giving the child everything they want (toys, sugar, TV, etc.), but not from giving them everything they need (like security by holding them when they are scared, and setting limits on unhealthy behaviors).

I disagree with the old school "spare the rod and spoil the child" style of parenting that promotes fear of authority.

Undisciplined discipline is not what the world needs. Respect for authority is needed, and that is based on trust.

Good attachment comes from the caregivers being a secure base from which the child can launch when he or she is ready. Sometimes children want to launch before the caregivers think they are ready. The key for healthy caregiving is to be supportive, sensitive, strong, and wise, without being intrusive.

Research shows that good attachment, bonding and positive involvement throughout the child's development leads to better-adjusted children (emotionally and behaviorally). Children perform better academically, have better employment records and are better able to make and maintain stable relationships. And they are better prepared to have and raise children of their own.

I have included this chapter on issues of attachment and bonding as important building blocks for the development of stable children which grow into stable adults who raise families and later generations. While I believe my parents did the best they could with what they had, I believe I have had to overcome some attachment issues in my development. In addition to attachment are issues of trauma in my family.

Trauma

As stated elsewhere, chronic trauma is any stressful event that is prolonged, overwhelming, and unpredictable. And when the events continue on unexpressed, unprocessed, and misunderstood, it leads to long-term trauma. Again, long-term trauma which is unresolved and integrated into a person's development is called complex trauma and affects our personality development and our worldview.

I encourage you to do further reading, research, and personal processing if this topic catches your attention, and/or if you are ready for it. Go find out more about what "Resilience trumps A.C.E.S." means (Adverse Childhood Experience Score), through books or the Internet. This can be powerfully impactful, so seek help from a qualified helping professional if you need support. It could change your life!

I include this information in this brief chapter as I believe it relates to my own development growing up with my older adopted brother, and it may affect you. There is hope, and there is a way out. If you've been impressed, find the right time and place to express it, or it may depress you (or affect you in other ways). Again, *impression without expression leads to depression. Pain not transformed is pain transmitted.*

We can do together what each of cannot do alone! There is hope!

Chapter 8
The Neels and the McCools Not the Hatfields and the McCoys

The Neels and the McCools are my father's side of my family. McCool is my paternal grandmother's maiden name.

Because Neel is my last name, I have a particular interest in this lineage. Maybe this is also a reflection that our culture in America shows that the man's name is more important than the woman's name - at least until Women's Liberation seemed to result in a lot of women hyphenating their last names after they got married. My wife, Mary, changed her last name to "Carson-Neel" when we got married, but changed it to just "Neel," after 14 years of marriage because of difficulty with airline tickets and photo identification due to increased security after 9/11/2001.

I wonder to myself sometimes, asking "What if I was a woman?" Or if the rules in our culture were different or I was more liberated, and I had changed my name when I got married as a man? Would I then have less ownership in the Neel name? What is it like for a woman to lose a part of her identity when she marries if she changes her name to that of her new husband? I know some women who struggle with the choice of their last name when they divorce. I wonder about all of the women who have done genealogy research in our family, and wonder if they have different feelings about their last name than I do? (It seems I find more women interested in doing genealogy research than men do, but it is not an exclusive women's club here. Here is a shout out of "YEAH!" to the Kootenai County Genealogy Society of which I am a member.)

I can trace the Neel name through documents from Betty Thorson and Doris Neel Groves, and from my Internet searches. They found "John Neel, an immigrant from

Scotland" in the 1700's without a specific date of birth or death, or immigration date. He was seven generations back from me. And I have since found Neel ancestors further back to 1560 since I started my genealogy searches. (It's not well documented, but Internet searches have found Neill, born about 1560 in East Lothian, Scotland, my 15th great-grandfather.)

As stated elsewhere, the McCool name comes from my paternal grandmother's maiden name, Estelle "Stella" Agusta McCool (1883 – 1981). This grandmother lived to be age ninety-eight, and I have aspirations to live that long! I remember this grandmother fondly. She was very kind. She had unique physical features that clearly stand out in my memory, with large ears with unattached earlobes, and a large nose - I remember my Dad called these "Jack ears" from the family of Lydia Jack. (Lydia Jack, 1815 – 1881, was my great-great-grandmother, and she was married to my great-great-grandfather, William McCool, 1809 – 1882.) I remember this Grandma was a tiny, petite lady, and I wonder if this may be related to why I seem to be attracted to petite-sized women. I wonder if we had a family reunion with the Neels and the McCools together at the same time if we would physically see the differences and similarities between the Neel lineage and the McCool lineage? I did notice some similar physical features between myself and my siblings with our relatives of the McCool lineage at the three McCool family reunions that I have attended - see *Chapter 23 - McCools are Cool.* I attended McCool family reunions in 2003, 2004 and 2017.

Suggestion/Hint - There is nothing wrong with your genealogy search looking for your ancestors with the last name that was given to you which is placed on your birth certificate. This will help you focus for a while. But be open also to look for branches of your family tree with other last names. It will add richness and color to your family tree and to your own identity! It may make things confusing and overwhelming sometimes, but you'll get over that. That's family!

As stated elsewhere, my great-grandfathers, John Robinson "Honest John" Neel and William Andrew McCool, ran against each other for Sheriff of Red Willow County in Holbrook and Indianola, Nebraska. I wonder what year that was? I wonder if there were some political posters? Were they Democrats or Republicans? I'll bet that could stir up some "dirt"! I haven't heard any colorful stories of conflict (some call it "family dirt") between the Neels and the McCools, like stories of them shooting at each other across the gully like the Hatfields and McCoys, but I wonder if there are other interesting stories about these two families. I would think there has got to be some "dirt" since they ran against each other for a political office. It gets my imagination going when I wonder about what their relationships were like.

Before my great-grandfather, William Andrew McCool, who was the incumbent Sheriff and then ran for office of Sheriff against John Robinson Neel, he was the Postmaster General for Red Willow County, Indianola, Nebraska.

When my cousin, Penny B. died in 2017, and my younger brother cleaned out her house, he found and brought me two amazing documents, beautifully framed and preserved. They look like original signed documents signed by two presidents of the U.S. One is dated 1906, signed by Theodore Roosevelt, and the other is dated 1910, signed by William Howard Taft declaring our Great-Grandpa as Postmaster.

Photo of one of these framed documents declaring my great- grand-father, William Andrew McCool, as Postmaster of Red Willow County, Indianola, Nebraska, signed by Theodore Roosevelt, dated 1906.

I do find this a very interesting story :

"*<u>Memories of Stella McCool Neel</u>*" written in 1976 when she was age ninety-three. She lived until about age ninety-eight. She lived with my parents and our family in Alberton, Montana until she was about ninety-seven.

"*William McCool* (her grandfather who lived from 1809-1882) *bought scholarships for his sons Robert* (Robert James McCool, 1846-1911), *Will* (William Andrew McCool, 1856-1926), *and Calvin* (John Calvin McCool, 1843-1929). (William Andrew McCool would be Stella's father). *Cal and Will did not appreciate their father's sacrifices for the scholarship and ran away from college. They went to Wilton, Iowa to work on a farm. Sarah Garber's family were farmers. Will met Sarah at a School Social. When Sarah started to stir the fire, Will asked if he could help, and Sarah (flattered and embarrassed) handed him the hot end of the poker. Sarah later became his wife. Sarah went to church in the "Little Brown Church in the Vale," about which the song was written.*

"Will's brother Robert and Bell (Isabella "Belle" Hamilton) were to be married in Davenport, Iowa. Will and Sarah wanted to attend that wedding, but Sarah's mother (her father had died when Sarah was very young) would not let them go unless they themselves were married. They contacted the minister, who agreed to come to perform their marriage ceremony and started toward the farm and Sarah and Will started out toward town. They met the minister part way, and they got out of the buggy and the marriage was performed right there by the road. They went on to Davenport to attend Robert and Bell's wedding.

"Sarah and Will remained in Iowa, probably farming, for a couple of years. Minette (a.k.a. Nette or Net) *Margaret Elizabeth was born there. When Net was about one year old they moved to Nebraska, stopping in Red Cloud, Nebr., where Sarah's uncle Garber lived. They planted a field of potatoes and built a little sod house. For reasons unknown now they moved out West and settled on the divide north of*

Indianola (on a tree claim). Later they moved closer to Indianola and homesteaded. Will would drive his horses and wagon to Plumb Creek, which is near Kearney, and haul supplies, which had been shipped in on the Union Pacific Railroad. This trip would take several days and he would camp out at night. One of his favorite camps was east of what is now Holbrook, across the creek, where an Irishman lived who would come out and tell stories way into the night.
"Will taught school at Red Willow. Sarah would stay on the farm with the children while Will boarded out after riding horseback to the Willow.
*"Then Will was deputy sheriff in Indianola, Nebr., and then elected Sheriff. The family lived above the jail. Will liked playing cards with the prisoners. It was the only jail for six counties. When his term as sheriff was up the family moved to Missouri. Mr. Peterson, a former postmaster at Indianola had moved to Unionville, Mo., and wrote how nice it was there, so Will decided to move there, but experienced a lot of difficulties. The adobe stuck to the wheel spokes and they had to stop and punch it out before they could proceed. Their neighbor Jim McClung, helped drive Will's cattle down to Missouri. The cattle were all stolen. A relative sent Sarah $100 with which she bought sheep which turned out to be diseased and all died. They had lost everything and had to return to Indianola, Nebraska, by covered wagon, crossing the Missouri River by ferry. (*NOTE: I remember when my grandmother, Stella, was living with us she told us she remembered traveling by covered wagon to Nebraska as a child.) *They returned to the farm and the sod house which was always kept whitewashed, and had sheets covering the ceiling so dirt would not sift down. When dirt collected, Sarah would let one corner of the sheet down and remove the dirt. Their children were Net (or Nette, or Minnette), Emmet, Stella (about 6 years old at this time), Lydia, Gladys. Their younger children were Paul, Jessie and Fay. When Lydia was small, the family had a pet goose. Will would put corn in his pocket and then, while he was milking the goose would eat the corn out of his pocket. One day Lydia crawled out in the yard and the goose almost killed her, beating her with its*

wings. Will killed the goose, which they ate.

"They had a good corn crop, but prices were so low that they had to burn corn for fuel. Charlie Hartman, a neighbor, bought corn for 5 cents a bushel, built large storage bins, and sold it later for $1 a bushel.

"They moved to a farm on the divide and built a frame house. Will built a reservoir to catch the rainwater, which he used to irrigate the garden. They had a large barn. One night, after Will had burned off some grass, sparks ignited the barn and got close to the house, where the furniture was removed until the fire was put out. All neighbors came and helped rebuild the barn.

"Will had to get a job to supplement farming, so he ran for Sheriff but was defeated by "Honest John" Robinson Neel. Indianola's Postmaster was using Post Office money so was removed from his job. Will McCool was appointed to finish that term and remained for 17 years as postmaster. The family moved to town. Net helped her father Will in the Post Office, but wanted to teach school, so Stella went to work as assistant, until she married Frank Neel (son of former mentioned Sheriff "Honest John" Neel – these are my grandparents).

"Frank Neel worked in the lumber yard and previously went with Miss Stevens, who stayed at Mrs. Hoag's and worked in the bank. Miss Stevens and Stella went on a trip to Los Angeles, where they visited the Dolens, former bankers at Indianola who had gone to California and bought in Hollywood, and then sold at the high prices and became millionaires. Stella and Miss Stevens then proceeded up the coast to Seattle, Washington where they visited Irvin Barton, formerly from Indianola. They also attended the World's Fair. John Donnelly, former telegraph operator, had gone to Alaska, but came down to visit. Stella and Miss Stevens started back to Nebr., but Miss Stevens got ill in Salt Lake City, and being a Christian Science believer would not consult a doctor, so they were delayed a week until she felt better.

(Todd's comment here: Ah, there it is - *the Soup of Life* -

germ bugs! Were they the downfall of Miss Stevens so my grandmother would marry my grandfather instead?)

"Susie Collins, Stella's friend, boarded with the Hume family while teaching. Humes were from Illinois and worked on the newspaper. Susie and Paul Hume and Stella and Frank Neel were married, not in a double wedding, but the same day and all took the train to Kansas City for a wedding trip. Stella and Frank bought rugs, which they used in the house Frank had rented from the Ensleys in the east part of Holbrook, where Frank worked in the Perry Lumber Yard. (Many years later Frank's father, the aforementioned Sheriff "Honest John" Neel, after his wife died later married Mrs. Perry, who had a daughter Ada who never married. John Neel and Mrs. Perry got a divorce).

"John and Floyd (Neel) were born while Stella and Frank lived in the Ensley house (Todd's comment: John is my dad and Floyd would be my uncle that I never met). *When the older Ensleys wanted to move to town Frank, Stella, John and Floyd moved to the Neel Hotel, which Frank's father* ("Honest John" Robinson Neel) *had taken in a trade, until the home they were having built in the west end of Holbrook by A.D. Lord, Bill Bible, and Mr. Lucky, was finished."*

(Todd's comment - My recollection is that my Dad told me that his Dad, Frank Neel, had such a nice house because his Dad, was part owner of the lumber yard. There is confusion about "The Neel Motel" and what this is referring to in the previous paragraph).

On the next page is a photo of what I think is the Neel home that was built in the west end of Holbrook, Nebraska referred to in the paragraph above. It appears to be an old black and white photo of the same home that I found in my Dad's photo box without any writing on it, and with the family in the front yard here. So that could my grandparents sitting on the front porch, and I'm assuming the tallest child on the left in the front yard is my Dad, as he was the oldest.

The photo, below, of the Neel home in Holbrook, Nebraska is taken in 1987. On the back is a hand written note which says: *"June 1987 - Tillie took these pictures of our old house and sent them to me. The house certainly looks well cared for doesn't it?"* (Does anyone know who Tillie is? If so, I'd like to hear from you).

And below is a photo I took of the Neel family home (with me in the photo) in Holbrook, Nebraska as I was traveling through in August 2004.

You can see there are differences between the photographs, as modifications have been made in the home. You can see the elimination of the upstairs deck, but half of the door left behind in the later photograph. (See *Chapter 20 - Saga of a Pilgrimage* later in this book for this story.)

(Todd's comment: Does anyone reading this remember the "Neel Hotel"? Does anyone have a picture of it? If anyone knows I would appreciate some clarity. If there is a "Neel Hotel" and has a photo of it, I would really appreciate a copy of it!)

Below are more comments from my grandmother, Stella (McCool) Neel:

"Frank Neel represented the Odd Fellows, and Susie Collins Hume the Auxiliary at a convention in Omaha. Mrs. George Scott was there from Holbrook, and Frank introduced Susie to her. Later Mrs. Scott said she had already met Frank's wife, who had mistaken Susie for Frank's wife in Omaha.

"James (Mac) Neel was born in the new home July 7, 1917, and Sarah on Nov. 29, 1918, and Vera Fay on July 3, 1920. (Todd's comments: These are my aunts and uncles that I got to know well.) *When Floyd was 15 he became ill. Dr. Minnick, who had grown up with Stella and Frank in Indianola, was practicing in Cambridge, the next town. Dr. Minnick was called. Floyd was bleeding internally and died in a short time. Floyd was a great mimic, and Mrs. Myrtle Coppom asked Stella once if she realized she repeated more things Floyd said and did than all the other children, and Stella said "He just says and does more things."*

(Todd's comments: I recall the story that Floyd was injured when the school janitor, Bill S's father, threw a basketball at Floyd which eventually killed him, and that it was an accident. Bill S. later married Vera Neel, Floyd's sister). (NOTE: I designate this "S." family with just an initial as I am currently unable to locate them for permission to use their name.)

"That same year, 1930, John graduated and was still home when Frank phoned Stella to send John to the lumber yard with the car, and he found Frank, his father, slumped on the floor. Somehow he got him in the car and home, where a neighbor, Mr. Charlie Burner, helped get him inside the house. Stella phoned for Dr. Minnick, who was on another call at the time, but his wife Flossie met him and sent him right down to Holbrook. At first he didn't think Frank would live, but after working over him awhile Frank revived. The doctor asked that a bed be brought downstairs and Frank should not move until his heart improved. A nurse was hired and Frank wasn't out of the house for a year except for a ride around the block one time for a bit of fresh air, and because of that, part of his insurance was cut off. Son John (my Dad) *was put in charge of the lumberyard for the time Frank was disabled. When Frank was able to return to work John applied to the Naval Academy at Annapolis and was accepted. Shon Land and Mac took John back to Annapolis in a Model "T" Ford Roadster.*

(Todd's comment: I have some recollections of my Dad's story about the trip to Annapolis in this car - I wish it had been recorded.)

"Earlier, a niece, Georgia McCool, came down from Indianola to stay with Stella and Frank to attend school. (She was in Bill W's class). At another time Betty Malleck, another niece, attended Holbrook school and stayed with the Neel family. One year Betty and Phyllis Hanson stayed with the Neels and went to school while Sarah stayed with their parents and taught in their country school.

(Todd's comment - Was this Bill W., mentioned in the previous paragraph, the father of Neal E. W., the author of the story "Bill: A Small-Town Nebraskan and His WW II Service"?)

"John Neel graduated from Annapolis in 1937, and the entire family went to see him graduate. Beth Keyes, John's high school girl friend and later his wife, also attended the graduation.

"Frank Neel died in April, 1938, of a heart attack.

"Note about the Jim McClung family who helped Will McCool move his cattle to Missouri. Dub McClung, Jim's son, went to the University and studied pharmacy and later took drugs. Mable _____(?) married him and brought him back to the farm, but he never straightened out. Jim had another son Jack. One day a lady came by and wanted to give the McClungs her baby son Cecil, who was dirty and sickly looking and covered with sores. First they said "no" and the lady drove away. Jim McClung ran after and agreed to take the baby. Their own son Jack was near the same age. Later both took whooping cough, and Jack died. McClungs were bitter that Cecil lived and their son died, so they gave Cecil to M/M Dutcher, who kept him a while. One day Jim McClung was in the Post Office and Cecil and Mr. Dutcher came in, and Cecil grabbed Jim around the legs and cried. Then Jim laid his head down on the counter and cried too. Then he took Cecil home again. Later Will McCool had

Cecil's mother sign papers and Cecil was adopted by the McClungs."

(Comment from Todd: I find this last paragraph fascinating, as I was a social worker with Idaho child protection services (CPS), and I have done adoption work. I wonder what CPS and the addictions fields were like back then.)
(Comment from Todd: I have a suspicion that my aunt Vera S. wrote the story of the Memories of Stella (McCool) Neel on these pages, maybe from interviewing my grandmother Stella, who would be my aunt Vera's mother.)

Below is an interesting newspaper story, the obituary for William McCool, my great-great grandfather, who is the grandfather of my grandmother, Stella (McCool) Neel, and the father of William Andrew McCool. From maps I found that Davenport, NE and Indianola, NE are 140 miles apart:

"The Davenport Democrat
Obituary of William McCool
September 8. 1882
Another Old Pioneer Who Has Crossed the "Dark River of Death"

"The heart rending intelligence was conveyed by a telegram from Indianola, Neb., last evening to Miss Allie McCool, of this city, that her father Wm. McCool, was dead. His death was very sudden, for he had been sick but a few days, when he passed away. The first intimation his daughters here had that he was dangerously ill, or even sick at all, was by receipt of a telegram last Monday morning, and on the same evening, Miss Lyde McCool started for Indianola, where she arrived, on Wednesday evening, only to find out that her father had died a few hours previously - or at noon on the same day. Through some mistakes she failed to take the right train, delaying her several hours, and thus, unfortunately, she deprived of the consolation of being with her father in his dying moments. The other two daughters-Allie and Margaret, were on the eve of starting for Indianola, when the sad news reached them. They were overwhelmed in grief, being doubly orphaned in less than a year - their venerable mother having died in October last. Soon after that event, the now deceased father went to visit his son William who owns a farm in Indianola, where he has tarried over since, and at whose resident he died. The nature of the disease is not known at the present, but it was startlingly fatal, as only last week his children received a letter from him in which he stated he was coming home next Monday.

"William McCool, was one of the old settlers in this county, and was well known, and respected by a large circle of friends. He has led a quiet and retired life all his days, devoting himself to home and family, but ever forward in the work of the church of which he was a member. Honest in all his dealings with his fellow man, a true friend, a good citizen, a kind neighbor, a devoted husband and a loving father, he enjoyed the esteem and respect of all who knew him. He was born in Allegheny County, Pa., in 1809, and at the time of his death was 73 years old. He came to Le Claire in 1846, near which place he bought a farm, on which he resided until 1863, when he removed with his family to this city, and engaged in the grocery business for two years thereafter. Since that time he has not been in active business of any kind. He leaves six children, besides a number of grandchildren and relatives to mourn his loss. Three of his children, Misses Lyde A., Maggie, and Allie are residents of this city, and well known as school teachers William, the son at Indianola, at whose house he died; John C., residing in Clarence, Iowa, and Robert J. McCool, living in Tyler, Texas. The nature of the disease was such that the body could not be brought here for burial, and his remains rest in the cemetery at Indianola. The stricken daughters have the sympathy of their fellow teachers and a host of friends in this hour of their terrible affliction."

Other Notes for WILLIAM MCCOOL:

Scotch families, McCool and Jack, settled in Northern Ireland and feuded with the Catholic peasant Irish. The trouble came to a head. Finally the Irish were going to run the Scotch-Irish out, but a friendly Patrick tipped them off. They had planned to come to America for some time, so that decided them. When they tried to reward Patrick he asked only that they name a baby "Patrick" for him. So there was a Patrick Jack and a Patrick McCool in the new land. Aunt Lyde also told of General Jack, Revolutionary War hero. (This would be a cousin)
(source: Shirley Ashburn)

(NOTE from Todd: This story was also verbally conveyed to me at the 2017 McCool family reunion in Oregon.)

Notes for JOHN CALVIN MCCOOL (born 1783 or 1787 in County Down, Ireland, and died February 16, 1841):

EMIGRANT PASSENGER LIST TAKEN FROM THE HANDBOOK ON IRISH GENEALOGY In Tri-County Researcher (Proctor, WV), vol. 8:1 (January 1984), pp. 911-912.

(NOTE from Todd: These are the kinds of records that genealogists dig deep into. For the purpose of this book for public consumption, I will not include all of them.)

In my records and Family Hunger books for family

consumption, I have many family photos which I will not include in this book for public consumption. If you were to document your own family story, these records would be treasures for generations to come.

NOTE: I want to acknowledge my appreciation for Betty Thorson and Doris Neel Grove and their books, "Neel Genealogy" and "A Continuation of the Neel Genealogy" as well as the many other family members who kept photos and stories and passed them on to the next generations.

Chapter 9
Sojourn into Montana, home of my heart

We head out of Coeur d'Alene, ancient home of the Schitsu'umsh - the discovered people. French fur traders called them this: *heart of an awl* (not owl, rather *awl*, a sharp pointed tool). These native people were described as tribal traders, tough businessmen, *sharp-hearted* and *shrewd*.

Seeking escape into the mountains, we look for sanctuary from the sharp edges of town. With me sits my friend, Bonnie, in a *sharp edged box* in the seat beside me.

Heading east and passing through the Silver Valley, we roll past historic mining towns where in 1895 Noah Kellogg's jackass found him precious metals. He had gone to sleep and during the night his mule wondered off. In the morning he heard her braying high on the hillside, and where he found her standing saw sunshine glittering on a huge outcropping of galena (lead ore). That was the discovery of the great Bunker Hill and Sullivan Mines.

We continue east and summit Lookout Pass on Interstate 90, leaving Idaho behind and flow into Montana, home of my heart.

Montana, where I lived from age ten, during the years of my developing consciousness like the image forming on paper in a tray of chemicals in a photographic darkroom.

Montana, the forming of my identity. Am I still that good boy that cares to please my parents? Or that seeker of my friends' approval, that sneaker of gin from my parents' booze cabinet? That story is now far behind me, black and white in my rear view mirror, for review. Or is it in front of me in full technicolor, waiting for relapse? I remember where I got the metal plate in my leg - my own precious metal, where as a boy/man in 1973 I discover the seeds of alcoholism in car vs. pine tree.

We roll down Lookout Pass into Montana, scanning for the first exit off I-90. There it is! The Hiawatha Trail, ancient railroad grade turned into commercial bike trail, managed by *sharp-hearted or sharp-witted* businessmen. (They may be more soft-hearted than I give them credit for, though.)

This road leads me off the pavement, where we slow down from highway speed to earth speed. I roll down my windows and drink in deep the intoxicating smells of fresh pine, fir and hemlock. I hear gurgling, rushing streams, and the crunch of my tires on gravel.

Leaving the crowd even farther behind, we turn away from cars full of families and friends heading to pay their fee to ride through historic railroad tunnels and lofty trestles soaring over creeks with the eagles.

We know a secret place. Or at least I'd like to think of it that way where few and fewer people travel, and I might go all day and not see another soul. Maybe I'm seeking my own soul. I envision Bonnie running around the peak, ears flying like wings in the wind. Nothing like a dog off leash, free to fly as she wishes!

We behold deer dancing, and eavesdrop on beautiful bird songs singing one another to bed. The woods smell so sweet.

We head to the top of the divide, straddling the Montana-Idaho border. There we find our home for the night as the blazing sun sets on the western horizon: Dominion Peak, where the bones of an old Forest Service lookout remain. Those rangers knew how to find a good view!

A hawk, cruising in the wind over the peak, holds steady like a kite tethered on a string, beholding us.

As the light fades, so do the distant frozen rollers of mountain peaks and ridges, like a sea of solid highland waves. They are frozen in my eyes, measured by my time. But by geologic time, they are actively moving, rising, falling. The earth is alive.

We have traveled all this way to stand in a special place as I sprinkle Bonnie's ashes in a circle around this peak. I feel the grit of her bones on my fingers. I sense our faithful four-legged family member in my heart and remember the softness of her fur on my face. I decide this is where I want my remains scattered, to flow north into Montana to the St.

Regis River watershed, and south into Idaho to the St. Joe River drainage.

I'm here because my heart is in Montana, and this jackass (me) is in Idaho – with my own precious metal in my leg – with tears in my eyes missing my furry friend.

Sojourn To Place Of Heart

(Note: This version of the chapter, below, won 1st Place prize for "Nonfiction Book Excerpt" in an Idaho Writers League contest. One of the judges commented that while they liked the piece, they did not like the last line of this version, and it might cause them to stop reading further. Along with other feedback from the judges and from friends and family members, I re-wrote it to create the version, above. There is nothing like "writing by committee." Below is the prize winning version, with apologies for redundancy. You make your choice.)

As I head out of town
and into the mountains,
I summit over Lookout Pass on Interstate 90,
leaving Idaho behind
and flow into Montana,
home of my heart.

Montana,
where I lived from age 10,
the years of my developing consciousness
like the image forming on paper in a tray of chemicals
in a photograph darkroom.

Montana,
the forming of my identity.
Who am I?
The good boy that pleases my parents?
Or that seeker of my friends' approval,
that sneaker of gin
from my parents' booze cabinet?

That story is now far behind me,
in my review mirror.
Or is it in front of me,
as I roll down Lookout Pass
into Montana

as I scan for the first exit off I-90?

There it is: The Hiawatha Trail.
It leads me off the pavement,
where I slow down
from highway speed to earth speed,
where I can roll down my windows
and smell the fresh pine and fir trees
and hear the gurgling and rushing streams
and the sound of my tires on the gravel.

I leave the crowd even farther behind
as I turn away from the cars
full of families and friends
heading to pay their fee
to ride the Hiawatha Bike Trail.

I know a secret place.
Or at least I'd like to think of it that way
where few and fewer people travel,
and I might go all day
and not see another soul.

Maybe I'm seeking my own soul.

To head to the top of the divide,
to straddle the Montana-Idaho border
to Dominion Peak,
which I find as the sun sets
on the western horizon.

Dominion Peak,
where the bones
of an old Forest Service lookout remain.
Those Rangers knew how to find a good view.

As the light faded,
so did the distant frozen waves
of mountain peaks and ridges.

Like a sea of solid mountain waves.
They are frozen in my eyes,
measured by my time.
But by geologic time,
they are actively moving,
rising, falling.
The earth is alive.

Scattering of Bonnie's ashes
in a circle around this peak,
I decide this is where
I want my ashes scattered,
to flow into Montana to the St. Regis River drainage
and into Idaho to the St. Joe River drainage.

I'm here because
my heart is in Montana,
and my ass is in Idaho.

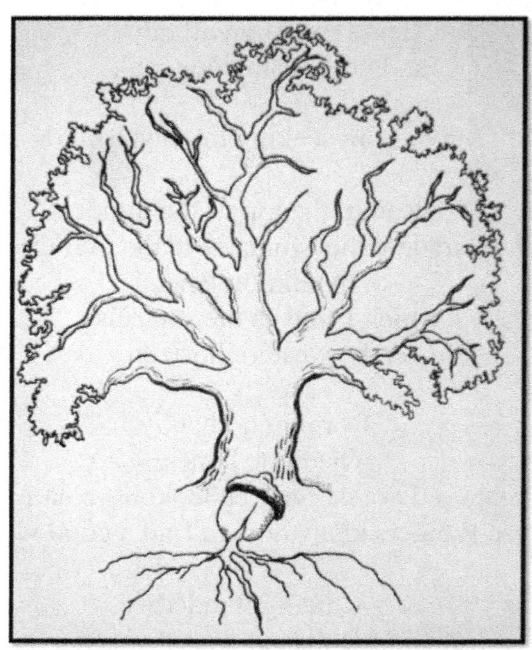

Chapter 10
John William Neel
My Dad

(d.o.b. 1/7/1914 – d.o.d. 5/24/1994)

Autobiography
(written for his sister Vera (Neel) S.)

"After graduating from Holbrook, Nebraska High School in 1930 I took over running the Lumber Yard while Dad (William Franklin Neel) was recovering from a heart attack. When he was well enough to take over, I went to Annapolis Prep School and then into the Naval Academy. After waiting the required 2 years after graduation I married my high school sweetheart Beth Keyes in Vallejo, California on June 4, 1939. After more schooling I was transferred to Destroyer Division as Paymaster on the USS Shaw stationed in Pearl Harbor when the Japanese attacked and the Shaw was hit.

"Families of servicemen were evacuated from Honolulu to the States. Beth was ill with cancer and it was arranged for Mom and Sarah to move from Holbrook to live with Vera in Richmond, California and take care of Beth, who died January 13, 1943. I had been sent to Naval Air Station (NAS) Jacksonville, Florida for a year. Then was sent out to the Islands Guadalcanal, Los Negros, Samar and the Cavite Navy Yard.

"After the war I was assigned NAS Alameda, California where I met a WAVE Alice Johnson, who became my wife Sept. 28, 1946. A tour at NAS Ford Island, then served on board the USS Oriskany. I was sent to Naval War College. Last 2 duties at Pensacola with Com Air Training and in New York City with Com East Sea Frontier. New York City is no place for a sailor, and after 3 years there, they were

going to send me to the worse place for a sailor, Washington, DC. So in 1966 I quit after serving 29 years, and headed west in a covered wagon (a travel trailer we called The Delicate Pioneer). After traveling around the country looking for that ideal spot to retire, for no good reason except that it was a long ways from New York City and it looked like a good place to raise children, dropped the hook in Missoula, Montana.

"It was a good place to raise children, but not to find that second career pot-of-gold. Since I had a lot of experience with computers in the service, I tried my hand in that field, but in 1966 Missoula was not ready for Computer Consultants (COMSYTEC). I then tried the rent-a-car business for a while (Budget Rent-a-Car), but that didn't make any money either. By then the children had finished school, so we moved a little ways out of Missoula and built our dream home in the woods above the river.
(Todd's comment - This was their "castle in the woods" near Alberton, Montana where they had 20 acres between the Clark Fork River and Forest Service land at the top of their property.)

"Alice died of cancer September 4, 1980. ... Living up on this hill in the middle of a beautiful Larch grove, with the river down below, and the children within Montana-commuting distance is nice. It is hard to remember having been a sailor for 33 years. Yet every so often the thought sneaks in. There was something special about being at sea. Shipmates were always special people. The job was always challenging. It was a good life."

Resume for John William Neel

John William Neel completed a thirty-three year Naval Career on 6/30/1966 with the grade of Captain, Supply Corps, U.S. Navy.

Decorations, Campaign Ribbons, etc. - Bronze Star Medal,

American Defense Service Medal, American Campaign Medal Asiatic, Pacific Campaign Medal, Philippine Liberation Ribbon, World War II Victory Medal, National Defense Service Medal, Korean Service Medal, United Nations Service Medal.

1930 Graduated High School, Holbrook, Nebraska.
1930-1932 Perry Lumber Co., Holbrook, Nebraska.
1932-1933 Cochran-Bryan Preparatory School, Annapolis, Md.
1933-1937 U.S. Naval Academy, Annapolis, Md. Midshipman Student. Bachelor of Marine Engineering Degree.
1937-1938 U.S.S. SARATOGA (Aircraft Carrier). Assistant Gun Division Officer. Assistant Communications Officer. Assistant Navigator.
1938-1939 U.S.S. DORSEY (Destroyer). Engineering Officer.
1939-1940 Finance and Supply School, Philadelphia, Pa. Student.
1940-1942 Destroyer Division Six, U.S.S. SHAW, Pearl Harbor, Hawaii. Division Disbursing Officer. Military payrolls.
1942-1943 Naval Air Station, Jacksonville, Florida.
1943-1945 Staff, Commander Air South Pacific, and Commander, Air Seventh Fleet, Guadalcanal and Philippines.
1945-1948 Naval Air Station, Alameda, California. Head, Stock Control Division, Senior Assistant to Supply Officer, and Supply Officer. 1100 employees. $250 million inventory of aviation repair parts and other materials.
1948-1949 Naval Air Station, Pearl Harbor, Hawaii. Head, Supply Department. 200 employees. Managed inventories of material for the support of operating aircraft and the industrial operation of aircraft overhaul; accounting and budgeting for station operating funds; operated mess for feeding of crew; operated retail grocery store. Conducted operation to pack and ship the inventories of material upon the closing of the Air Station.

1949 Air Force comptrollers School, Selma, Alabama. Student.
1950-1953 Aviation Supply Office, Philadelphia, Pa. Head, Planning Division. 30 employees. Systems and procedures development for the management of the Navy's aviation spare parts, i.e. an inventory of $1.2 billion (400,000 items) located at 63 stations. Collection of statistical data regarding the deployment and hours of operation of aircraft to be supported and the effectiveness of the aviation supply system in supporting them. Development of system to report number of aircraft grounded for lack of parts.
Head, Stock Control Division. 600 employees. Management (budgeting, determining requirements, distributing material) of the aviation repair parts inventory. Participated in development of programs to use Univac I computer in the management of the system inventory of parts.
1953-1954 Naval War College, Newport, Rhode Island. Student. Strategy and Logistics Course.
1954-1956 U.S.S. ORISKANY (Aircraft Carrier), Pacific Ocean. Supply Officer of the ship. 200 men, $2,000,000 inventory. Procurement, stowage, and issue of stores and repair parts for ships and its aircraft; accounting for ship's material inventories and funds; payment of bills; payment of crew; operation of retail store, clothing store; feeding crew; feeding officers and operating wardroom.
1956-1958 Headquarters, Commandant, 11th Naval District, San Diego, California. Assistant to District Supply Officer. Inspections of supply and accounting functions of the 39 activities of the Naval District. Initial studies to place supply and accounting records of a Naval Supply Depot on IBM 650 machine.
1958-1960 Naval Shipyard, Pearl Harbor, Hawaii. Head of Supply Department. $90,000,000 inventory of supplies, 230 employees. Primary function was to provide the repair parts and raw materials to the industrial operations of the shipyard. Developed system to mechanize the translation of material planning for ship work into card form requisitions. Initial studies to place inventory records on IBM 1401 computer.

1960-1963 Headquarters, Chief of Naval Air Training, Pensacola, Florida. Development of decentralized supply system for the smaller stations of the command. Development of problem parameters for design of a pilot training/resources programs. Development of new concept for organization of retail sales/food service/clubs/recreation functions of a large Naval Air Station.
1963-1966 Headquarters, Commander Eastern Sea Frontier/ Atlantic Reserve Fleet, New York, N.Y. Logistics planning for the coordination of sources and supply and transportation from U.S. to the Fleet and overseas bases. Organizational alignments of supporting shore stations. Supply system redesign to take fuller advantage of computer capabilities.

Here is a photograph of my father, Capt. John William Neel, U.S. Navy

He was born on 1/7/1914, and died on 5/24/1994. This photo was taken on 2/8/1963 when he was age 49. He attended the U.S. Naval Academy in Annapolis, Maryland. He was at the bombing of Pearl Harbor, Hawaii on 12/7/1941 when the Japanese were dropping bombs on his ship, the U.S.S. Shaw, while it was in dry dock and he was home mowing the lawn watching these "funny looking planes" fly overhead. He used computers to keep track of inventory in the Supply Corp after his eyes went "bad" and he couldn't do "watch" as an officer on a ship wearing glasses (those were the rules in those days, he told me).

Here is a photograph of my father, John William Neel, as an infant.

He appears to be in a baptismal dress. I'm wondering if this photo was taken on the same day as the next photo because of the baptismal dress. I look at this picture and I think, hmmm, those hands look familiar …

Here is a photograph which has written on the back: "1914 Grandfather Neel, Frank, and John. Our first home in Holbrook, Nebr."

This picture is of my father as an infant sitting on his grandfather's lap - that of John Robinson Neel (5/17/1847 – 5/29/1931), and my grandfather William Franklin "Frank" Neel (4/14/1876 – 4/30/1938) - whom I never met. I'm assuming this note written on the back is in my paternal grandmother's handwriting, Stella (McCool) Neel, who may be standing in the doorway. It appears that my father may be wearing his baptismal dress, and this photo may have been taken on the same day that photo was taken on the previous page. I wonder who took this photo and what kind of camera they had used? (I wish that camera was in my collection.) I ponder history and consider that my great-grandfather here was born before and lived during our American Civil War. My grandfather here was born about ten years after the end of the Civil War (which lasted between 1861 – 1865), and he lived during the time of World War I (1914 – 1918). My father was born at the beginning of WW I. The historical context of our ancestors' lives help us appreciate the fragility of life.

John W. Neel
My Dad

by Todd W. Neel
and other family members

NOTE: This chapter was originally written about the year 2000, after my Dad died, and has been edited and added to as the years go by.

With the anniversary of Pearl Harbor Day occurring, I was sharing stories with co-workers at my office about my Dad being in Honolulu on the date of the attack on Pearl Harbor by the Japanese on 12/7/1941. I shared stories that were clear in my memory about Dad and his stories, and I realized that I had not committed them to print - to try to make the record a little bit more permanent. I'll try to do that here.

On that Sunday morning, Dad said he was home mowing the lawn when these "funny looking planes" flew overhead on the way to Pearl Harbor to bomb his (and others') ships. His ship, a destroyer named the U.S.S. Shaw, was in dry dock. Japanese bombs hit the ammunition magazines in his ship and there were resulting large explosions which were made famous because of pictures taken. Dad told the story about driving around the island and having his car headlights painted out so it couldn't be seen as well by the enemy after that. He said he went down to his ship later with divers, who went down to his office which was then underwater, and his office had been split open by the explosions. The divers went under water in the "dry" dock and found the safe had been blown open. Dad was the paymaster for the ship, and they paid sailors in cash in those days. The divers brought up remains of cash, which were put in a box. He tried to find a bank in Hawaii that would accept this cash, but none would accept it. He had to send the remains to the mainland, and he was given credit for (what I recall) was $100,000 more than he calculated was in the safe.

Dad also told the story about his first wife Beth. He said she was diagnosed with cancer in Honolulu, and the way the doctor gave them the bad news was to go to his shelves, pull down a book and open it, and pointed out an entry. The doctor told them "This is what your wife has" and left the room and let them read it. Because it was war time, Beth was shipped stateside, and died in California on 1/13/1943 being cared for by family members. In my Dad's papers I found a letter from him to his commanding officer requesting permission to be relieved of duty to be able to go and bury his wife. I also found another letter from Dad written very soon after that to his commanding officer requesting permission to return to duty.

Another story about my Dad was when he lived home with his parents in Holbrook, Nebraska. His father, Frank William Neel, ran a lumber yard and while at work his father had a heart attack. My Dad had to go to the lumber yard and bring his father home. The doctor was called for, but he was away for another patient visit in another town, and the doctor's wife found him and told him to go to the Neel home in Holbrook. The doctor said my grandfather needed to stay in the home with bed rest for recovery, and they brought a bed downstairs into the front room for his rest. Later in recovery, they took him for a car ride to get out of the house, and the insurance company found out about it and stopped insurance payments because it was against doctor's orders. My Dad ran the lumber yard for a while as his father recovered from his heart attack.

Christmas 1979 in Alberton, Montana with my Mom (Alice, center in back) and Dad (John, front on right), my grand-mother (Stella (McCool) Neel, center in front), myself (back, on right) and my two bio-siblings.

Chapter 11
Todd William Neel
My Life

(d.o.b. 7/25/1955 to d.o.d. - not yet!)
Autobiography

As I stated in the introduction of this book, this work is inspired by those living and those who have passed away. These include my family, friends, and also the "Soup of Life!", the mix of human and non-human beings that are part of the mix (sickness and premature death are part of my story).

I had been intending to compile my family history for a long time, and there have been a few people and events that pushed me over the edge to generate the inertia that I can't seem to stop, like white water over the lip of the falls.

As with my Dad and Mom, so much of our lives go on without being noticed, without being recorded, or without being remembered. I hope my life has been significant, that it has made a difference for someone, and that it will be worth remembering. I wish that my life will be thought of as constructive rather than as destructive, with positive reminisce and not recalled by the factory as a defect.

My parents' lives mattered and made a difference for me. I wouldn't be here without them! They had a positive influence on me, and any errors are forgiven. There are things about them I can recall, things that I know I forgot, and things I am distorting in my memory. There are inquiries unanswered, unasked, and questions were forgotten. But they aren't around anymore to ask. Lives fly by!

Have you ever wondered if your life mattered? Have you made a difference? How will you be remembered? Does this cause you to consider the questions you think others might have for you? Have you written your life story yet, your autobiography?

In case you want help remembering my life (as someday I will need help in recalling it), here it is:

I was born on July 25, 1955, in San Diego, California. My family left for Hawaii when I was quite young. According to my Dad's resume, he was at sea for the Navy when I was born, then in San Diego from 1956-1958. As my younger brother was born in Hawaii in June 1958, it is not clear when we moved. I have no conscious memories of California as a child.

I did research later and found the home and the owner of the San Diego house that we lived in - see *Chapter 21 - Finding the home of my parents and the hospital where I was born – Welcome Home!*

When my younger brother was born in Hawaii he had significant medical problems at birth (some sort of growth around his windpipe), so he had to stay in the hospital for quite a while. He had a tracheotomy, and he still has scars on his throat. I have a vague recollection of hearing the news the day he was born when I was about three.

I have some conscious memories of Hawaii - like images of our yard, the street in front of our house, and the sweet smell of flowers, but I don't know how accurate these memories are.

Now, as I re-write this chapter, I wonder how many readers of this book will care about how sweet the smells were, the colors of my favorite toys, or the magic of when I saw my first snowfall, etc. I am now using those memories in a separate, more personal journal, and leaving the highlights for you, here. (You might try a brainstorming exercise for yourself, trying to remember as far back as you can from your earliest memories using as many of your senses as possible to access details and emotions, and making choices about what you share with others as it might make or break your relationship with your audience.) I hope I am not losing you here.

According to my Dad's resume, it looks like we lived in Hawaii for only about two years before we moved to Pensacola, Florida in 1960.

I have more memories of Pensacola, likely as I was

developmentally a little older. One of the two houses we lived in there was on "Captain's Hill" in a lovely brick house with screened in front porches and a huge yard with palm trees and long hanging moss like old men's beards blowing in the wind.

Photo of our family home on Captain's Hill" in Pensacola, Florida.

We moved from Florida to Mountain Lakes, New Jersey in 1963 where my Dad had his last tour of duty for the Navy on the island of Manhattan in New York City. He commuted to work daily ninety minutes each way on public transportation (by train and subway) so we could live in a friendly suburban community instead of the big city. Wow, how my life would have been changed if we had lived in N.Y.C.!

I was in the Third, Fourth, and Fifth grades in New Jersey. We could run freely and feel safe through the neighborhood until after dark in the summertime. I still have a mental map in my head of where our house was, the path to school, how to pass under the railroad bridge to get to the gas station, soda fountain, and the bakery. The abundant lakes and canals in between offered ice skating on deep, thick, black ice in the winter.

I remember our older, adopted brother, "Bob," starting to get into trouble with the law in New Jersey, and a story about him in the newspaper because he stole an expensive painting from a vehicle which he presented to one of my parents as a birthday gift. I got a bloody nose from him, the only one I ever remember from a fight. "Bob" and a friend of his convinced me that it would be cool to go into their underground play fort when they threw a smoke bomb in after me and slammed the door shut. I recall my sister being so mad at him that she threw an ashtray at him and locked him out of the house.

In 1966 my Dad had a choice of doing another tour of duty in Washington, DC, but instead, he decided to retire early at fifty-two years of age. My parents bought a travel trailer, and upon his retirement, we took off across the country in it. We drove up through New York state, into Canada, over to Montana, and down into Missoula were we lived in our trailer in a KOA campground while our house was being built up the Rattlesnake Creek in a new sub-division called Lincolnwood.

I had the first newspaper route in Lincolnwood with eighteen deliveries of The Missoulian. When we moved out of this home in 1976, my younger brother had the paper route with over two hundred homes to deliver to.

I finished grade school at Rattlesnake Elementary (sixth through eighth grades), completed Hellgate High School, and obtained my Bachelor's degree in psychology at the University of Montana.

I think of Missoula as more of my "home" than anywhere else, in my heart. This is because of the many significant developmental milestones that I achieved when I was more conscious in my development, and maturing emotionally on some levels. More lifetime friends and first-time experiences were planted here, with wonderful memories as an Eagle Boy Scout and hiking in the wilderness, running whitewater rivers in the family canoe, the thrill of downhill skiing, the thrill of a first kiss, first date, and other indicators of growing up. (I later learned about boys moving out of Scouts because of "fumes," meaning perfume, exhaust fumes, and for me marijuana fumes.) My first intoxications on alcohol and drugs occurred here (see *Chapter 16 - My Alcoholism – A Family Deal* about my chemical dependency and recovery – thirty-seven years sober now as of this writing in 2018).

Picture of our family home in Missoula, Montana, with Mt. Jumbo in the background.

In 1976 my family moved from Missoula to twenty acres on the side of a mountain near Alberton, Montana, about thirty miles away. This was the year my youngest brother graduated from high school with his friends (the timing such that he didn't have to leave his supports). In building the home we had a construction crew do the foundation, and they framed and enclosed the house. My Dad and I stayed out on the property in the travel trailer working on electrical, plumbing, insulating, sheet-rocking, and finishing the home. Everyone in the family came and helped, of course, but I remember spending a lot of time alone with my Dad and learning how to build a house - an important part of my development and my relationship with him.

Photo of our family home in Alberton, Montana. Both of my parents died in this home.

About 1978 my Mom was diagnosed with cancer. My paternal grandmother, Stella (McCool) Neel, was living with us at the time but she had to leave because it was too much for my Dad to care for both Grandma in her aging years, and my

Mom with cancer. Grandma went to live with other family members in California where she finally died at ninety-eight years of age in 1981.

My Mom was able to attend my college graduation from the University of Montana (UM) in 1980, but in a wheelchair because of her illness. I recall looking up for her in the UM Harry Adams Field House and realizing she had to leave before the graduation ceremony was over, impacting my awareness that this was a great hardship for her. After I graduated, my parents asked me to stay home and not look for a job so I could help Dad in taking take care of Mom. She finally died at home on September 4, 1980, at the age of fifty-nine – way too young.

Both of my parents' ashes are scattered on the mountain behind their "castle on the hill" near Alberton, as my Dad waited fourteen more years, alone, for his end in 1994. (He wasn't really alone as I'm grateful for my brother and sister and their families in caring for our Dad. Our father just didn't have any other friends besides his wife.)

All of my living siblings still reside in Montana as far as I know, as we haven't heard from our older adopted brother for about 15 years now as of this writing. (As stated elsewhere in this book, as of September 2018 we may have found that he's still alive, and where he may be.)

My identity is tied up with Montana. I was ten years old when we moved to Missoula, and I was twenty-nine years old when I left Montana for Spokane, Washington to attend graduate school. I met Mary Carson in Missoula (who is now my wife), and she also says she misses Montana.

We moved to Coeur d'Alene in 1987, got married here in 1989, and raised our children here in Idaho.

After graduating with my MSW (Masters of Social Work) in 1986, I had a few different jobs until landing in my career job in 1990 in Coeur d'Alene with the Idaho Department of Health and Welfare (see Resume below). The benefits and security of working for the state of Idaho allowed me to raise a family here. Mary has been working as a social worker at Hospice of North Idaho for over 30 years now (as of this writing in 2018).

Our firstborn son, Nathan, arrived in 1992 and our second son, Joshua, was born in 1994. Both boys were born in Spokane because Mary had a doctor she liked who practiced in Spokane, which is only 30 miles from Coeur d'Alene. We purchased our first and only home in 1992, and we're pretty comfortable here except for a few gripes about not enough space in the house and the neighbors' noise at times.

Right now, I'm trying to thrive instead of just survive. We're getting through the tasks of daily living, family life, watching our kids grow up and participating in their development as best we can. I know our time with our children is very brief before they become independent, so we try to cherish it. They are young adults now, as of this writing in 2018.

I have been busy with recovery, work, friendships, men's work, photography, genealogy, and recreation here in the northwest (camping, whitewater canoeing, skiing, etc.).

I was on the volunteer Ski Patrol at Silver Mountain in Kellogg, Idaho from 2004 to 2012. (The red coat is like a Superman cape!)

I was pretty impressed with my Dad's resume, so I share mine here, without the intention of being boastful. (They can be helpful in gathering facts for family timelines.)

Resume for
TODD WILLIAM NEEL

EDUCATION
B.A. Psychology - University of Montana (6/1980)
M.S.W. - Eastern Washington U. School of Social Work (6/1986)

HUMAN SERVICES EXPERIENCE

Idaho Department of Health and Welfare, Children and Family Services, Coeur d'Alene, Idaho (3/1990 – 12/2017). Held job titles as Social Work Specialist Senior, Clinician, Social Worker 2, and Social Worker 3. Working with individual clients, families, and systems in the areas of child protection, children's mental health, permanency, adoptions, guardianship, fatherhood, courts, computers, substance abuse, juvenile justice, attachment, trauma, independent living, etc.

Excelsior Youth Center, Spokane, Washington as Treatment Coordinator (11/1987 to 3/1990). Supervised staff, provided individual, group, and family treatment to residents and their families.

Mountain View Hospital, Spokane, Washington as Contract Speaker (10/1987) providing lectures on addiction and recovery issues.

Pine Crest Hospital, Coeur d'Alene, Idaho as Psychiatric Social Worker (9/1986 to 1/1987) and Chemical Dependency Counselor (1/1987 to 10/1987), working with adults, adolescents, and families in the area of mental health and chemical dependency issues.

Eastern State Hospital, Medical Lake, Washington as temporary Psychiatric Social Worker (7/1986 to 8/1986) providing case management for mental health patients on the Intake/Triage Unit.

Veterans for Sobriety, Spokane, Washington, as group facilitator of a support group for children of alcoholics (4/1986 to 5/1986).

Center for Drug Treatment - Program of Community Mental Health, Spokane, Washington. Student practicum placement for MSW degree doing individual, group, and family therapy, co-facilitated a support group for children of alcoholics, and assisted in preparation of education materials (1/1986 to 6/1986).

Shodair Adolescent Chemical Dependency Unit, Helena, Montana - Counselor in Aftercare Program (11/1983 to 8/1984) for adolescents and their families.

Helena Attention Home, Helena Montana - House Parent/Child Care Worker in crisis oriented adolescent group home (3/1983 to 8/1984).

Hospice of St. Peter's Community Hospital, Helena, Montana - Volunteer Group Co-facilitator for bereavement support group (1/1984 to 8/1984).

Western Montana Regional Community Mental Health Center -- Riverhouse, Missoula, Montana - House Manager in transitional living facilities for chronically mentally ill adults (8/1982 to 10/1983).

Attention Home of Missoula Youth Homes, Inc. - Assistant House Parent (6/1982 to 8/1982) providing supervision for adolescents in crisis oriented group home.

Transitional Living Facility of Missoula Alcohol and Drug Program. - Substitute House Manager (6/1982 to 7/1982) providing supervision of adults in residential housing facility for recovering alcoholics/addicts.

Battered Women's Shelter, Missoula, Montana. Volunteer Peer Advocate (11/1981 to 5/1982) providing support for women in shelter coming from domestic violence situations.

Missoula Crisis Center. Volunteer Phone worker, Trainer, Outreach Worker, member of the Board of Directors, Temporary Coordinator (salaried) (5/1979 to 12/1980 and 10/1981 to 5/1982).

District II Alcohol & Drug Program, Glendive, Montana - Counselor Trainee under CETA program (1/1981 to 6/1981) providing individual and family counseling and education.

Junior Citizens Camp, Chico Hot Springs, Montana - Cabin Counselor for troubled youth (6/1980 to 7/1980).

Missoula Youth Court - Counselor Internship (9/1979 to 6/1980) for juveniles on probation.

Big Brothers & Sisters Program, Missoula, Montana - Volunteer (2/1978 to 8/1978) match with youth.

INTERESTS

Skiing, canoeing, backpacking, outdoor sports, photography, computers, philosophy, men's groups, personal growth, genealogy, writing.

CERTIFICATIONS & LISCENSES

-L.C.S.W. (Licensed Clinical Social Worker) - Idaho (12/2013)

-L.M.S.W. (Licensed Master Social Worker) - Idaho (1986)

-Outdoor Emergency Care (OEC) certification (for Silver Mountain Ski Patrol) (2004 - 2013)

-Eagle Boy Scout (Troup 3, Missoula, Montana, 1972)

Chapter 12
<u>Who am I? ... And how did I get here? (Psychology and Genealogy)</u>

By Todd W. Neel
March 9, 1979

The following paper I wrote for a class I took at the University of Montana during the winter quarter of 1979 while working on my Bachelor's Degree in Psychology. I was twenty-three years old at the time I originally wrote this paper, and I'm now sixty-three years of age. (My, how times flies!) The class was called <u>Roots A Psychological Analysis</u> (Psychology 395-1), taught by Dr. Balfour Jefferies. I fondly remember this class. We watched videotapes of Alex Haley's <u>Roots</u>, and the professor provided us with a structure to interview our family members and a framework to write a paper on our own families. He even taught us how to use Family Group Record sheets from the LDS Church. From this, I wrote the following paper (with apologies for the big psychological words that I was probably using to impress the professor).

Roots are an important need, as in Maslow's hierarchy of needs for an actualized life, and help to recognize and avoid maladaptive behaviors. The needs at the lowest, most basic level of the hierarchy must be at least partially satisfied before those at the next level become important determiners of action. (Need leads to motivation or drive.) He claims basic primary physiological needs such as food and water must be met, at least to the point of being out of danger before other needs are tackled. The next most basic need is safety, where explanation, order, and stability are found. Security in your environment is obtained in familiar surroundings, where you know what is expected of you, and you know what you can expect from your environment without being threatened. The next need that can be dealt with is belongingness and love need. To know you have a right to be, that you as an individual are of value. To be accepted. A need to be affiliated with something. When this is missing, depression, rejection, and rootlessness occur. To find your roots, your origins, is one way to attempt to satisfy this need, to know where you come from, to have something in common with the rest of the world.

This paper is a presentation of my own roots. Working on it has given me a feeling of belonging, of being closer to my parents where there was a gap before, because of a rebellious disrespect I had. Maybe bitterness on my part for their attempt to control my life, and not wanting to belong to them but to myself. Belonging to others means something different to me now.

To report where I come from entirely, genetically and psychologically, is practically impossible. The vast number of my ancestors, whose lives were each equally important for my existence, is impossible to accurately trace because of a lack of written record of who they were, and where they came from. And the vast number of peoples' actions and reactions that I have observed or have personally experienced are, obviously, not recorded except in my memory, which is not only imperfect in recall, but is victim of my perception, logic and previous conditioning.

I will begin with a presentation of my genetic roots, as far as I was able to gather from documents and interviews with my family. I was fortunate to have easy access to my father's mother, Agusta Estella (McCool) Neel, though for an unfortunately short period of time for interviewing. My grandmother, though 95 years old, has a very good memory, and I, being an inexperienced interviewer, was at the mercy of her direction of topics. She provided me with quite a few names of importance, and many interesting stories. Having time for only one formal interview, I was overwhelmed by writing names down, so placing people and stories together where I might attempt to apply learning principles and personality characteristics didn't succeed very well. I will try to apply examples of learning directly to the forming of my own personality with reference to my own experience.

The interview with my grandmother gave me names of ancestors four generations previous to me, and a document I obtained from my father confirmed her accuracy. That document is a syllabus of the Neel and allied families, written in 1940 by Doris Neel Groves, a cousin of my grandfather, William Franklin Neel. The author is obviously proud of her background, as illustrated by this quote "There are no lame nor halt nor blind in these generations; no bow legs, knock knees nor hunchbacks. No crooked eyes, no inebriates, no suicides, no epileptics, no insane; a heritage of parents with high ideals, and clean lives."

"The name Neal or Neil is believed to be of Irish origin, possibly coming from other spellings where ni means "daughter" and aille means "cliff," probably referring to a place of residence of the progenitor of the family name." The author of the syllabus (Doris Neel Groves) found different authorities give three different origins for the name - Normandy, Scotland, and Ireland - but she choose to favor Normandy. But who is to say where our real origins are? (Who can say who the first "human" was?) Bearers of some form of the name were among the first colonists in America, and the syllabus mentions some predecessors who have distinguished themselves as authors, educators, historians, painters (artists, I assume), a statistician, a biologist, a university president, and a U. S. Commissioner of Labor. The author reports many people who changed or dropped parts of the original name, but didn't give any reasons. (Maybe they weren't tuned in to how important their roots are, or maybe by changing their name they thought they could avoid being associated with any deviant predecessors.)

The few distinguishing physical characteristics I have observed in my family are mostly on my father's side of the family. His nose resembles his mother's only in being large, his more round while his mother's is more long. He has fairly large ears, as his mother does, with unattached ear lobes which his mother attributes to "Jack blood" of four generations before me (see pedigree chart). My mother's father had dark eyebrows, as my mother and I do. I have not observed any other distinctive physical traits in my family that may result from dominant genes, possibly the result of a lot of outbreeding preventing the accumulation of strong phenotypes. My sister has red hair as I do, and the only other red head we have found in the family is an aunt of my father's in Tacoma, Washington.

Having some facts about names and dates of births and deaths of my ancestors doesn't tell me much about their personalities, and how they might have influenced me in the long run. To get an idea of what my predecessors were like, I had a talk with my parents and asked them what their parents were like.

I found some characteristics of my grandparents that were similar to my parents, and some I found in myself. My mother describes her mother as demanding, strict, stubborn, and not very warm, but generous to people she cared for. She was neat, orderly, and meticulous, and valued doing things in her usual formal way (possibly a sign of compulsiveness). She also didn't like to wash the dishes - which she trained her children to do. All of these traits I see in my mother. Mom's father was community minded, loved kids, had a good sense of humor, was honest, and did not have strong political opinions. He was a career Army man, spending a total of 46 years in the service. My mother explained that military people of that time didn't normally vote in elections because they felt they owed loyalty to the commander-in-chief, whoever it was. I don't recall any occasion when either of my parents voted, but I recall plenty of occasions of complaints of the democrats in office. The other above mentioned traits of my grandfather I also see in my mother.

My father's mother didn't socialize much as he remembers but that may be because of the isolated conditions they grew up in, relative to today, because to me she seemed very open to visits and liked to talk. Other than that, Dad said it was hard to picture her as he was a child. His father was warm, quiet, enjoyed reading, didn't socialize with people outside the family much, and may have been slightly achievement oriented as far as his personal comforts went. He was the first in Holbrook, Nebraska to own an Edison record player, and my dad has said that he sees striving to better his comforts as worthwhile. Idealistically, I see striving for a constant rise in standards of living as ridiculous, but I still enjoy new material objects. I find that I am at a point of changing in my life where some of my own values are changing, and I find myself acquiring or accepting some values of my parents that I used to reject. I mentioned the above characteristics of my father's parents because I see them as part of his personality also.

My own parents' orientation towards physical and emotional nearness, or warmth, is not homogeneous, but maybe compatible. (I recall my mother said that a marriage should be made of two people who are opposites.) Neither of them showed much physical affection in front of the kids, except when friends of the family were visiting. Emotionally my parents are quite different from each other. Mom is controlling, dominating, possessive, and helpless at times. She seems to want to direct you to your goals, rather than to leave you to find your own way, as if she feels she is making it more convenient for us to learn from her experiences. She seems to try to control you with her helplessness and complaining, but this may be due to her poor health. She is very caring of her family, but expresses it by being directive. She wants you to be happy and healthy, but unfortunately, by her methods.

My father is a well-disciplined man, maybe partially a result of his 33-year Navy career, and seems to be innately warm and concerned of others. He shows his concern by showing respect for others, in allowing them to be and do as they wish, rarely asking for a favor or help. I learned a lesson from my father when, on several occasions when I was being insensitive and aggressive toward others in my family, he sternly told me that golden rule "Do unto others as you would have them do unto you" to which he added "BEFORE they do unto you. Be kind to others, and they will be kind to you."

Neither of my parents freely express their emotions. Maybe that just comes about as a result of age, where they try to protect their vulnerable parts by not exposing it. I remember an occasion when we got a kitten for a mouse chaser, and it didn't survive even the first afternoon home because our dog killed it. We had been playing with the kitten while our dog expressed a jealous curiosity. Mom, who treats the dog like a child, told us to leave the cat alone and let the two get used to each other. We turned our backs for a short while, and the dog bit the cat, breaking its' neck. My younger brother was upset for a while, trying to hear if the cat's heart was still beating. Mom was coldly upset, and told us to take the cat out to the garbage, and apologized for not showing much concern, because if she did she would start crying.

I consciously feel that I try to model after my father, as I admire his personality very much. I appreciate my mother very much also, for the concern she has for me, but I am not very fond of her dominating personality. I have had to acknowledge this conflict within myself when I was once living a distance from my parents, and I had received news that Mom had cancer. I felt very guilty for a while, until I realized why. No one who is a big part of your life has only good or only bad feelings about you, and vice versa. (This is called ambivalence – you CAN love and hate someone at the same time.) When I am in control of myself, that is when I'm not under stress, I try to perform as my father does, that is take on his actions and attitudes. I feel I am most comfortable with myself when I have a calm, concerned attitude, as my father exhibits most of the time. But when I'm under stress, I see myself behaving like my mother, short tempered, easily frustrated, and uncomfortable with myself.

For observational learning and performance to take place, and for instrumentally learned behaviors to be performed and maintained in the absence of those primary rewards and punishments of parental sanctions there must be some internal, personal control, or motivation for your actions. You must see the behavior as attractive in itself, or you must be attracted to secondary rewards (or repelled by secondary punishments). I have tried to express here some examples of repulsive and attractive stimuli that effected my personality development. I did not show the whole picture of my personality, because I don't have a very good view of myself. It's like living on top of a mountain all of your life, and trying to determine how high the mountain is without being able to stand back to measure it. My own personality, as well as my genetically caused traits, come from a great many confounding sources. Many psychological influences are especially hard to find because of painful emotional barriers.

I feel the writing of this paper has been an important learning tool for me, and has sparked interest in the continued search, of the opening of my eyes, to the past and possible future influences that make me what I am.

Update – Post UM Paper

An update as of 2018: Regarding Doris Neel Groves' comments on " … no lame nor halt nor blind in these generations … no inebriates, no suicides … no insane …," I wish to disclose some facts. I identify myself as a recovering alcoholic/addict with thirty-seven years of sobriety as of 1/2/2018. (My last drunk was in Butte, Montana for New Years on 12/31/1980 - 1/1/1981.) I believe I have found others in my family who were alcoholic. I do not disclose this to embarrass or shame anyone, or to make moral judgments. It is better known these days that alcoholism is a disease, and it is sometimes passed on genetically. I tell my own children this, explaining it is like an "allergy." They have to make their own choices about consumption of alcohol later in their lives. I am grateful that I do not have to drink anymore, and my life is better for it.

I have found entries in Neel Genealogy by Betty Thorson, Oakland, Calif, 1979, A Continuation of the Neel Genealogy prepared by Doris Neel Groves in 1940 of a family member who died in an institution, and this makes me wonder the cause of that. I have a recollection of my own mother having a "nervous breakdown" and going away (to a hospital?) in New Jersey when I was growing up. My older, adopted brother has had multiple serious problems in his life, and he still had struggles, the last time I saw him. (It is not yet confirmed but he may still be alive, as I have not been able to locate him for about 15 years until just recently.) (See chapters *5 - A Mother's Story* and *6 - A Brother's Story* for more on my adopted brother).

Regarding my own developmental issues as it relates to this writing: As stated above, I was twenty-three years old when I wrote that paper. I am now sixty-three years old as of this re-edit in 2018. I am now married (since 1989), have 2 boys (now ages twenty-four and twenty-six), had a stable career (twenty-seven years as a social worker for the state of Idaho, just having retired in December 2017). I have completed 2 college degrees since I wrote this paper. I have lived another life time since then! Both of my parents and my grandmother are now deceased as well as other important relatives have passed away- aunt Sarah and uncle Ted, aunt Babe and uncle Bill, among others many of whom I haven't met but are no longer available to us to answer my nosy questions. I don't remember my grandfathers - my paternal grandfather died well before I was born, and my maternal grandfather died a few months after my birth, and I know they have affected my development.

I have an active interest in my roots that I pursue voluntarily, and with a passionate appetite (this is my "family hunger"!), and I do this not to please a professor for a grade (although I wouldn't have signed up for that class if I hadn't had an interest in my roots at the time).

I now recognize traits of my family of origin that are "dysfunctional" that I now have choices in (back then, I didn't have much insight). I do believe that the difficulties my older brother had growing up in our family created some dynamics in our family that caused us to be a "dysfunctional family" - (traits that negatively affected our development - not everybody likes this term, and this is just my opinion). There is the argument of the "chicken and the egg" - which came first - my adopted brother's problems, or our problems? I could write another whole chapter or maybe another book on these issues, but I wonder sometimes if he could have just identified and addressed his issues related to his adoption and his genetic family of origin that he might possibly be able to resolve some of his problems instead of "puking" them on others. (Some of the information in this chapter is redundant, but is relevant to the material in this chapter if it is read alone.)

This ability to survive - and most importantly, <u>TO THRIVE</u> - in spite of hardships, is also called "<u>resiliency</u>." There are many traits of "functional" healthy families that are within mine as well as dysfunctional traits.

I write about this not to blame anyone else. We all do the best we can with what tools and abilities we have at the moment. In spite of any dysfunction or disease that any of us have, it is balanced with healthy traits and survival skills - the ability to get up and do what we have to do, in spite of or because of the difficulties we encounter.

When I wrote the above paper at age 23, I was probably feeling the invincibility of adolescence and young adulthood at the time. Now I feel the signs of aging and my own mortality - my joints feel rusty at times, and sometimes I forget what I walked into a room for. Writing about these issues is my attempt to preserve my immortality, to take a snapshot of my life and dip it in lacquer for safekeeping (I know there is folly in this).

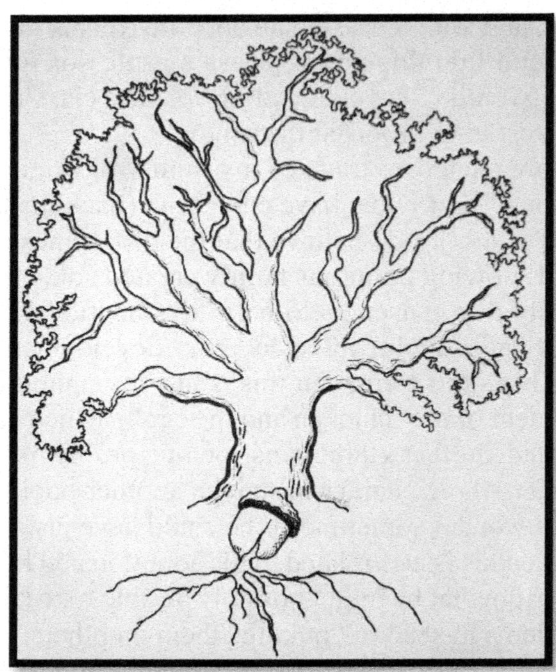

Chapter 13
We're all part of a bigger whole
- Spirituality and Genealogy -

As I do this work, I am reminded of how transient we all are. Anything put in writing is only temporary. Anything printed on paper or a computer screen is only momentary, as we all are.

Undertaking this work is an opportunity for me to do some of my own spiritual work: to be a part of something much more significant than myself - generations past, present, and future. This is a chance to extend that brief moment of my life a little longer, to receive, appreciate, and to pass on the light that was given to me.

When engaging in this work, with the proper attitude and conditions (like a clear sky needed when searching for stars at night), I learn about and come to appreciate the Bigger Picture and my place in it. If you or someone else in the future pick up this writing and reads it, with the right conditions of a proper attitude of an open and clear mind, it can affect you (or them), and history is made! I will be seen, remembered, and I am giving you, the reader, light to pass on to the next generation when/if you do your genealogy work. This is a chance for <u>you</u> to be seen and remembered. (Don't forget the offspring of our thoughts, words, and deeds are also part of the deal, here.)

> **... with the proper conditions, like a clear sky that is required to see the stars ...**

Am I worthy of being seen? Yes, I have something important to say! <u>You</u> have something important to say!

I am a very tiny part of a much Bigger Whole. I see it when I am out in the woods, and I look up at the Milky Way and see just a small slice of our own galaxy, one of many, many, many galaxies! Consider the HUGENESS of it! Of course, sometimes conditions like a cloudy sky interfere and don't provide us with a clear view. Or a cloudy mind.

One of those conditions will be that the reader will care about their genealogy. Will our children and grandchildren or others be looking for us? Do they have a clear view, or is it cloudy for them?

When we can see them, those stars in the sky appear permanent, but they are only brief flashes of light. "Brief" is a relative term, cosmically speaking. Some of them have actually burned out long ago. The constellations, so far away, appear stable to us year after year since it takes so many light years to travel the immense distance before their light energy reaches our eyes. It's an illusion that they form a pattern that we recognize, and we try to capture them by naming them, like the Big Dipper.

We name them as it reminds us. They each have a story!

Our parents tried to capture us by naming us. Each of our names is a chapter heading, or a book title.

Humility tells us that even though we are small, we are also BIG! There is a universe inside each of us, a microcosm of the big picture!

When everything lines up, this brief moment of my life may extend beyond the time of my heartbeat. Somebody may be looking at me from the distance of time through their telescope.

Random? Planned? Purpose!

Was it random chance, a roll of the dice, that brings me to this keyboard, struggling with these words in this next sentence up to the point of hitting "Send" and final publication, and finally you holding it in your hands and reading this with your own thoughts? (Like John Hartford says in the song "I Would Not Be Here" if I hadn't been there if… That's a good song. I suggest you look it up.) Or is it some part of somebody's bigger plan that we might, or might not, have some choices in? From my viewpoint, I see that we are part of a larger roadmap, not all of it charted, which is at least four-dimensional in space and time. And we have some choices.

I digress here for a second: Two-dimensional is left-right and forward-backward like on a flat sheet of paper. Three-dimensional involves the illusion of movement with perceived depth like in a 3-D movie, or like our two eyes see because we have stereo vision. Four-dimensional involves changing through time which is more flexible than we think. We change over time, and if our histories are written down, someone in the future might read about us in the past. In the space-time continuum, Stephen Hawking theorizes that if we travel through space at the speed of light and we return to earth in ten years, we will have aged at a different rate than our friends and relatives that we have left behind. Have you noticed that your perception of time seems to have changed as we get older? I do not perceive time as an adult the same way I experienced it as a child.

Opportunities are presented to us that we have choices in. Every path available before us is all important if we pay attention to it. (Do we turn left or right, go forward or backward, down to the lower elevations or up to the mountains, living in the present moment only or considering ourselves in the space-time continuum and aware of past and future history?)

But know that we don't have time to follow all of the trails before us. I do not believe someone, or something has a specific dramatic plot for me, like God dangling me on strings as a puppet (although I do have some residual beliefs from my childhood along these lines – control issues). I have grown to believe that I am not powerless but also not all powerful! (And the flipside is also true – that we are powerless and powerful at the same time.) I have some control, but at times I get confused about what I have control of. Mostly, I do have confidence that I have a purpose, with

I believe not so much in a plan for me, but rather that I have a purpose!

some control in fulfilling that purpose, that destiny.

Coincidence and Commitment - Belonging

Along with the synchronicity of events that seem to link things together, a sense of belonging and connectedness are also part of my spiritual path. What series of events led up to your considering my words here? What motivated you to read this far, and what will keep you going? Can you tolerate this if it gets messy or distasteful or uncomfortable or confusing or painful or if this sentence is too long and I lose your attention? Or if you are too full for the moment and you need to chew on this for a while? Will you say "Enough!" or will you remain committed to your own genealogy and to your family?

As this section is full of questions, I will present it this way for your consideration:

- Can you stay committed to this genealogy path, to this process that is never finished? Will you keep eating your literal and metaphorical fruits and vegetables and nuts and grains, and all of the food groups for a balanced diet, even when you get tired of chewing before you can get the dessert that you deserve?
- How does this translate to your family life? Maybe you don't want to eat your vegetables and fruits right now. Perhaps later you will understand how important they are to a balanced diet, a well-adjusted life. Do all of the food groups, the nuts as well as fruits and vegetables belong on your table? Do you have any of these in your family?
- Do you belong in this sport of genealogy? Do you belong on the field of this game? Are you one of those nuts? (If you ask my family members, they will probably say I am one of them.)
- Do you have any allergies or other sensitivities to these types of nutrition, including emotional nutrition? (Do you like hugs, or are you repelled by

them?)

- Do you feel that you belong at your family table and in your family tree? Why are you here? Why this family? Why me? How did we end up here? Just a coincidence or by design? Or do you feel like you don't fit, that you are not included?
- Do you feel welcomed by your family? Do you mutually welcome them into your home?
- Do you respect and value that others also belong in your tree and at your table? How do you tolerate or deal with them if they are distasteful?
- Do you feel you have a right to sit at your family's table and/or to state your need and your right to do so? Are you committed to claiming your place and sitting at the table and in the conversation of life? Does your opinion and do your feelings matter?
- Who is at the head of your family table, and who is in charge? Who lets members in? Who is the gatekeeper?
- Besides belonging at the table, are you welcomed into the *kitchen* as well, to help co-create the menu and nutrition that we all need?
- Are you and your family mutually *committed* to each other? Are you there for each other through the joyful times as well as through the challenging times?

If you find answers to these questions for yourself, you may discover peace-of-mind, or at least the path towards it.

Desiderata

Go placidly amid the noise and haste, and remember what peace there may be in silence. As far as possible without surrender be on good terms with all persons. Speak your truth quietly and clearly; and listen to others, even the dull and ignorant; They too have their story.

Avoid loud and aggressive persons, they are vexations to the spirit. If you compare yourself with others, you may become vain and bitter; for always there will be greater and lesser persons than yourself. Enjoy your achievements as well as your plans.

Keep interested in your own career, however humble; it is a real possession in the changing fortunes of time. Exercise caution in your business affairs; for the world is full of trickery. But let this not blind you to what virtue there is; many persons strive for high ideals; and everywhere life is full of heroism.

Be yourself. Especially, do not feign affection. Neither be cynical about love; for in the face of all aridity and disenchantment it is perennial as the grass.

Take kindly the counsel of years, gracefully surrendering the things of youth. Nurture strength of spirit to shield you in sudden misfortune. But do not distress yourself with imaginings. Many fears are born of fatigue and loneliness. Beyond a wholesome discipline, be gentle with yourself.

You are a child of the universe, no less than the trees and the stars; you have a right to be here. And whether or not it is clear to you, no doubt the universe is unfolding as it should.

Therefore be at peace with God, whatever you conceive Him to be, and whatever your labors and aspirations, in the noisy confusion of life keep peace with your soul.

With all its sham, drudgery and broken dreams, it is still a beautiful world. Be careful. Strive to be happy.

Found in Old Saint Paul's Church, Baltimore; dated 1692

Immortality

Carl Sagan writes in Cosmos (1980): "*A book is made from a tree. It is an assemblage of flat, flexible parts (still called "leaves") imprinted with dark pigmented squiggles. One glance at it and you hear the voice of another person - perhaps someone dead for thousands of years. Across the millennia, the author is speaking, clearly and silently, inside your head, directly to you. Writing is perhaps the greatest of human inventions, binding together people, citizens of distant epochs, who never knew one another. Books break the shackles of time, proof that humans can work magic."* ...

"Books are like seeds. They can lie dormant for centuries and then flower in the most unpromising soil." ...

"If I finish a book a week, I will read only a few

thousand books in my lifetime, about a tenth of a percent of the contents of the greatest libraries of our time. The trick is to know which books to read." (from his Chapter XI "*The Persistence of Memory*" Copyright © 1980 by Druyan-Sagan Associates, Inc.)

Is this book you are reading now one of them?

I am not a dead person, yet, and I don't want to be one of the "walking dead" like in the zombie movies, or like some practicing alcoholic or addict like I once was.

This is about who I am, my right to speak up and state what is important to me and to claim where I came from. This book is about me finding my voice, and planting seeds of inspiration to help you find yours. I want to help you understand and claim who and what was necessary to get us here, and consider what remains of us after we are gone. We have more conscious choices when the light is just right, and we can see more clearly. Rather than writings on a dark cave wall, I would like some remnants of my time here to live on in the form of this book, beyond my heartbeat. What about you?

... like writings on a dark cave wall?

In my genealogy work as I search for and find headstones or other traces of my ancestors, I sometimes feel a strong emotional response and tears about those I have studied and actively sought. Like when I found the headstone of my great-grandfather, John Robinson Neel, in Nebraska. I choked up and had difficulty in getting my breath. I have a photograph of him with my father as an infant sitting on his knee. (See *Chapter 10 - John William Neel - My Dad*) For others, I feel less attached and have less personal emotion, like with Niall of Nine Hostages (or Niall Noígiallach from the fifth century), who I still search for my emotional connection with. (Grandpa Niall has a great story, so I want to feel more connected with him – See *Chapter 28 - Ireland – "Banter and Chat and Laughter*

Between Cousins" - Irish DNA Cousin Tom Molloy.)

As I re-visit my family's stories, I find my own appreciation growing, and I experience my ancestor's immortality alive in my hunger for them.

Do you consider these issues of mortality for yourself?

The problem with Religion

I was raised in the Episcopal Christian church as a child where my Mom was the church organist and choir director. My wife and I are currently members of the Unity Spiritual Center of North Idaho.

It was not until later in my life that I learned that Religion and spirituality are not the same thing.

I am not always mindful of a Higher Power, and I sometimes need reminders of my place in the big picture. Without this, I can think and act like I am my own creator (and <u>your</u> Creator, acting like I'm your boss!), and my false-ego gets too big. I can get a fat-head attitude like "Get out of <u>my way</u>!" in the traffic jam of life.

I have periods of time when I am less than spiritually conscious.

Sometimes I falsely think I am accountable for the outcome as well as responsible for the footwork. It is important to me to know that I am NOT responsible for the results. For example, whatever I write, I am not responsible for your reaction as the reader, although I do need to be as response-able to other people's needs as I can. I need to be able to respond to other people's needs for privacy if they are still alive and I want a good relationship with them. I need to be responsible for my potty-mouth language to not offend you as the reader, particularly if I care about what you think about me. (Response-able <u>to</u> you, not response-able <u>for</u> you – able to respond to you, but I'm not able to respond for you and your needs.) If I am stepping on your toes, please let me know, and I will try to

There is a difference between my being response-able <u>to</u> you, and response-able <u>for</u> you.

back off and correct my actions if I need to. But I cannot assume that I know what you need or want, like when I talk about spirituality or Religion. (This can be such a touchy topic, someone can be turned off very quickly.)

One of the things that attracted me to Unity is that they honor all churches. I would request that you respect and honor my choice about what church I attend, or even that I do attend and am a member of a church. That doesn't mean we have to agree.

I don't want to impose my spiritual beliefs or force any religious beliefs on anyone. I also don't want you to discount my words because I believe in God (but, again, I'm not responsible for your reactions).

I believe in a Higher Power, I believe in something that is greater than my self, and I do believe that we are all part of something bigger than ourselves and we are all interconnected. As with the trees and other plants in the forest, under the soil, we do not readily see how our roots are entwined.

I do believe in God, but it isn't necessarily an exclusive Christian God. Jesus was one of many teachers. We are all the children of God. I am working on trying to understand the Sufi concept of "99 names of God." Even though these are my thoughts, this does not mean I have a right to impose my beliefs upon you. I try my best to respect your beliefs. It's easier for me to say this than it is to practice it 100% of the time.

I do have trouble with some churches and religions that impose dogmatic belief systems upon people (on members of their congregation and on "outsiders") and then teach their followers to pass judgment on those who don't believe the same way. This can lead to the followers who don't think for themselves, who are hypocritical (i.e., forgiveness and judgment), and promote disrespect and harm and death upon others who do not believe the same way. I don't like the promotion of belief systems that say: "I'm right, and you are wrong." We all have our own points of view (p.o.v.) that are right for us, and our p.o.v. is unique for each of us. We have the freedom of choice.

I'd like to reflect on words that Nelson Mandela used in a famous speech which are inspirational to me. It was written by Marianne Williamson. Use it as a prayer:

> *"Our deepest fear is not that we are inadequate. Our deepest fear is that we are powerful beyond measure. It is our light, not our darkness, that most frightens us. We ask ourselves, Who am I to be brilliant, gorgeous, talented, fabulous? Actually, who are you* <u>*not*</u> *to be? You are a child of God. Your playing small doesn't serve the world. There is nothing enlightened about shrinking so that other people won't feel insecure around you. We are all meant to shine, as children do. We were born to make manifest the glory of God that is within us. It's not just in some of us; it's in everyone. And as we let our own light shine, we unconsciously give other people permission to do the same. As we're liberated from our own fear, our presence automatically liberates others."*

(Marianne Williamson, <u>A Return to Love – Reflections on the Principles on A COURSE IN MIRACLES</u>, text from pp. 190 – 191 © 1992, reprinted by permission of HarperCollins Publishers)

As I walk through life in doing this genealogy work, I sometimes find people who are reluctant to let their "own light shine." I am this way myself sometimes. I struggle with balancing those different parts of myself that make up my own psychology, both my true and false ego parts, and also my honorable self that comes from my spirit. On the one side is that part of me that feels small, insignificant, and unimportant at times, which can be covered up with false bravado and appears not at all what it really is. There is this part of me that questions whether or not I really have anything of value to say, and I sometimes question my self-worth. I can shame myself, and I can project this self-doubt on others and perceive that they just want me to sit down and be quiet, disappear, or just go away. (Find the poem "*Please Hear What I'm Not*

Saying.") On the other side is Spirit trying to speak loudly, shouting "Yes! You do have something of value to say!"

The false face or front that I can put up can attempt to cover up when I'm really feeling scared, small, or inadequate (like when I'm acting with my "Get out of my way!" attitude). There are places in our culture that support an authoritarian posture, i.e., "You are the boss/teacher/parent/expert/etc. Now make that happen!", or some variation of this where I buy into a distorted sense of will about what I truly have the power to change.

The truth is probably somewhere in between these polar opposites, and if I don't travel back and forth, then I don't get perspective. From time to time it's good to be on the mountain tops, and once in a while it's good to be in the deep canyons or even to visit the dark caves, in the shadow. Occasionally even camouflage is good.

I question at times whether or not my storytelling is an effort to get attention for myself at someone else's expense. That is not respectful, and that is not how I would like to be treated. I don't want it to be my camouflage.

Then there are times when I am clear about my own opinion and my own needs, and I know this part of me that has a right to speak up - to feel my own feelings, to think my own thoughts, to express my Self without imposing myself upon others. To know myself confidently means I do not always have to speak up, though. This is the part of me where I can be secure enough to be quiet and to listen to another truly.

Sometimes, by speaking my truth, I sense sometimes I am imposing myself on others. (Like when I'm singing and dancing too loudly in the morning and my wife hasn't had enough coffee yet!) And there are times I know I am withholding my truth because I don't want to step on other people's toes.

On some occasions, it is proper to share my own opinions, thoughts, and feelings. Yet, when I speak my truth to others, a sense of resistance can form between us, making me wonder if I'm imposing myself on them. I prefer to be fully present in a relationship without losing my Self. I want to cultivate relationships where you (or the other person) are also present in the relationship, and you do not feel judged by me, and you (or they) feel safe in our "us."

I am still in "recovery" from my arrogance – still working on this. Working my boundaries. Working on figuring out where I end and where you begin.

While I have had religious influences in my life that have affected my consciousness about spirituality, I may (or may not) sound confident that I know what the truth is about this topic. There is beauty to keep some truth about spirituality still a mystery. There is still some unknown, and that mystery can be wonderful and exciting when I embrace it.

Mystery!

In my Internet "travels" I was sent this reflection written by an anonymous author about those who have this "family hunger" out of respect for our ancestors, who have walked the paths before us:

We are the Chosen

"We are the chosen. My feelings are that every family has one who seems called to find the ancestors. To put flesh on their bones and make them live again, to tell the family story and to feel that somehow they know and approve. To me, doing genealogy is not a cold gathering of facts but, instead, breathing life into all who have gone before. We are the storytellers of the tribe. All tribes have one. We have been called as it were by our genes. Those who have gone before cry out to us: Tell our story - so, we do.

"In finding them, we somehow find ourselves. How many graves have I stood before now and cried? I have lost count. How many times have I told the ancestors, "You have a wonderful family. You would be proud of us." How many times have I walked up to a grave and felt somehow there was love there for me? I cannot say.

"It goes beyond just documenting facts. It goes to who am I and why I do the things I do. It goes to seeing a cemetery about to be lost forever to weeds and indifference and saying, "I can't let this happen." The bones here are bones of my bone and flesh of my flesh. It goes to doing something about it. It goes to pride in what our ancestors were able to accomplish. How they contributed to

what we are today. It goes to respecting their hardships and losses, their never giving in or giving up, their resoluteness to go on and build a life for their family.

"It goes to deep pride that they fought to make and keep us a Nation. It goes to a deep and immense understanding that they were doing it for us so that we might be born who we are, and allow us the ability to remember them. So we do. With love and caring and scribing each fact of their existence, because we are them and they are us. So, as a scribe called, I tell the story of my family. It is up to the one called in the next generation to answer the call. In so doing, they will take their place in the long line of family storytellers.

"This is why I record my family's genealogy, and this is what calls those young and old to step up and put flesh on the bones."

Author Unknown

Debbie Dlouhy worked with me as a social work intern in my office, and she worked in my wife's office as a Bereavement Counselor at Hospice of North Idaho. She passed away at a very young age of forty years. She designed a t-shirt for Hospice which said: "Hope is like a path in the countryside; originally there was no path. Yet as people walk in the same spot, a way appears."

Again, I say, hug your family, those you can reach. Love your family, those you can find (including your ancestors). If it weren't for them, we wouldn't be here. They are waiting for us. They have important, meaningful stories, just as you and I are writing our own important stories now.

Translation of Aramaic version of the Lord's Prayer
by Mosheed Samuel L. Lewis –
(Dances of Universal Peace tradition)
(transcribed from Mark Stanton Welch's CD
"Riding the Sound Current"):
NOTE: due to Copyright and intellectual property rights, these words are not included in this book, but I encourage you to seek them out on your own. Buy Mark's CD!

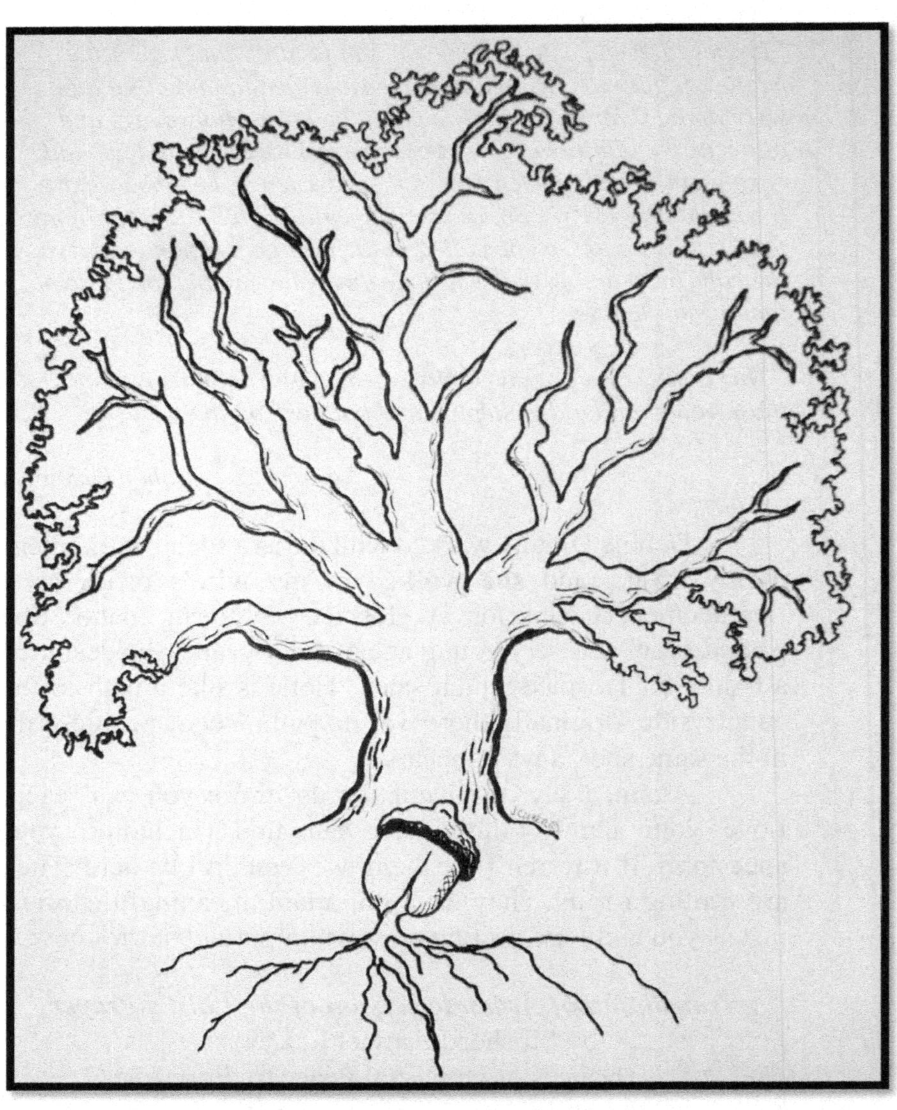

Chapter 14
My Chosen Family
vs.
Family of Obligation

I think it may have been Tim "Tool Time" Allen on television that argued with his son about family obligations around the holidays. The boy didn't want to go to his grandparents for the holiday, and the dad said something like "Holidays are not when you spend time with the people you want to be with. It's about spending time with the people you have to be with." Or something like that. (Sorry if I misquoted you, Mr. Tim Allen).

I have a friend who said he's not so sure about this "family hunger" stuff, as he was invited to his family reunion that he's not interested in. He said he might be more interested in my family than his own. There are many families like that. There are parts of my current family that are like that, and the reactions to invitations to family reunions from my own are like that (" … no, you go ahead … What would I say to them? They are strangers to me … I'm good …").

I do have some friends who are divorced or separated from their spouses. Thinking about not having a family to come home to, to check in with every day, I am so grateful that I have my "nuclear family" to come home to. Some days it's not so easy, though, to come home and negotiate and compromise and live in one household. In my new retirement, I wish the house was quieter for my lovely naps.

Some have said, "I didn't choose my family, they choose me." Others say we did choose our family to be in even before our birth. Who knows? Whether the Buddhists are correct or not about the afterlife and reincarnation, I know I have choices every day, about some things. (The good old Serenity Prayer helps me be clear about that.) Right now in this physical life I choose to honor my commitments to my wife and children with whom I live, to my extended family with whom I am in touch, and to be as respectful as I can be with them. And I choose to honor my ancestors and potential descendants through stories that I gather and write.

I also have a "chosen family" that I spend time with because I want to. I refer to them this way as we may not related in the "family" sense, at least not that we can prove. These are *my friends*, the people I hang out with by choice. I have several circles of people that are like family to me, but we're not related. Some I hang with regularly. Some I see only occasionally.

"Chosen family" are those that I spend time with because I want to.

A note to my birth family: Don't get me wrong, I do want to be with you. Sometimes, however, it doesn't feel mutual. I have learned to meet people where they are at because if I wait you won't meet me where I am at. This is my hunger. I have learned that my expectations are a set-up for disappointment.

I am a reasonably active social person, but I wasn't always this way. I was very shy as a young person, and I believe I have since learned better skills to recognize and fulfill this social need (or want or desire) that I have to make connection. There was a period of time in my life I self-medicated by using drugs and alcohol to help me feel more comfortable in social situations – greasing the wheels with social lubricants. But for me, in some of those occasions I was like as I've heard as an explanation for addiction: A man on fire that runs into the sea to put out the fire, and ends up drowning. (Do you need to see my scars to prove my addiction to you? The addiction model works very well for me.)

I am now sober and very active in several community activities that get me out of the house a lot. Work circles. Music circles. Dance circles. Drumming circles. Men's group. Recovering addict/alcoholic groups. Genealogy groups. Writing groups. Church groups. Board meetings. I seek out group time. I also seek out individual time with friends over coffee or a meal. I also seek alone time.

Brene' Brown states in her book The Gifts of Imperfection (2010) that it is scientifically proven that we need relationships and connection. She defines "connection as the energy that exists between people when they feel seen, heard, and valued; when they can give and receive without judgment; and when they derive sustenance and strength from the relationship" She also says "Connection begets connection," and "… we are wired for connection. It's in our biology. From the time we are born, we need connection to thrive emotionally, physically, spiritually, and intellectually. A decade ago, the idea that we're "wired for connection" might have been perceived as touchy-feely or New Age. Today, we know that the need for connection is more than a feeling or a hunch. It's hard science. Neuroscience, to be exact." (p. 19).

Some people stay connected with other people through social networking on computers, like Facebook, Twitter, Instagram, etc. While I have a Facebook page (as well as my own website for this book), I prefer face-to-face time with real persons in the same room with me. Brene' Brown, in The Gifts of Imperfection, talks about false connections through technology. She states "If you need to refuel and losing yourself online is fun and relaxing, then do it. If not, do something deliberately relaxing. Find something inspiring to do rather than something soul-sucking. Then, last but not least, get up and do it! I closed my laptop, said a little prayer to remind myself to be self-compassionate, and watched a movie that had been sitting in a Netflix envelope on my desk for over a month. It was exactly what I needed."

> **" … find something inspiring to do rather than something soul-sucking …"**

Recent research in attachment and trauma-informed practice shows that direct face-to-face contact is too uncomfortable or threatening for some people, and that "parallel interactions" (activities that are side-by-side rather than face-to-face) are safer and less threatening for some. Robert Bly talks about men and women generally being different in relationship styles, and that men (generally) often prefer "shoulder-to-shoulder" activities (i.e., watching TV or talking about sports or doing mechanical things together, etc.), while women more often prefer "face-to-face" activities (i.e., sitting down for tea and crying over family or relationships stories, etc.) Bly also suggests that if a marriage is going to last that the woman sometimes needs to be willing to compromise and go for a walk in the woods with the man, while the man at times needs to be willing to compromise and sit down, face-to-face, and be in close relationship with the woman. (Keep in mind these are generalities, and do not fit all relationships.)

LGBTQ+ (homosexuality) issues throw a whole new wrench into the formula regarding gender issues and relationship styles. I won't go into detail about that here.

I have family members that have a diagnosis of Aspergers (on the Autism spectrum), and I see other family members that have traits of this diagnosis without the severity. Some of these traits appear in myself at times. Some of my addiction issues in the past may have been related to my efforts to self-medicate my discomfort with relationships until I learned more skills to fulfill my need for connection in a healthier way.

By my professional training and practice, I am a social worker, and this affects the lens I see the world through. I acknowledge this bias. I recognize that I am a social animal. I identify this need, and I seek ways to keep my life in balance to fulfill this need or desire, including alone time as stated above.

There was a paper called "Why Men Don't Have Friends, and Why Women Should Care" by an anonymous author I received many years ago. (You can Google it on the Internet today). The main message I got from this paper was: "Don't put all your eggs in one basket," which I take to mean it is not fair to your partner that you expect them to be your everything for you. We need multiple social connections.

Besides issues of homophobia, competitiveness, socialization, and other issues in this paper that I relate to, there are other concepts in this article that I disagree agree with. But it has a lot of useful information to consider, and I recommend that you look it up.

It's a known fact that we learn basic issues about relationships in our family-of-origin, and we take that out into the world and apply it to our chosen families after our parents are gone. And with education and insight (or not), we make conscious or unconscious choices about it.

I do find myself at times critical of my parents and their relationship style as a role model for what a marriage should be. I have a metaphorical image of them sitting in chairs, back-to-back and not communicating, strangers living under the same roof. I have very few memories of them being affectionate. I saw my Dad had put "all of his eggs in one basket" (which was his relationship with his wife), and after my Mom died it seemed he just waited fourteen more years for his body to quit as he didn't seem to have an identity except through his relationship with my Mom. He didn't have friends, and he didn't have any passions that he pursued. I try to take from them what works for me and remain open to continuing to learn new ways all the time.

I love you, Mom and Dad!

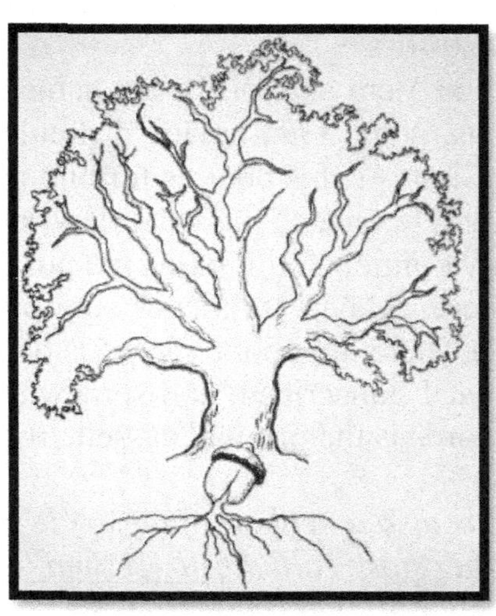

Chapter 15
<u>My aunt "Babe" and my uncle Bill</u>

My aunt "Babe" (Vera Fay Neel) passed away in June 2004. She was the last surviving sibling of my father's. She was called "Babe" in her family because she was the youngest. (My wife, Mary, was also called "Babe" by her brother, Gary.) I have many fond memories of my times with aunt Vera and her husband, uncle Bill. Babe was always very sweet and generous, very attentive toward others, and was very much a caretaker and caregiver. She had a great commitment to caring for her husband, Bill, who had MS (Multiple Sclerosis) for many years. Uncle Bill was very funny with a dry sense of humor, and we were often left scratching our heads about whether his story was fact or fiction.

I really enjoyed sharing our genealogy stories with my aunt Babe and uncle Bill. In my <u>Family Hunger – A Neel and McCool Family History</u> books is a transcription of a taped interview I did with Vera and Bill at their home in Medford, Oregon on 5/18/2001.

I am not using Vera and Bill's last name as they have a son (my first cousin) and I am having difficulty locating him to get his permission. As this book is for public consumption, I am only making reference to this interview for brevity, but it is priceless in my opinion and it pains me not to share it with you in entirety here. (Maybe it relieves your pain that it is not in entirety here!) There are about 15 pages of interview with Babe and Bill that I transcribed, and somewhere in my piles of genealogy records is the original cassette recording.

NOTE: *Neal W. is also a nephew of my uncle Bill, and he wrote a fascinating story called <u>Bill - A Small-Town Nebraskan and his WW II Service</u>*

Chapter 16
My Alcoholism
A Family Deal

11/12/2002
Tuesday

Dear Aunt Vera and Uncle Bill,

I am now getting back to try to finish this letter to you that I started last Saturday. Thinking about your question about my alcoholism and recovery, I think that documenting this story can also be useful for my genealogy record.

I've learned that alcoholism, addiction, or chemical dependency, are diseases that are partially genetically inherited, or rather, one has a tendency towards becoming an alcoholic or addict if there is a family history of it. Genetics is a pre-disposition, but you have to add fuel to build a "fire," and if you pour "gas" on the fire it makes even bigger flames – the more alcohol one consumes, and the more powerful the drugs one consumes increase the risk of addiction as well, which is what happened with me. Once you've crossed the line and become an alcoholic, it is a brain disease and a whole-person disease, though. It is a family disease as well as it affects everyone in the family.

Because of the genetic pre-disposition, I tell my boys that I am a recovering alcoholic, that I used to drink, and that for me it is like an allergy. I try to be careful to tell them drinking alcohol is not a moral issue, and all alcohol is not bad for everyone, just bad for alcoholics. I want my boys to have this information because they have to make their own decisions to drink or not to drink someday. If we tell them that all alcohol is bad, and then if they try it someday and find out it is good for them (if they find it tastes good, feels good, doesn't cause them problems, etc.), then they might throw out everything we've taught them because they would think we lied to them.

Research has shown something like this: If one of your parents was alcoholic, then you may have a 50/50 chance of becoming an alcoholic; and if both of your parents were alcoholic, there is an 85% chance of you becoming an alcoholic. (This is an old statistic, and it may not be accurate anymore.) This doesn't mean you will ever pick up a drink, but that if you do drink then your body may not handle it the way other people's bodies handle it. People who can handle alcohol responsibly are called social drinkers. Some people just don't drink either for moral reasons, or because they don't like how it feels, they know they get out of control with it and they don't like it, so they abstain - they might be called teetotalers.

I remember when my Grandma (Stella, Vera's mother) lived with us in Alberton in her 90's, she said she had never drank alcohol.

I don't know if my Mom or Dad were alcoholic (I knew they drank), but I didn't see them as being out of control with it. I think I may have found other family members in the Neel history that I think were alcoholic (an uncle), but I don't think it is fair for me to diagnose other family members and potentially embarrass them or their relatives. But being an alcoholic is nothing to be ashamed of. In our culture, there is still a lot of misunderstanding about alcoholism and addiction. Many still think it is only a moral issue, an issue of will power, and/or that an alcoholic does damage to himself or herself and others by choice because of his or her inherent weakness.

My own personal substance use/abuse story goes something like this: I first drank alcohol when I was in the

8th grade. I stole gin from my parents' liquor cabinet on a dare from a friend, wanting to fit in and be accepted by my friend. I got so drunk that I blacked out and don't remember how I got home. Then I didn't drink for a while until later in high school.

I also experimented with marijuana in high school, got scared and didn't use it for a while, then started using it again later in high school and college. Most of the people I hung around with drank alcohol and smoked marijuana like me (we probably chose each other as friends to party together).

When I was 18 years old, in September 1973, I was driving home after partying with friends. (This was the fall after I graduated from high school – it's funny but I never thought I'd forget the exact date, but now I can only remember the month and year of that event.) I had just dropped off my last friend at his home who was in the car with me up the Rattlesnake, and I was driving home and passed out. (My parents told people I just went to sleep at the wheel.) I went off the road on a curve and smacked straight into a large pine tree. I was driving my first car - a 1964 Buick Skylark convertible, V-6 engine, 2 speed automatic transmission, with no seat belts! I was a mess. Someone who lived nearby heard the crash and called for help. I broke my leg and messed my face up badly on the steering wheel, which required surgery to wire my jaw shut. The doctors screwed a metal plate on my right thigh bone with 8 screws. (No, it rarely sets off metal detectors at the airport in case you were wondering - too deep in my body, I guess.) I still have the plate screwed on to my thigh bone, and I can still feel a notch in the bone around my eye socket because my facial bones were broken when I hit the steering wheel. I was in the hospital for a week and then was laid up at my parents' home for months afterwards. (A question to any readers who knew me back then: Do you remember that event? If so, I would appreciate hearing from you and hearing your perspective.)

Well, I was 18 years old at the time of that car accident, and even though I could have died from that accident, I still didn't get it. I started partying again, and experimented with other drugs, although I didn't use the other hard drugs as regularly as marijuana and alcohol - which were my "drugs of choice." (Alcohol is a legal drug, with the chemical symbol ETOH, although many people don't think of alcohol as a drug.)

When Mom got cancer and was really sick (when my paternal grandmother Stella was living with us), her doctor said he couldn't prescribe this for her but suggested her children might know where to get marijuana for her to help her with her symptoms. Mom asked if I used marijuana, and I lied and said "no," but we got her some for her symptoms, and it helped her. It was weird seeing my Mom smoke pot. (And my recovery from addiction was partially motivated because of my guilt from when I stole my mother's marijuana.)

Missoula being a college town, it was also a party town; and I thought everyone who was "normal" smoked pot (actually, I probably chose my friends based on whether or not they smoked). I chose psychology as a major, and Mom lived long enough to see me graduate with my Bachelor's degree in June 1980. My parents asked me to delay looking for a job after college because Dad needed help taking care of Mom with her cancer, so I moved home. Mom died the following fall, September 1980.

I found my first job using my psychology degree when I got a CETA (Comprehensive Employment and Training Act) training position as a counselor in Glendive, Montana, in an outpatient alcohol/drug treatment program. Having driven all the way across the state for the job interview, I figured I had nothing to lose by being honest with them in the interview when they asked about my alcohol and drug usage history. I told them I drank and smoked marijuana like other college students. I agreed with them that if I got a six month training job that I wouldn't use drugs or alcohol in that small town because I might be using with potential clients. So I got six months of sobriety there, starting out with my first 24 hour period of sobriety on January 2, 1981. (My last party, last drink, last time I smoked marijuana was New Year's Eve 1980 and New Year's Day 1981 in Butte, Montana, with a friend who lived there as I was driving across the state to my new job.)

On the job, I had an "intervention" of the educational sort. I learned about what alcoholism and addiction were. I met with clients. I attended open AA meetings to find out what they were about. I remember visiting with a man in the hospital whose liver quit working because of his alcoholism, and his stomach was swollen up with fluids and poisons because his liver wasn't cleaning out his blood as it was supposed to do. He looked like he was pregnant or had a football in his belly. He said the doctor told him if he drank again that he would die, so he told the doctor to let him go drink his last six pack. (I sometimes wonder if he did die - I don't know the outcome.) I remember another man who said he wanted to drink so bad as he was going out the door that he grabbed a hammer and smashed his hand to stop his compulsion.

On the job in Glendive, people would ask me how I was doing, and I would often say "fine," but I guess my face said otherwise. I was probably scared, sad, depressed, lonely because there was a lot going on for me - my Mom had recently died and I was stuck in my grief; I didn't know anybody in this new town for me; and I was learning information that was affecting me strongly. However, I was emotionally "constipated," and I couldn't get it out, and couldn't express my feelings very well. Because of my behaviors, my employer sat me down and asked if I was drinking or using again because I guess I didn't look so good, but I wasn't using.

At about five months into the job there a week-long training on addictions that was brought into town (called "Community Interventions"), and there were "learning labs" or groups where we talked about what we've learned, and the emotional impact on us. I had been holding back a lot of emotions, and this gave me an opportunity to let a lot of it go, and it felt good, like getting a jump start. At this training, a co-worker (who was a recovering alcoholic) disclosed that he had not been honest and that he had been drinking again. He checked himself into an in-patient (hospital based) treatment program. I stayed in touch with him, and visited him at the hospital.

The things I was learning were confusing to me. I was not drinking or using other drugs as I had agreed, but I was learning about the patterns of use and abuse, and I was confused about whether I met the criteria that made me an alcoholic. I didn't know whether or not I could safely drink again or not after I finished my six month training job there and left Glendive (which ended my commitment to not drink or use other drugs during that time). So I used the medical insurance I had on the job, and the last of the sick leave I had and I checked myself into the same hospital that my friend/co-worker had just finished at St. Joseph's Hospital in Dickinson, North Dakota. I did the standard 28 days of inpatient therapy (based on the Hazleton model), did testing, attended educational and process groups, and did the first 5 Steps of the AA 12 Step program. I came to the conclusion that I was "chemically dependent," that my former chemical usage was getting in the way of me growing up, and that it put me and others at risk (especially if I was under the influence and driving a car).

So I left Dickinson, ND, and Glendive, MT, and came back to Alberton, MT, and lived with my Dad for a while. But that's another chapter to my story.

I have worked in various jobs in the helping

professions, some of which were in substance abuse treatment facilities, doing counseling. I am still learning, and I still attend my self-help support groups after 21 years, now almost 22 years (as of the date of this writing in 2002), and I still have a sponsor.

Love, Todd

(NOTE: I have shared these writings with my sponsors, who said they didn't feel I was violating the principles of anonymity by publishing this. I understand there may be other members of these programs that disagree with this.)

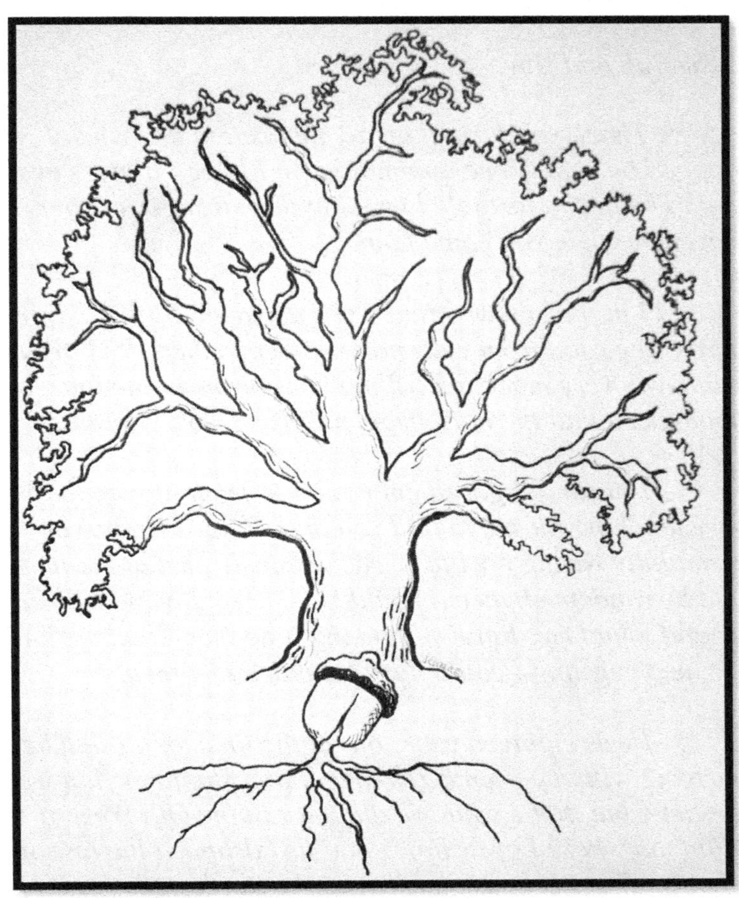

Chapter 17
Dear Bob and Kay

1/14/2015
Wednesday

Bob and Kay
Missoula, MT

Dear Bob and Kay,

Thank you for talking to me last Sunday when I stopped by your home unannounced. I hope I didn't cause you to be uncomfortable by seeing this stranger in your driveway when you came home.

I'm the guy who had a car accident, hitting a tree across the road from your home in September 1973. Again, thank you very much for calling 911 for me at the time, and I apologized that the noise from my crash woke you up.

I'm sorry I got so emotional in front of you, but it is very touching for me to find you and to say "Thank you" for essentially saving my life. I was seriously hurt at the time, and by random chance it could have been anyone who came by and found me. But I'm thinking if no one found me until the next morning I could have been dead by then.

I was eighteen years old at the time, and I had been partying with my friends (as illegal and stupid as that was at the time, but that's what we did back in the Old West of Montana where I grew up). I had just dropped the last of my friends off at his house further up the Rattlesnake, and I just as easily could have hurt or killed him or any of my friends who were in my car that night (or on many other nights that I drove in that condition) or I could have hurt or killed anyone else if I had crossed the center line. I am so grateful for my sobriety that I have now, and that I don't have to live a life filled with any remorse about such possibilities.

My dad, John Neel, retired from the Navy as a Captain in 1966 and we moved to Lincolnwood then. My mom, Alice Neel, did various volunteer work in Missoula (Red Cross, typing Braille, etc.) and she was also a bank teller at First National Bank. I don't know if you knew them or if you ever talked to them after my accident, but they are both passed away now.

That accident was a life changing event for me, as it should have been. I did not get the full lesson at the time, because I kept drinking and partying for about seven more years after that until I was age twenty-five in 1980 or 1981when I went to treatment and I have now been sober for about thirty-four years (at the time of this writing in 2015). I have worked in the addictions recovery field as well as the mental health field, and I am now an MSW social worker for the state of Idaho working for child protection services and children's mental health for about the last twenty-four years. I have two young adult boys (no grandchildren yet), and I've been married for twenty-five years (at the time of this writing). So I think my life has been worthwhile, worth living, and that I have made a difference in the world by helping others and making it a better place.

I do genealogy work as an interest and a hobby and searching for my ancestors and searching for and telling my own story has been a passion and past-time for me, which is part of why it was so important for me to find you and to tell you "Thank you."

I was visiting with my brother in Missoula over last weekend. He and I were driving around the Rattlesnake last

Sunday on the way to go X-C skiing that day up the Rattlesnake, and we took some side roads, reminiscing about our times here growing up, talking about memories. That's when I noticed you in your yard that morning taking care of your horses, and I had been wondering about your home over the years, as I have occasionally been looking for you to say "Thanks." I had been going to the Missoula library a few times to look up possible newspaper articles that might have reported my car accident, and to see if the reporting party was listed so I could express my gratitude.

So, Bob and Kay, I again hope I am not being a bother to you. I wanted to express these feelings I have. If by any chance you would like to tell your side of the story, I would appreciate hearing it. I appreciated hearing when you said that good has come for others because of that experience, because you have told other people of that story as well. I am also curious about another part of our story, in that did I hear and remember you correctly when I thought you said you had just moved into that house in September 1973, the same month of my accident?

Again, thank you for being there for me. I wish you well!

Sincerely,

Todd Neel

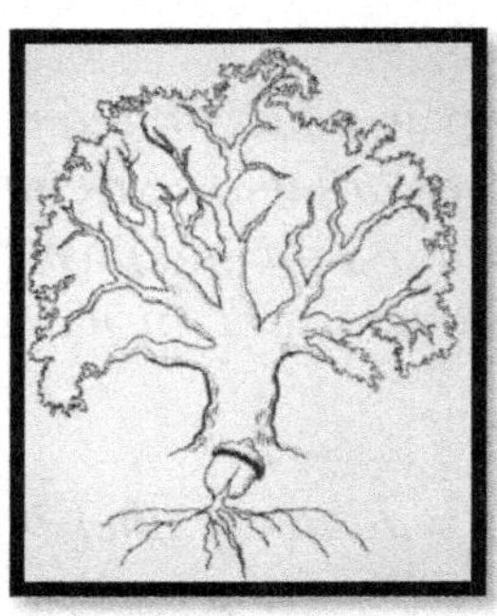

Chapter 18
The Role of Emotions

What are emotions? What role do they play in genealogy?

According to Karla McLaren (The Language of Emotions © 2010 Karla McLaren, excerpted with permission of publisher, Sounds True, Inc., on page 29 of her book), she states "*... we truly need our emotions. We can't live functional lives without them. Without our emotions, we can't make decisions; we can't decipher our dreams and visions; we can't set proper boundaries or behave skillfully in relationships; we can't identify our hopes or support the hopes of others; and we can't connect to, or even find, our dearest loves.*" For me, those parts of her words about relationships and our ability to connect with, or even find our dearest loved ones is vitally important to survival (individually and as a species), to thriving (being the best you can be), and having a life worth living!

Kahlil Gibran said …

"And a woman who held a babe
against her bosom said,
Speak to us of Children.
And he said:
Your children are not your children.
They are the sons and daughters of
Life's longing for itself.
They come through you
but not from you,
And though they are with you,
yet they belong not to you.

"You may give them your love
but not your thoughts,
For they have their own thoughts.
You may house their bodies
but not their souls,
For their souls dwell in the house of tomorrow,
which you cannot visit,
not even in your dreams.

"You may strive to be like them,
but seek not to make them like you.
For life goes not backward
nor tarries with yesterday.

"You are the bows from which
your children as living arrows are sent forth.
The archer sees the mark upon the path of the infinite,
and He bends you with His might
that His arrows may go swift and far.
Let your bending in the archer's hand be for gladness;
For even as He loves the arrow that flies,
so He loves also the bow that is stable."

(from The Prophet by Kahlil Gibran, 1923)

These words cause me to reverberate with emotion. Deep in my being, I know that this is true. These words are so good, so palatable that I hunger for more. Is it folly for me to have dreams about my children's futures and about my place in their dreams by writing this book? (I hope not.) Gibran says I cannot visit them in my dreams in the "house of tomorrow," which makes me want to argue with him! (Arguing with him will be a little difficult since he died in 1931.) Did he have dreams of having readers beyond his physical life? By my reading his words does he not have immortality? Like with a good poem or other challenging words you might read, I invite you to re-read this passage, turning them over in your mind, chewing on them to get at the richness in the deep marrow of the bone … his words, your thoughts, your feelings … still vibrating with echoes …

We need to explore. We need to seek out one another. We need to find one another. Our children depend on it! We must connect, and then we need to release. We need one another whether we have offspring or not, (in the past, the present, or in the future). And if some of us don't have offspring, our species won't survive.

We are social animals. We need to be able to find one another. Our emotions are like radar, getting pings echoing back from others as we fly through the universe.

Our species needs to propagate! Or, maybe our species has too many offspring right now. Perhaps we are propagating ourselves to death with over-population and related symptoms of pollution, global warming, war, genocide, terrorism, school shootings and other mass shootings, family domestic violence issues, poverty, child abuse, neglect and abandonment issues, mental health and addiction issues, etc. Are these signs that we are just lemmings following one another in a suicidal leap over the edge of the cliff and into the sea? Maybe. But, I choose to have hope rather than hopelessness!

And, if we choose not have children, remember that our thoughts and behaviors are also like our children. Our actions are also our offspring.

We need relationships with people like the baker who makes bread for us, the butcher who prepares our meat, and/or the farmer who grows grains, fruits, and vegetables for us to eat. Maybe we don't have a direct, face-to-face relationship with some of these people, but we do reach into each other's pocketbooks! We need the grocer that we buy these goods from. (By the way, do you know the name of the store manager, the cashier, or other staff at your neighborhood grocery store that you regularly shop at? How far does your relationship with them go?)

We need a relationship with our boss to get a paycheck, or to get our retirement pension from if we are at that phase of life. And we need the government who protects us and regulates our behaviors with laws and regulations, and that we pay taxes to. (Or not! Are you that independent? Can you do it all on your own without an over-reaching government? If you are, I salute you! But I do appreciate it when you pay your taxes!) I do appreciate the roads that we drive on, and I do enjoy some aspects of our governments that keep us safe. And I do have some resentments about the governments of the world, including our own at times.

Anyway … what was I talking about? Oh, yeah … emotions and genealogy!

Feelings and Emotions and Genealogy

A common term that many people use for emotions is "feelings." Yet, some people differentiate between feelings and emotions, stating that one is a noun, and one is a verb. We "feel" (a verb) our "emotions" (a noun). Most people use the terms "feelings" and "emotions" for the same thing, and I still use them interchangeably. But I like to consider the concept of "feeling my emotions."

Can you feel your emotions? Can you accurately name them and interpret them? Can you express them in a healthy way that increases the chances of getting your needs met, including your need to have successful relationships?

Can you feel your emotions? Can you accurately name them and interpret them?

As a practicing and as a recovering alcoholic, there were times in my life when I did not "feel my feelings" or "feel my emotions" very well. There were times that I was numb when I did not listen to the wisdom of my emotions (or "instincts" or "intuition"). And this got me into trouble when they came "squirting out sideways" (meaning they were not clearly recognized or honored or expressed respectfully or responsibly). This can still get me in trouble. When I "puke my process," I am "dysregulated." I can over-react to a situation, maybe cussing or screaming or using a non-verbal gesture at someone that didn't deserve it. Sometimes my emotions are expressed indirectly (i.e., passive-aggressively), dumped on the wrong person (called "projection"), let out at the wrong time, for the wrong reason, or in the wrong place, or in the wrong proportions that the situation didn't call for. And this can cause damage. Like a bull loose in a china shop.

Sometimes it seems some people don't know how to "handle" me, and don't know how to react or respond to my expression of myself, or my expression of my emotional life. I don't need to be "handled," yet I know I can be overbearing sometimes, and I am sometimes dysregulated.

It may appear that I am trying to show that emotions can be destructive. But they can be used for very positive and constructive actions as well if used for the good. Even anger can be valuable if used productively. Some think that there are good emotions and bad emotions, but this isn't accurate. Some emotions may feel good, and some may feel bad, but it's what we do with them that makes them good or bad. If we push away the emotions that feel bad, they may "come squirting out sideways." They are trying to tell us something. There is great wisdom in our emotional life.

There is great wisdom in our emotional life.

And in regard to genealogy and our ancestors and descendants, if we can't behave skillfully in relationships (including how we manage our emotions), it will probably be difficult to create and raise healthy offspring who have an active interest in where they came from, where they are going to, or thinking about things beyond themselves.

Apathy or Energy - What is Your Tipping Point?

Do you ever "feel like" doing something or not doing something? Without any rational thought processes, or without logical calculations about the costs and benefits of doing that "thing"? Do you ever "not feel like going to work," or "not feel like doing the laundry"? Do you ever feel like grabbing the remote control and turning on the TV? How about just having a big bowl of popcorn with lots of butter on it? Or if that's too hard because you have to cook the popcorn, how about just grabbing that bag of chips? This can be our emotional life talking to us.

Do you feel like following this thread of thought that I'm trying to express here, and will you read further about what I'm trying to get at, or do you feel like skipping this or avoiding this topic altogether? Or do you "feel" like I have something to say here, and you are "hungry" to get at what I'm trying to express here? Stop or go?

Consider the concept of your "tipping point." What moves you into action of getting up, moving, taking a step, and turning left or right at this decision point of your life? Or will you just sit there?

Feeling my emotions can lead me to motivation and to action, some trigger that will move me in one direction or another. (And I do have some emotions that lead me to apathy and procrastination on many days. Some days I do go for that bowl of popcorn and the TV remote!) Sometimes I am conscious of my emotions and I can name them, which may lead me to a "tipping point" of action in one direction or another, preferably in a constructive direction. And sometimes my emotions are just under the surface and I'm not conscious of them, and I'm following my feet in a direction that I know I should, or shouldn't go, and I don't precisely understand why I'm doing this.

Right now, do you "feel" like reading this book about my genealogy journey? Do you "feel" like pursuing your own family history? Do you have emotions that cause you to approach or avoid doing your own genealogy work? (Or doing or avoiding your own emotional deep-process work?) Can you name these emotions?

Do you ever "feel like" doing something or not doing something? Do you feel like pursuing this search?

Do you feel like following the tracks, the footprints of your own ancestors? Do you feel like consciously and deliberately leaving hints or clear tracks of your existence for your descendants to find someday? Are you worthy of this mission? Do you have something to say? (This is a self-esteem question.) Do you think they (your readers, or even your relatives who are looking at your pictures that came out of a cardboard box) will care about you, and care about whether or not you were ever alive? Do you want them to be curious about you?

A note to the Redundancy Police (as some readers have commented that I go on and on too much trying to make my point), I'm trying to drive my point home here: GET OFF THAT COUCH AND DO IT! Write that story, or even just that note about that thought that might turn out to be a great novel! LABEL those photos and that photo album!! ORGANIZE those notes! LEAVE YOUR MARK AND LEAVE A GOOD MARK!!! I do believe that ***WE ALL HAVE SOMETHING IMPORTANT TO SHARE*!** (I apologize for "yelling" at you here with my capital letters in this paragraph.)

I am trying to help you find that emotional fuel inside you, and I'm trying to light it off with the spark of my passions!

Are You Out of Touch?

We have more than just the 5 senses.

I like to think about our traditional five senses (touch, taste, smell, sight, and hearing) as an incomplete list of our senses. We use these physical senses to look out at the world. They provide vital information necessary for our <u>survival</u>.

We also have other senses like our emotions, passions, and intuition which we can use to look inward also to provide us with vital information. There is a lot of wisdom we can get from our emotions if we can listen to them, interpret them accurately, and express them constructively. They provide vital information necessary for our <u>thriving</u>!

It is useful, and in some cases essential, to know the difference between what is healthy to approach or to touch, and what we should avoid. We use our senses to figure this out, and being in touch with our senses helps us get our needs met.

Our senses are our connection with our world.

But sometimes it is confusing as to what is pleasant and what is healthy for us, and what isn't. Sometimes what is pleasing is not healthy. Think about that example of popcorn with lots of butter on it. (What exactly is "comfort food"?) Is it in our best interests to go for that thing that makes us comfortable at this moment? Think about alcohol or other drugs or medicine for the alcoholic: How do we know what is good for us, and what is dangerous or otherwise not in our own best interest? How did some of these things get so confusing, so cunning, baffling, and powerful?

How do we know what emotional food is good for us? (What is emotional food? See section below on "Comfort Food, Emotional Food.")

And is this genealogy work in our best interest? Is it necessary for our survival? Or is it for our thriving, helping us to be the best that we can be? What if it pushes other family members away? (This is not my intention, but sometimes it seems like that is the result.) Can we use just our 5 traditional senses to figure this out? Do we need our emotions also? (YES!)

The A's
(Addictions, Autism, Attachment, Abandonment)

For persons with ***addictions***, what should we avoid putting in our mouths if we are going to get clean and remain sober and healthy? Also, for persons with addictions what kinds of people do we need in our relationships? As a recovering alcoholic, is my family good for me? Substance abuse is just the tip of the iceberg for the alcoholic or addict. If the alcoholic or addict can get clean, then to maintain sobriety it is essential that we work on healthy relationships. Should we isolate ourselves and give up relationships or avoid them? (NO! This eventually would lead to physically or emotionally starving ourselves to death.) Should we re-examine our social networks of support? (YES!)

Our senses, when healthy, tell us this vital information like radar in a war zone and we're trying to find the enemy, or like a social situation of entering a room full of strangers or even a room full of family members. Who can we find that are good for us, and who will not be in our own best interests?

Discernment, judgment, and evaluation can be useful like the green, yellow, and red lights of a traffic signal at an intersection (although the term "judgement" can have a bad reputation). Our senses, including our emotions, can help us with this skill.

Consider the sense of physical touch (and think about it as a metaphor for our emotional senses): Do I feel the irritation of this thing from my shirt that's rubbing the back of my neck? Do I feel it and can I interpret it correctly because it's out of my reach and I can't see it, or will I just squirm and get irritable and take it out on someone who doesn't deserve it? Should I come closer to this thing I feel and embrace the problem as a challenge and an opportunity, or should I try to ignore it and move away and avoid resolving it, maybe just having an irritated or angry look on my face and be grouchy with other people? I "feel" with the sensory nerves in my skin, one of the largest "organs" in our body. If I can accurately "feel" the thread from the label on the back of my new shirt, the discomfort might lead me to try unsuccessfully to ignore it or move away from it, or to examine where the irritation is coming from and do something about correcting the problem.

NOTE: I use the example of the paragraphs above and below because I have a family member who has a diagnosis on the ***autism spectrum***, and I suspect other family members of mine may also have this diagnosis, or at least symptoms of this diagnosis. I recognize traits or characteristics of autism in myself sometimes. There are other people out there in the world that I suspect have traits of autism or other mental health or medical disorders but are not diagnosed as such. There are people currently in positions of great power and influence who seem to have traits of undiagnosed conditions that affect many of us, and there have been famous persons in history who were diagnosed with a mental health or a medical disorder long after their death. Sometimes such people have these issues with "***sensory processing***", like a person with autism.

Consider the sense of vision (and also consider this example as a metaphor): Some people are uncomfortable with direct eye contact with others. This may also be just one aspect of a whole spectrum of issues of difficulties with relationships, like ***attachment*** or ***abandonment*** or other ***intimacy*** issues. (Refer to *Chapter 7 - Attachment, Bonding, and Trauma* for more on this topic.) It may be hard to identify why one has difficulty looking at someone directly in the eyes, and so they may avoid direct face-to-face interactions, leading to avoidance and isolation. Or that person might embrace this problem, reframe it as a challenge and an opportunity, and say to themselves "I know I get uncomfortable looking at others directly in the face, but I'm going to try to work on this as a social skill that I want to improve."

Sometimes I just have a feeling about a person or a social situation that makes me feel very strongly (either comfortable or uncomfortable), and I just can't figure out why. Our emotions talk to us about relationships. Can I feel that irritation (or attraction) when that person walks into the room? Can I name what I'm feeling? Can I interpret it accurately? Can I take responsibility for my emotion, and not blame them by my passing judgment upon their character? Can I use my emotion constructively? Can I be mature enough to be calm, patient, and "sit" with that emotion (even if I'm just appearing calm on the outside until I figure it out)?

Love or Lust?

In relationships, we might sometimes experience our feelings of interest or excitement about another person and maybe think that it is "The Big L" (or love). Or we may even feel disgust or revulsion which later turns out to be love, as the passions of love and hate are actually not that far apart because psychological defense mechanisms can cause our emotions to be very deceptive.

At other times we might feel bored with the calmness of a healthy relationship. Some of us thrive on chaos or control issues, but we don't recognize it as such. We might not recognize that we can work on this and change our thinking and feelings about a particular relationship, or about our patterns in relationships. ("Why is this happening to me, again?") Some of us may not understand our part in the dynamics of relationships. Maybe I like having a partner that I can push around, or perhaps I like a partner who will make decisions for me and tell me what to do. Both of these might be variations of "control issues".

Are we part of the problem, or are we part of the solution? Ask yourself the question: "Where do I end and where do you begin?", which is a question about emotional and psychological boundaries.

How many love songs are about "How can I tell you that I love you?" Can there be genealogy without love? (I don't think so.) And what is the strongest emotion related to genealogy? LOVE!!! (That's my opinion!)

Yet some people disagree that love is an emotion. I like the saying that "*love, the feeling, is a result of love, the verb*" (meaning that emotions follow actions). Of course, we might be distracted by "*eye candy*," meaning that another person's hair or some other attribute might be turning us on. Or off. It can get confusing.

Have you ever been distracted by "eye candy"?

Karla McLaren says "*The truth about love is this: love is constant; only the names change. Love doesn't just restrict itself to romantic relationships. Love is everywhere – in the hug of a child, in the concern of a friend, in the center of your family, and in the hearts of your pets. When you're lost and you can't seem to find love anywhere, you're listening to love in human language instead of listening to the language of love. Love is constant; it's not an emotion*". (Page 124 from The Language of Emotions, © 2010 Karla McLaren, excerpted with permission of publisher, Sounds True, Inc.) I encourage you to check her out!

Healthy/Unhealthy Nervous Systems, Including Emotions

What is healthy or unhealthy is not always black and white.

For some of us, our nervous systems (including our emotions) are unhealthy and are not working properly and don't give us accurate feedback about the world around us and we put ourselves in dangerous situations. I know that as a recovering alcoholic that I didn't always feel and interpret my emotions correctly. Sitting in support groups with other recovering alcoholics and addicts, we sometimes compare our stories about the wreckages of our past, and compare our stories about the hostages we took, or the scars or the metal parts on or in our bodies because we were not "feeling our feelings" in a healthy way, and we put ourselves (and other people) in dangerous situations, and we had "accidents" and/or committed crimes. (Hostages, scars, metal parts, accidents and crimes can be taken literally here, or as metaphors.)

For some of us, we may have unresolved ***trauma*** that leads us to misinterpret our feelings or emotions about a certain situation (or patterns of situations). Sometimes we sought, or created, or contributed to chaos. Or sometimes we avoid things that weren't really there because we thought we saw ghosts from the past (called projections). Is that pain or discomfort I feel from the situation right here and now? Or is it something left over from my history and it really doesn't apply to this current situation? (NOTE: This may also apply to other persons with traumatic histories, and they may be reacting to their own ghosts because we remind them of someone else.)

Pathology and dis-ease and relationships can get messy. What is healthy and what is unhealthy is not always clear. ("Dis-ease" can mean "not at ease.") Health and recovery can get messy.

Reality Check

We can use our five senses to look out at the world, and if we're lucky, we can compare notes with others and do a "reality check" to see if the other person saw what we saw. (It takes reasonably healthy individuals to do such reality checks without it turning into a gossip session.) But what about our senses that we can use to look inward, what some people call our sixth sense? Do other people feel what I feel who experienced the same situation? If so, would that be healthy? (We all approach situations with our own personal histories, and therefore we each have our own baggage about large people, small people, loud people, quiet people, etc.)

What about our filters or our "rose-colored glasses" that affect our five senses? Do we recognize our lens or worldview from which we look out through? Or do we just know that what we see/hear/taste/touch/smell/feel is reality? (***Hint***: It's not reality!) How do we know what our emotions are (which affect our perceptions), and what they mean? How do our emotions relate to reality? How do we know who and where we are in relation to other people in space and time? (This can be the space-time continuum that I talk about in *Chapter 20 - Saga of a Pilgrimage.)* We each have our own histories and experiences which affect our perceptions.

The people we have relationships with can be in close physical proximity, and we can have relationships with people from afar. Can I feel my emotions about my family, near or far, whether they be my biological, legal, or chosen family? Do they have feelings about this also? Can we compare notes by doing a reality check? Do I have emotions of interest and excitement about them, or do I have feelings of disgust and revulsion? How about them – how do they feel about me? (These people I'm talking about can be either living people or dead people.) Do I currently have relationships with living people that I have access to that I can compare notes with?

Did you see that, too? Am I going crazy, or what? (If you're comparing notes and doing a reality check with dead people, you might want to get a mental health check-up, though.)

And what does this have to do with genealogy? Think about the relationships that have had to occur in the past for our ancestors to have propagated offspring who had offspring that had offspring that got us here to feel these emotions and think these thoughts and see these things right now. Did our ancestors understand that each of our unique perspectives is just a point of view? Did they have thoughts about the nature of reality? And what about our descendants, if we have any? Are they (or will they be) capable of having relationships and having offspring that care about other people's points-of-view? Will they (or did they) have the capacity for compassion, sympathy, or empathy? Did our ancestors and will our descendants have good boundaries, and understand and be clear about where each of us ends, and where the other person begins? And do we have a part in that? (YES, by golly, I think we do have a part in our descendants' mental health and their grasp of reality, but we do not have complete control – I believe we do have an influence on their mental health! No matter what Kahlil Gibran says!) Our descendants are watching our behaviors, and the results of our behaviors – we are role models!

Motivation and Emotions

I know that my emotions move me, like the wind, like the currents of a river. And I have a choice in how I respond to their wisdom. How will I set my sails? Will I go downwind, the easy way, or will I tack and work my way up into the incoming storm? I will conclude this chapter (soon) with a section on "What? So what? Now what?"

Motivation, Intention, Needs, Wants (redux from Introduction)

... Some of my emotions about your pursuit of your family, even if I don't know you, is trust and hope! (Some people don't believe "hope" and "trust" are emotions, though. The emotion related to "trust" might be about safety and comfort. I'm having difficulty in naming this emotion, but

it's warm and fuzzy.) My hope is that you can feel passion for your ancestors, about your current living family, about your chosen family, and about your future family - your descendants or your readers if you decide to write or to leave some writings, photos or some markers behind. If you can feed this passion, then the future of humanity is looking brighter! I encourage you to care about the future! Be conscious about what happens seven generations from now, like our Native American brothers and sisters teach us!

Again, can I sit with these feelings, listen to them? What are they trying to tell me?

Emotional Vocabulary and Other Emotional Skills

Another essential aspect about emotions is that if we pay attention to them, we can work to broaden our emotional vocabulary. By doing this we can learn skills regarding what we do with our emotions, how we communicate them, and take responsibility for ourselves and be less of a victim of someone else's words, thoughts, and deeds. We can get better at feeling and listening to our emotions and where they come from. We can do our own personal work. We can do our own genealogy work and seek out our ancestors, or not, but at least we can make a more conscious choice about it. (Our emotions drive us towards or away from something.) With a better set of tools (like an increased emotional vocabulary, learning about assertiveness and non-violent communication and applying these skills), the world can be a better place! With more consciousness about our behaviors, thoughts, and emotions, and with a willingness to take more responsibility for ourselves, we can be more deliberate in our choices instead of just reacting to and being at the mercy of other people, places, and things.

What does it mean to "broaden our emotional vocabulary"? Like an artist who may have more words than the average person to describe various shades of colors on their palate of paint they are using. Or like an Eskimo who may have many more words than the average American to describe snow and weather conditions because their lives are much more dependent on it. If we value our emotions, if they are important to us, we can broaden our emotional vocabulary to describe what we are feeling. With this we can better meet our needs and our wants. We can read and write and sit and meditate and be in relationship with ourselves and with others more than we are doing right now. As a result, we can feel better about ourselves. We can have better relationships.

Many Americans might have fewer words in their vocabulary to describe emotions, especially heterosexual beer-drinking males, than a French poet, for example. (I apologize if I am stepping on any toes here!) I know that when I was a practicing (i.e., drinking) alcoholic, my emotional vocabulary was fairly narrow and limited. In my recovery from alcoholism, and with the help of treatment professionals, I learned to pay attention to my emotions more, and I have learned to express them in a better way to increase the chances of getting my needs and wants met (for example, using assertiveness skills, and learning about and applying non-violent communication skills). I'm still learning about boundaries (i.e., "Where do you end, and where do I begin?") and I'm continuing to learn about the difference between my needs and my wants.

Taking Responsibility ...

We have choices in our thought process, and therefore we have some choices in our emotions, i.e., "I'm bored - this doesn't interest me" (which can be a Victim attitude), or we can choose to say, "I feel grateful for the hardships that our ancestors went through, and I'm grateful and appreciate the very hard and heroic work they did to provide for the needs of my parents, grandparents, great-grandparents and others so that I could be alive today with the comforts and challenges that I have been gifted with." Or even, "I'm glad this guy, Todd, is doing this work for me. I'm glad I bought his book!"

There are whole books and workshops on taking responsibility for yourself, on relationships, communication, emotions, assertiveness, and non-violent communication that say it better than I can. You can seek these out on your own, and I encourage you to do so.

I have hope for those whose lives may have been positively affected by the work I do. I hope that my words and deeds have not been destructive. My intention is to take responsibility for my own thoughts, words, deeds, and emotions. And then I release, and I let go.

I have hope that with my words and deeds from my journey to take more responsibility for myself that it might help you improve your life. I hope that I have communicated in a responsible way so that I am clear that I am taking responsibility for myself. And I trust that you can take responsibility for your own self. I know that some of my words might be provocative, and might be pushing your buttons. I invite you to take responsibility for your own stuff, and not be a Victim to me.

Mystery

The role of my emotions in relationships can be mysterious. What is it that causes me to be "comfortable" or "uncomfortable" with another person? What might cause me to approach them, or to avoid another person? What might cause another person to approach or avoid me?

It's still a mystery, and that's the sweetness of it.

As I've said elsewhere, I want to leave the world a better place than I found it. And to do no harm. I hope I am being successful at this. I know that I have made errors in my being human and being a student of humanity. Does this feel good?

Comfort Food, Emotional Food

Getting back to the question: What is "comfort food"? Do you have some of these? Mine are things like popcorn with lots of butter and salt on it. Homemade chicken and dumpling soup like my grandmother and my mom made. White rice with butter and salt and pepper on it. Cream of Wheat hot cereal with brown sugar, butter, and milk. Rich home-made vanilla ice cream and chocolate syrup! And under some circumstances, like when I'm under stress, I love good chocolate and hot black coffee with it. Many of my comfort foods are physically unhealthy for me, except maybe a good, crisp, juicy apple, which is both comfortable and good for me.

Why don't I go for fruit and vegetables as a comfort food?

What emotion am I feeling right before I reach for that food that comforts me? What am I really hungry for? What a great mystery! Only you can answer that question for yourself! Sit with it for a while …

What? So what? Now what?

This is a simple framework that I learned in graduate school. With these questions, I can fairly easily access my emotions and figure out what to do with them. I can fairly easily access this simple model and adjust my thought processes which will adjust my emotions: ***What*** is it that I am looking at? ***So what?*** What does it mean? What does it matter? ***Now what?*** What am I going to do about it? What is the next step?

To the reader: What is your action plan? What are you going to do next? How are you going to accomplish it? When will you start it, and when do you intend to finish it? How will you measure your success?

By the way, if you're still reading this, congratulations! You've shown a commitment to feed your family hunger!

Chapter 19
What it's like to lose a father and gain a son?

March 2002

In 1994, I sat in a circle with Dominican Brother Joe Kilikevice on Lake Coeur d'Alene at Camp Lutherhaven in one of his Creating Male Spirit retreats. Our men's group had discovered that there were many similar groups of male gatherings around the country where there are familiar themes of father and son wounds. We found Brother Joe who was well respected in facilitating such gatherings.

Earlier in that same year, my youngest son, Joshua, was born on March 8, and my father died on May 24. Brother Joe wrote to me after the retreat suggesting I write an article sharing my thoughts and feelings on the love I have for my sons and on the loss of my father, especially since the two very significant events occurred so closely together. And so I did, finally, eight years later (in 2002), thanks to Brother Joe for the motivation. Sometimes we need a catalyst to take action.

What it has been like for me is … busy, very busy! I'm motivated to finally respond to Joe's suggestion because he will be here again later this month for another retreat. I have thought about writing these significant events numerous times, but I was distracted by the many roles and activities of my life, including being the executor of my father's estate. How do you clean up after the loss of your father? It's a big deal!

And being a new Dad for the second time also took a lot of time and energy. (My first son, Nathan, was born in 1992.) Add to that my marriage, full-time job, friends, family, health, recreation, volunteering, homeowner responsibilities, etc. I have had a very full plate.

I have a passion for writing, and I am using Joe's suggestion as motivation to follow through with documenting that time of my life around these significant events surrounding my manhood. (Like pulling out the photographs and labeling them before we forget.) There being just two months between my son's birth and my father's death is not insignificant. And it is very connected with my family hunger.

As I re-read Joe's letter from September 1994, I appreciate his comment about "the love you express toward your sons …" This is true. I do love my sons, and I'm glad that it is evident. I also love my father just as I know he loved me. But the love for my father and the love for my sons is different. I have to admit that I love each of my sons differently as well.

When my first son, Nathan, was born, overwhelming feelings I experienced were: "It's a miracle! A life created! What a beautiful child!" I cried tears that literally took my breath away!

When my second son, Joshua, was born, I remember hearing myself saying "It's just another miracle." I cried at the birth of Josh, but there was something different. I think I was in a different place, mentally, spiritually, developmentally. I may have been taking life more for granted. Perhaps I was more calloused or numb or distracted or otherwise less present at the time. I had been making many trips back and forth between Idaho and Montana to see my Dad when my wife was pregnant with Josh. I was aware that my father was near the end of his life as this new boy was being created at the hospital in Spokane.

Before the birth of my second son, I recall loving my first son with thoughts of "How could we love another child any more than this?" But when my second son was born, as we all grew up together (I grew up, also), I came to love each of my sons in their own unique way. It was like each of our relationships was a separate person with its own unique personality and characteristics of its own.

I've heard that a relationship is made up of you, and me, and a third being some call our ***"spiritual child"*** that is born of our relationship, and it is bigger than you and me alone. Greater than the sum of the parts.

When I found pictures I had taken of a cat we used to have that had died, I was looking at them, and Josh saw the pictures and commented "What a cute kittie! I almost forgot what he looked like." Josh talked about his idea of "pet heaven," and he wondered if he will see Willy (the cat) again. He cried about how much he missed the cat. Sweet, very sweet tears - embracing the memories. Joshua was still very easy to reach, to touch, to hug, to talk with at that time (when he was about seven). I loved it when Josh was playful and said "Let's play! Let's tickle play!" Josh and I together have tenderness, sweetness, and playfulness as part of this spiritual child born between him and me. Like the opposite ends of a magnet that attract one another.

My relationship with Nathan is different. At age nine (at the time of this writing), he was getting harder to connect with. When I reached to him for a hug, he would quickly duck and dodge and run away, looking back with a smile on his face. He will still reach out to touch me, but it is on his terms. Sometimes he "zones out" and it is harder to get him to respond to emotions, to "hello," or to anything else. I still find him sneaking up behind me and grabbing me, and with a growl, he will say "Let's wrestle!" (He knows I could squash him and tickle him every time, and that sometimes I let him win.) Evasiveness and distance is part of this spiritual child born between Nate and me, but we still orbit around each other. Like the similar ends of a magnet that repel each other, but remain close.

When we were looking at the pictures of Willy, feelings of sadness came up for me looking at my boys, thinking "I hope I never have to bury one of my sons." I feel sad reading this again - tears in my eyes, tears of gratitude and of grief. Gratitude for what I have right here and now. Grief for things already lost.

Growing up I took my parents for granted. I had security that they would always be there for me, and therefore I could ignore them and go on with other things. An experience in my adolescence when the parents of one of my friends got a divorce, I was shaken up. How could that be? Parents are supposed to be there forever, together, for their kids. Parents don't get divorced! (How naïve I was. Divorce is way too common these days.)

My parents didn't divorce, but my mom died at a relatively young age of fifty-nine when I was twenty-five years old. And then my father died at eighty years of age when I was about thirty-nine years old. Still, that's too soon!

I don't take my parents for granted anymore. The scabs after their acute loss have fallen off, but I can still find the scars.

I know now this physical life is brief. The emotional experience of our "spiritual children" still echoes of my parents' lives. They are still there for me in my memories, photographs, artifacts, stories, etc. And my parents are "there" (or "here") for me spiritually now, if I am open to receive that. (I still see the ghost of my mother on the streets of Spokane from when she was a child as she grew up there, and I clearly know this is my imagination. Or is it?)

Emotionally my parents provided security for me, a secure base from which to launch into the distant and sometimes difficult waters of life (in the language of attachment and bonding). With some scar tissue left where I'm not as resilient as I'd like to be at times.

In hindsight, one of the qualities of my relationship with my father was "distance." While I knew there was love, there was little physical affection between us. I rarely remember hugging my Dad. I certainly don't have any memories of wrestling with him when I was a little boy. In his elder years, I passed behind him while he sat in his kitchen chair, and I physically reached out to touch him on the shoulder but couldn't bring myself to close the gap of just those few inches. I regret that we did not share such closeness, and I am trying to keep those ways of connecting with my sons open.

One of the realizations I have about the loss of my father and my mother is that I am now an orphan. Not that I need to go away to an orphanage, but that there is no one, no parent figure, left for me to lean on if I need it. They were the gatekeepers to heaven, the beyond, to the afterlife of this physical life. I looked up to them. I could call on them for answers even though somewhere beginning in my teenage years or before I discounted their answers more and more. I could call on them to bail me out of trouble that I got myself into.

I have since developed my own understanding of a Higher Power, a being or force that I can and do lean on (which I now refer to as God as I understand him/her, sometimes I call Mother Nature, or the mysterious "99 Names of God"). Mother Nature or Higher Power is now my secure base. But I am now a gatekeeper to heaven for my boys. They now look up to me - which I am reminded of when Josh says he misses me, or when Nathan takes my glasses and puts them on and says he wants a pair himself.

And my sons rely on me to take care of their needs. They lean on me. And I like it.

And it keeps me busy. Very busy.

Chapter 20
Saga of a Pilgrimage
Written November 2004

My father-in-law, Ralph St. Clair Carson, Jr., died in November 2003. My mother-in-law said she wasn't interested in keeping any of the tools from his shop and she would appreciate having that part of her basement cleaned out. So in August of the following year my wife, our sons, and I flew to Missouri for our usual summer visit with Phyllis. I made arrangements to rent a truck to clean out his shop and haul his detritus back to our home in Idaho. As I looked on a map to plan the return trip, I realized that Nebraska, the state my father was born and raised in, was right on the path back to Idaho. So I planned a pilgrimage to find my father's hometown like my ancestors did.

Is there a relationship between my father and this mission about my father-in-law?

There was still a sense of sadness about these losses, and in a way, this was part of the cleaning of the emotional wounds of grief. My sons really loved their grandfather, Ralph, as we all did. They never really knew their grandfather, John. Maybe through this story they can build attachment to my father.

Can attachment to stuff make up for our attachment to family?

We left home on a hot August Saturday, flying out of Spokane heading for St. Louis in the hot, steamy, humid Midwest. What a great month to visit that part of the country.

We then took our customary shuttle to Rolla. On Sunday I packed and cleaned Ralph's shop, and on Monday I rented the U-Haul and hired some muscle, Bob and Joe, from a local moving company to help me load the truck.

I reset the odometer to "0".

Guys and their workshops – Ralph's is a gold mine!

I saw this as an opportunity for myself, acquiring a assemblage of very fine tools and supplies that Ralph collected over his lifetime, making our shop a better-off place. Or from the Carson's expressed point of view, a chance to "keep it in the family." My brother-in-law, Gary, said he was not interested in his Dad's tools.

It was an opportunity for me to reflect on items that represented a lifetime of hobbies, interests, and callings – symbols of a lifetime of an interesting human being who was important to me – my father-in-law, who gave life to my wife, and whose DNA remain in my sons. Do genetics speak to such interests?

These are the very tools and supplies that Ralph used to build and keep his home running smoothly, spend his free time with, and to do whatever else guys do in their shops. The family built this home when Mary and Gary were just little kids in the 1960's, and I'm sure some of these tools were used for that.

Out of his shop, Ralph cultivated hobbies of model railroading, ham radio, painting, chess, computers, electronics, and other various interests. As a Ph.D. and professor of Electrical Engineering at the University of Missouri – Rolla (UMR), Ralph was definitely interested in "stuff"!

Phyllis looked at all this paraphernalia and made statements like "What a bunch of junk!" Mary said something similar and added "You aren't going to bring that home are you?"

There was a repair man who came to Phyllis' home and saw Ralph's shop that summed it up best, in my opinion, when he said something like "What a gold mine!"

Phyllis said that when Ralph got interested in something, he really got into it! It looked like he went on spending sprees, purchasing some very fine quality tools, some of which looked like they had been used very little if at all. Sometimes he kept receipts showing the original purchase price, reflecting inflation. And if you know about the build quality of American tools, these were definitely better built than the tools I have in my shop, which were mostly made of plastic in China. So, I drooled over Ralph's stuff!

As a guy, I know all about our shops. Mine is an opportunity for escape from the noise in the house, and a chance for creative outlet. Ralph made a chess set, a beautiful model railroad layout, furniture for their home, and many other pieces of evidence of his existence. I have made some very nice toy boxes for my sons using dovetail joints, a kitchen cabinet for my wife, and have done other repairs in the household. I plan on doing more, but I have to negotiate my time with Mary. She says she has to be a single parent when I take on projects in the garage. (Evidence of abandonment issues? I know I demonstrate a pattern of unfinished projects. Am I running from something? What am I really building for my family? Pathology or resilience?)

As I pack and clean Ralph's shop, I reflect on my own mortality, considering what evidence I would leave behind of the workings of my mind when I'm gone, wondering who would clean up after me, what they would reflect on, etc.

Preparing for the pilgrimage
- contacts with relatives -

In preparing to leave for home in Idaho, I make a phone call to a relative, Paul Malleck in Washington state to tell him I am leaving the next day to drive cross-country, and that I plan to drive through Holbrook and Indianola, Nebraska. (Paul Malleck is Shirley Ashburn's father.) I call him because he grew up in these towns in Nebraska. I want to visit with other relatives who are there, and I need help finding them.

I had met Paul and Shirley for the first time in August 2003 at my first McCool family picnic. Shirley is a relative that we found on the Internet, and we shared a lot of McCool information with each other. (See *Chapter 23 – McCools are cool!* for more details on the McCools, the Mallecks, and a photograph of Shirley and her father. Thank you, Shirley, for your permissions.)

From Rolla, I make another phone call to Lester "Bum" Malleck in Indianola. I introduce myself, trying to convince him that I am family and not a salesman. I tell him I that I am going to drive through Nebraska, and I hope to visit him. He kept saying "I can't hear you … Who is this? … I won't be there ….", typical tactics I use when solicitors call me. This was a frustrating phone call for me.

I then call Hazel Malleck in Indianola. I introduce myself, explaining who I am - a relative, not a salesman. I tell her that I tried to talk with Bum and that I want to visit him but had a hard time communicating with him on the phone. We talk about family members and begin to build some trust. She said that Shirley Ashburn had just called her and said: "Someone was coming through town," (referring to my visit). Hazel didn't know my grandmother, Stella (McCool) Neel, but she knew some of the individuals that I have in my genealogy records. I harvested data from her, getting names and dates of birth and death of relatives that I wasn't aware of. My grandmother, Stella (McCool) Neel was sister to Fay (McCool) Malleck (Catherine Mona Fay McCool, not Fay Marie Malleck who would be Bum's sister). Two McCool sisters had married two Malleck brothers. Therefore, Bum's aunt my grandmother. Fay is my great-aunt, sister to my grandmother. (If you want more specific genealogical information about how our families are connected, please contact me. Isn't this fascinating?)

UPDATE: During another visit to the area in 2017, I speak on the phone with the son of Hazel Malleck, and he reported that she had passed away since I came through the area in 2004. Another sad loss of a family member that I didn't get to meet, and therefore more family stories lost.

Hazel offered to help me connect with Bum by calling him and explaining who I was. She said he was forgetful, but couldn't tell me why. She said he was not doing too well.

The Road Trip begins

I leave Missouri with the rented U-Haul truck, and start to have mechanical problems within the first 70 miles. This was frustrating because I had less than a week to get home and unload all of this stuff, and I have to get back to work by the next Monday.

Crossing state and county lines in the dark, I lose my sense of place and time. Sleeping in the truck at odd hours I feel disoriented, creating a sense of something out of the ordinary. Passages through doors, some warp in a time machine – approaching some ghosts or mythical stories. Here I am moving into the state where my father was born and raised, where the Neels and the McCools and Mallecks and other family members mingled, mixed blood, multiplied, expired, buried one another, and from where their offspring left for other parts of the country in a diaspora. This is where so many stories came from. This is why I am here at this time, and why I walk the earth.

Cornfields and the old man

My usual sleep patterns are messed up by driving for hours on end in the dark. I am under many stressors: isolation, speculation about turns on the right roads, worrying about the truck's mechanical problems, and more. I listen to the drone of the engine and its weird little noises and go into a trance. In the dark, I turn off the radio and reflect on stories of my family history which add to this mythical sense of family hunger that I feel. Am I starting to hallucinate? Are my ancestors talking to me?

With the light of the new day, I begin to see some physical features of Nebraska – endless cornfields in their deep green colors. Highways and smaller roads are straight and perpendicular to each other along sectional lines, and I try to imagine what they were like when my ancestors were here.

I reflect on my grandmother's stories about living in a sod house, crossing the Midwest in a wagon as a child when the wheel spokes got plugged with mud - they had to stop and punch it out before they could proceed. I see the doctor hurrying from a nearby town to treat my grandfather, Frank, after his heart attack. I visualized my uncle Bill hitchhiking in his soldier uniform here during WW II. I imagine their ghosts along the road as I sped by them at modern highway speeds.

As I approach the town of my father's birth, I pass a bent-over, gray-haired old man hitchhiking and wonder "Is he a relative of mine? Am I supposed to pick him up? Is his name Destiny?" I look over at the front seat of the truck and see all of my junk, figuring it's too full for a passenger. I want to be alone with my thoughts and feelings. I don't want to be distracted by the talk of a stranger, and I pass him by with my busy-ness and excuses.

Maybe I am passing up an opportunity for good karma.

Holbrook, Nebraska

About noon I arrive in "Holbrook, Pop. 233." I stop and take photographs of the evidence, including an old water tower that each little town seems to own. I am traveling in time like Dr. Who.

I drive slowly through town without much competition for traffic. I see a rusty old Chevy stopped in the middle of Center Street, watch the driver get out leaving his door open. He walks over to the Post Office while others drive around the empty, abandoned vehicle in the middle of the road.

I easily find my grandparents' home as I randomly turn down the streets. I recognize it from pictures in my parents' collection. I have a black and white photo of the house with a family outside that looks like my grandparents sitting on the front steps with their little children in the yard, maybe my father, aunts, and uncles, in the front yard. I take lots of pictures to put in my time machine.

Is that my Dad as a kid with his family in the same home?

I knock on the door, but nobody answers. A neighbor comes home for lunch, and I follow him to his door, introducing myself. I show him the picture I have, hoping he will recognize my family. His name is Dale. He tells me the name of the lady who lives in my ancestors' house now, Luella. She has daughters elsewhere, and she may be gone visiting them. I take down the address so I can write her.

I take pictures and hang around the house for a while. I organize my thoughts with a shopping list:

1) Home of my grandparents, Frank and Stella Neel
2) Cemetery with headstones of family members
3) Perry Lumber Yard where my grandfather had a heart attack
4) Library (there was none!)
5) School with trophies from my uncle
6) Phone book (got one at Barney's Hideaway)
7) Any living native residents in their 80's or 90's who still could talk and might have memories of my family

This was a tall order. Need more time. Never enough time. If you have family hunger, there is never enough time. There ought to be a song about this.

The neighbor, Dale, gives me directions to the former lumber yard. It's now a hay company, which I easily find by the railroad tracks. I drive across the tracks and imagine trains in the old days bringing passengers through Holbrook, with lumber and supplies that went through my grandfather's business, the enterprise that built this town. I drive across a parched riverbed thinking "This must be the Republican River!" Some relatives that told me they had learned to swim here - who was that? I stop and take pictures of the dry river bed, then turn around and go back into town and park by the hay company, formerly the Perry Lumber Company.

I knock on the door of the hay company office. It appears also to be used as someone's home now, and a lady answers the door. I explain who I am, show her the advertisement I had for "Holbrook Lumber Company" selling "Peacock Coal" and their contact info at "Phone 23." She shows me a similar advertisement on her wall.

I get permission to look around their business and take pictures. She reports that one building had been knocked down by a storm and replaced, but another original building is still standing. I look around and take pictures, and try to imagine my Dad and my grandfather here many years ago.

I have a great lunch at Barney's Hideaway: an old-fashioned fried chicken dinner with mashed potatoes and gravy made with real fried chicken drippings rich with fat, jello, canned vegetables, and ice tea - all for $4.50. I talk to people in the restaurant/bar. Carol there remembers Beth Ann Keyes, my Dad's first wife. She comments that Beth "must be Dr. Keyes' daughter" and pointed out his old house across the street, and pointed to where the hospital had been.

In Barney's Hideaway, I get names of people I should contact in Holbrook, and they give me a local phone book with addresses. I wonder if anyone in town has access to the Internet so I can e-mail them? It's now 2004, but it feels like I'm in another century. Carol's brother, Dennis, is in the bar also, and he shares memories. Dennis cautions me that I should avoid one man who smells badly.

I don't have time to find all of these people, but one of them, Connie G., answers her door. I leave her a copy of my book, Family Hunger – A Neel and McCool Family History, in case of any relatives or someone interested in genealogy or my family could see it and contact me if they wish. Connie is a member of the local Historical Society.

Later in the day at the old school, I find a picture labeled "Dr. Neel's residence and hospital" which must be a mistake as there was no Dr. Neel that I knew about. They must mean "Dr. Keyes residence ….". This is fascinating, as I don't have any family background on my Dad's first wife. I want to find someone to ask about the picture and to tell them to fix the mistake, but I don't have time.

"Dr. Neel's residence and hospital" which must be a mistake

In the school, I find a trophy from the 1930 basketball team with the name of Lester S., who was my uncle Bill's brother. I am specifically looking for a trophy with my uncle Bill's name on it, as he and my aunt Vera said that he was a good athlete and that I would probably find his name on a trophy here.

I could spend a week here meeting people and asking questions.

The cemetery

I visit the cemetery and find headstones for my relatives: grandfather Frank William Neel, my dad's first wife

Beth Ann (Keyes) Neel, and uncle Floyd Franklin Neel.

My grandfather died in 1938 at the age of sixty-two after a heart attack he had earlier while working at the lumberyard. My Dad was called to bring him home, and they had to wait for the doctor, who was in the next town. He had a long recovery at home, and they moved a bed down to the front room so he could stay there. One day they took him out of the house for a ride and some fresh air, and as a result, the insurance company didn't make payment as he was supposed to be housebound.

Beth Ann died in 1943 at the age of thirty from cancer, diagnosed in Honolulu after the bombing of Pearl Harbor. She was shipped stateside because of the war and her illness. She then lived in California with my aunts Sarah and Vera, and my grandmother until Beth passed away. Her body must have been shipped from California to Nebraska for burial if it lay under these markers. My parents didn't tell me that Dad was married before Mom until I was about 25 years old when Mom was terminally ill with cancer.

Beth Ann (Keyes) Neel, my father's first wife. Rest in peace. Thanks for keeping my Dad available and ready for my Mom!

Dad's brother, Floyd, died in 1930 at the age of fifteen from internal bleeding after being hit in the stomach with a basketball thrown by the school janitor, Ernest Howard S., who was the father of my uncle Bill S. (No photo shown.)

Grandpa
Frank William Neel.
Rest in peace.
Your life was too short!
I have your middle name,
a reminder for us so you
live on.

Life essential, and spacing

I had never met any of these people buried here. For one of them, my grandfather, it was essential for him to have lived and passed on his genetics for me to have a heartbeat. For another of them, Beth, it was essential for her to have died and to get out of the way for me to be standing here. She was a place keeper. If she hadn't kept my Dad available and then died at the right time, my Dad wouldn't have met my Mom and gotten married and given birth to 3 children, including me, and raised a fourth adopted child – vital to my development and identity. Beth was part of the lessons about family for my Dad. For my uncle Floyd, it wasn't essential for him to have lived for me to be standing here, but his life story certainly added color to our family tree.

The S. family had headstones nearby, including the school janitor who threw the ball that killed my uncle Floyd. I considered the spacing, timing, and the emotions they must have experienced when that dramatic story occurred.

Standing in front of these grave markers, I feel like I'm stepping into a time machine, providing a real spiritual and physical connection. I imagine strings of light following our paths through the histories of our lives, back down the highway I came from today, coming full circle to our conception and births, through all the complicated relationships and stories, back to this moment to be standing here now at my grandfather's grave. Is there any genetic material still in the ground that would prove we were related? I have no doubts. I kneel down and touch each of the Neel headstones. I say "Hi Grandpa" and feel sad, not remembering any direct experiences with any grandfathers of mine, but I still feel a loss.

Spacing - Have you heard of the "space-time continuum" from Stephen Hawking and others? Have you ever been on a narrow highway driving the exact speed limit in the right-hand lane and you are approaching another driver going the same direction who is driving one or two MPH under the speed limit and you can't get around them, and you want to yell "HEY! You are in my space-time continuum!" Or, have you experienced this one: "HEY! When are you going to get out of the bathroom? You are in my space-time continuum!" Some of my relatives that I share DNA with had to be in each other's space-time continuum and have relationships with perfect timing for the miracle of biology to happen if I was going to be standing here now. Now that's something to ponder!

Social psychologists call this "proximity." For there to be a relationship, people have to be in close proximity to each other … in each other's "space-time continuum" … at the same crossroads at the same time. Plus a few other details for the miracle of life to occur.

The spacing of these headstones makes me wonder if the cemetery plots were purchased so other family members could be buried here. I wonder if other markers could be placed here to remember other relatives who had died, like my grandmother, my father, and my mother. *That would be striking to me seeing the markers for my father, his first wife, and his second wife in the same place.*

I consider the possibility of whether my children or grandchildren would ever be standing here in this cemetery, or if they will ever stand over a marker of my grave. I wonder if they will ever read these words I write now, with their hearts open, and I wonder what their thoughts and feelings will be.

I am in Holbrook for about five hours, leaving about 5 pm for Indianola, just down the road.

Indianola, Nebraska, and Bum Malleck

I arrive in Indianola about 6 pm, and can't get Hazel Malleck to answer her phone. I get Bum on the phone, and he continues to be not very friendly, saying he was going to bed. I forced the issue saying I just wanted to leave him a gift, my book, Family Hunger. I promise I won't stay very long, so he said he wouldn't start dinner and gives me directions to his home. He answers the door and is more friendly in person. He apologizes at the end for starting out on the wrong foot. I don't blame him for being mistrustful – how many times does someone who claims to be a distant, unknown relative try to make it into your home as I did?

But here he is, wearing overalls and looking just like those Mallecks in Olympia that I met when I was a little kid in 1966. (I think it was Buster Malleck, not Bum, that I met when I was a child. Buster is the grandfather of Shirley (Malleck) Ashburn. Are you taking notes here? Drawing a family tree?)

There are those familiar facial features: ears and nose that looks like my Dad! How did that happen?

I again explain who I am, trying to make a connection with him. It seems something subtle has changed in our relationship. It appears that he had talked to Hazel because he says: "You're aunt Stell's grandson." He said he remembered my Dad, saying, "He was nice … he didn't let his (Navy) commission go to his head". Bum said he was in the infantry in the Army in Africa and Italy in WW II. He got his heel blown off by flak shot at him by the Germans in a foxhole, and they almost blew his leg off. He spent eleven months in the hospital after that.

I ask him if he was proud of his time in the military, and he said: "Yes, I'm proud of my time in the service." I thank him for the time he served our country.

I feel the tape recorder in my pocket, but I don't want to turn him off by being too intrusive with a microphone in his face. It was hard enough getting this far in conversation with him. Therefore I'm limited to my memory and the notes I wrote down after I left there. But those words are priceless to a genealogist like me. I bet his surviving relatives wish they had such a recording. Maybe they do? Hmmm …

Bum said: "They're trying to make me move into a nursing home," and he talks about the difficulty he has driving into town every day for lunch.

Some neighbors come by while I am here, saying they saw my U-Haul truck outside and ask if Bum was moving. I introduce myself, explaining what I am doing on my trip, and we visit awhile. I told them I thought Bum looked like my Dad and show them a picture of my Dad. They agree there is a similarity. They said they thought I look like one of Bum's sons, David, and they got a calendar off the wall with family pictures on it to show us. We tried to figure out why Bum and my Dad looked alike. I said I thought it was "because your aunt (Stella) is my grandmother, and those ears are Jack ears" (from Lydia Jack, according to my father).

Bum doesn't work the farm anymore. Instead, he rents it out for others to work. He says he can't get around very well, as he falls down as he doesn't have a heel bone.

I ask him why they call him "Bum." When he was born his parents said "Well, the little Bum is finally here," and the name stuck.

I get a couple of pictures of Bum on his front step as I am leaving. I probably stayed less than an hour. His phone rings, and he goes inside as I am taking pictures and saying "goodbye." His daughter calls him every day at this time. (Another family member I can meet and interview! Is there enough time?)

I wish I had more time with him. I call Hazel again when I get back to Indianola. It is late, and I am exhausted. She also lives out in the country, and sounds disappointed that

I can't visit her. Now I have regrets and wish I had. But I have many miles to go in a truck with mechanical problems, and this had already been a long, grueling day. So unfortunately, I didn't meet her face-to-face. I also wish I had time to meet with Bum's daughter who lives in Indianola, but there was not enough time.

On the road again, and another cornfield - A visit by the Sheriff -

It is after 8 pm that I leave Indianola. I add another gallon of water to the radiator. The drone of the engine hypnotizes me again. The adrenalin rush from the feast I just had for my family hunger fades and exhaustion sets in. (It's better than a sugar rush!) I pull over in the dark and intend to sleep just a few hours. I find a muddy dirt road between rows of corn. I am awakened at about 11 pm by the Sheriff. The farmer who owns the field is nervous that I am here. The officer tells me I can't stay. He asks for my U-Haul contract and asks me to open up the back end of the truck and looks inside. He asks if I was doing anything "illegal." I claim my innocence, but consider Ralph's guns that I am transporting.

So I drive some more and sleep beside the road until 6:30 am. I wake in the middle of nowhere … no crossroads or proximity to <u>anything</u>! Not in anyone's space-time continuum!

I cross a time zone line somewhere in the night, so keeping track of the time gets confusing. In Scottsbluff, Nebraska I fill up with diesel fuel and find an auto parts store to swap out the radiator cap as the engine is overheating. I cross into Wyoming, stopping at a truck stop and spend about two hours draining the radiator and put in a "Stop Overheating" product. I have lunch while waiting for the hot radiator to drain, and a guy in the bathroom commented he saw me having problems with the U-Haul. He tells me about a U-Haul dealer nearby who is also a mechanic and gave me directions. After finishing up at the truck stop, I drive to the U-Haul dealer, who agreed that from the symptoms that the radiator was probably plugged up, and offered three options:

1) Continue driving 50 – 60 mph down the highway (up to 20 mph below the speed limit, delaying my arrival time home).
2) Switch trucks (taking considerable time to transfer the stuff).
3) "Boil out and rod" the radiator, also taking considerable time that I didn't have.

I continue to drive with the truck that Destiny gave me. (Please don't judge me. I take responsibility for my decision. I am not a victim, and I am not stupid, although that is how I feel.) I take a nap at a rest stop and add another gallon of water.

BREAKDOWN!

At about 7 pm, 1085 miles from Rolla, I am driving up a long grade. The engine light comes on again, and I have a sudden loss of power. Looking out my rearview mirror, I see a LOT of black smoke. I make it to the top of the hill and then coast down the other side, and get off an exit.

BREAKDOWN! It won't start again.

I have a cell phone borrowed from my mother-in-law, and the battery is running low. I get a U-Haul operator who sounds like she is reading questions from a book: "Is there fuel in the tank?" She doesn't ask for my location. I get frustrated, telling her my phone battery is running out, and tell her to send me a tow truck, but she can't authorize that. She reads from her operator manual that she will send a mechanic to decide whether a tow truck is needed.

After several more phone calls, the tow truck finally arrives after about two hours. He tows me into Casper, Wyoming, leaves the truck at the U-Haul dealer, and puts me up in a hotel.

The next day I walk to the dealer. They diagnose that the engine is "blown" and cannot be driven anymore. We negotiated the exchange for another truck.

Newer truck, same company, same problems?

I need to say that U-Haul is a good company. They have been in business for a long time, and in the end they took good care of me.

The dealer says they can move the stuff from one truck another one, or I can move it myself and they will pay me $150 for the labor (which I chose). This is called "transloading," so they must have done this before. I spend about 4 hours moving stuff from the 14 ft. broken down truck to the 17 ft. replacement truck. I have time to think while I'm moving the stuff, and I ponder my future. I miss my "muscle," Bob and Joe that I had hired in Rolla. I wonder what mechanical condition this newer truck is in. As I move the stuff, which can be quite a meditative process, I calculate that the breakdown saved me $150 off the total rental bill, and got me a night in a motel with a hot bath. Thank you, U-Haul! What a great company!

I leave Casper, Wyoming about 1 pm, and start with a new odometer reset at Mile "0" again.

In the early evening, I fill up with diesel fuel in Lodgegrass, Montana. MONTANA!!! MY ROOTS!!! I'M HOME!!! (Well, almost home in Idaho, but Montana is where my heart is.)

It's dark again as I pull off Interstate 90, cross railroad tracks, and park next to the Yellowstone River. Again, my roots! I have paddled these rivers so many times, their currents are deep in my bones. My parents' home is on the Clark Fork River near Alberton. I start to pitch a tent, thinking "Is someone going to kick me out of here before morning?" (as I was clearly visible, in plain view of the highway). I stopped pitching the tent and took a little walk, trying to find a more secluded spot. A freight train roars by blasting his horn, making it clear this was not a good place to sleep. I'm in a fairly narrow canyon with no place to go to get farther away from the highway or the railroad, so I throw the tent in the back of the truck again and drive a little further down a frontage road.

I find a rest area in an unlikely spot off the Interstate near Livingston, Montana, and I backed the U-Haul in. While I was setting up the back of the truck for a spot for my sleeping bag in the dark, a large Native American family pulls into the same rest area, towing a van with another car. They push the dead van in backward into the parking spot and pull their other car in next to it. And then they started partying!! Why me?!?! I pull my sleeping bag up over my head and go to sleep.

About 6:30 am, they are still there. There must be about a dozen of them, with sleeping bags all over the ground. I leave as quietly as I can in my diesel truck which is not very quiet – it does not sound like the state bird, the Meadowlark, singing its morning call that I hear before I turn the key.

Early on this Saturday morning, I roll down the road again. I fill up with diesel fuel in Bozeman, Montana, thinking about one of my favorite books Zen and the Art of Motorcycle Maintenance, about a father and son having an adventure that includes this location (a great book by Robert M. Pirsig – highly recommended). Around noon I reach Missoula – the town where I lived from age ten on through age twenty-five. I go to the home my brother, Tim, and his wife, Karen. They take me to lunch at 3 Sisters' Café and we have a good visit.

About 5 pm I arrived in Coeur d'Alene, Idaho – home, after driving over 1897 miles.

Welcome home!
Welcome to Holbrook!
This saga is over!

Chapter 21
Finding the home of my parents and the hospital where I was born – You're a Mercy Babe! Welcome Home!

It's early Monday morning in late March 2010. I am fifty-five years of age. With my birth certificate in hand, I leave my wife and sons behind at the motel. It has the name "Mercy Hospital" on Hillcrest Drive in San Diego. That street is no longer here, but I still am. The hospital was torn down and re-built, re-named Scripps Mercy Hospital. The people I talk to as I search say "Yes, this is Mercy Hospital."

I was born here on July 25, 1955, at 9:56 am, about this same time and same day of the week over half-a-century ago. I tell the receptionist at the front desk that I was born here. She is a large, older, black African American woman with salt and pepper hair and a beautiful smile. With a twinkle in her eyes, she warmly says: "Welcome home!" I get emotionally choked up and can't talk.

There is history in stories about and pictures of the old hospital on the walls I find in the basement. I am looking around, taking pictures, and a lady is sitting, waiting with a professional looking camera in her hand. We get talking, and she says she has a great job as the hospital photographer. Her daughter was born here also. I tell her my story, and she says: "You are a Mercy Babe!" She shows me around, talks to me about the hospital's history, and makes copies of "History of Scripps Mercy Hospital" for me.

Upon leaving the hospital, I reflect on the ancient

black and white images in the basement while taking high-res color photos with my modern Nikon. I focus on people and notice that while this is a modern hospital in a clean suburban neighborhood, the contrasting economics of poverty of the patients that transition from birth to death here is evident.

Young adults and the old roll in and out in their wheelchairs to smoke cigarettes, some with amputations. I think about their lifestyle patterns and wonder about their stories. How many of these lives go up in smoke and ashes, lost forever? Don't they know that those cigarettes put them here? I remember my Dad with COPD turning off his oxygen so he didn't blow himself up when he lit a cigarette for comfort.

After the hospital, still with birth certificate in hand, I find the house that Mom and Dad lived in after they brought me home from Mercy Hospital. (Did they put me in a car seat buckled in for the drive home? Not likely. They were probably smoking cigarettes on the way. Was my father present or absent at my delivery? Where was he during the length of my Mom's pregnancy with me?)

My wife and our boys are with me now, as I went back to get them because of check-out time at the motel. We drive to this address, and I knock on the door. The lady who answers is initially reluctant to open the door, and she just talks through the massive screen door for security, which has iron bars and a heavy metal plate the length of it with small holes drilled in it for light and air. I tell her my story, asking permission to take pictures of the house. She said: "You must be wrong because we bought this house new and we're the only ones who have lived here ...." I try to show her my original birth certificate with the address.

She says her husband was also in the Navy, and they went to Hawaii for two years and had rented out the home to a Navy family. Realizing this must have been my family, she then says that our parents were nice, clean, that Mom liked to garden, and that I threw milk on the wall. I suggested it might have been my brother or sister who did that as I was just a newborn infant. I apologize for the milk on the wall, half a century overdue.

The lady says she can't stand very long as she is getting over being sick and she has to go, so I start to leave. As I walk away, she opens the door and starts telling more stories.

She says her husband was at Pearl Harbor the same time as my Dad when the Japanese attacked on December 7, 1941. He had a habit of waking early, so he had gone up to the top side of the ship before the Japanese started bombing. His vessel was critically hit and went down in eight minutes, and if he had still been below decks, he wouldn't have escaped. He helped release the lines so the next ship didn't get pulled down with his. He was rescued from the waters, and she still has the dungarees he was wearing at the time which have never been washed. They still have the smells of oil in them from the waters he was thrown in. Her husband is passed away now.

She didn't know her husband at the time of the attack on Pearl Harbor but met him later in the war when he was stationed in Australia where she lived.

As we get talking more, I share the story I knew about my Dad's time at Pearl Harbor on that infamous day.

She invites me inside, asking if I want to see the room and the corner where my crib was, and I take pictures. How does she know that was the corner where I cried for my needs to be met, forming my early attachment strategies? Was I securely or insecurely attached? Did I begin to see my worth here, or were seeds of self-doubt planted? Had my mother been given what she needed as an infant so she could give me what I needed as a newborn?

After a while, I get uncomfortable as this little old lady is clearly in jeopardy from this stranger (me) that she had never met before. She took a risk letting me in, and my family is still out in the car waiting for me.

As I try to leave the home, she asks why I am interested in this home and her story. I tell her I research genealogy and family history, and that I am writing a book. She says that she writes and helps other people write. We exchanged business cards. She offers to send me her work about her husband's story, and I offer to send her some of my words.

I finally slip outside, take pictures of the exterior of the house, and Mary takes photos of me in front of it (not included here because of privacy issues, but they sure are sweet in my private collection).

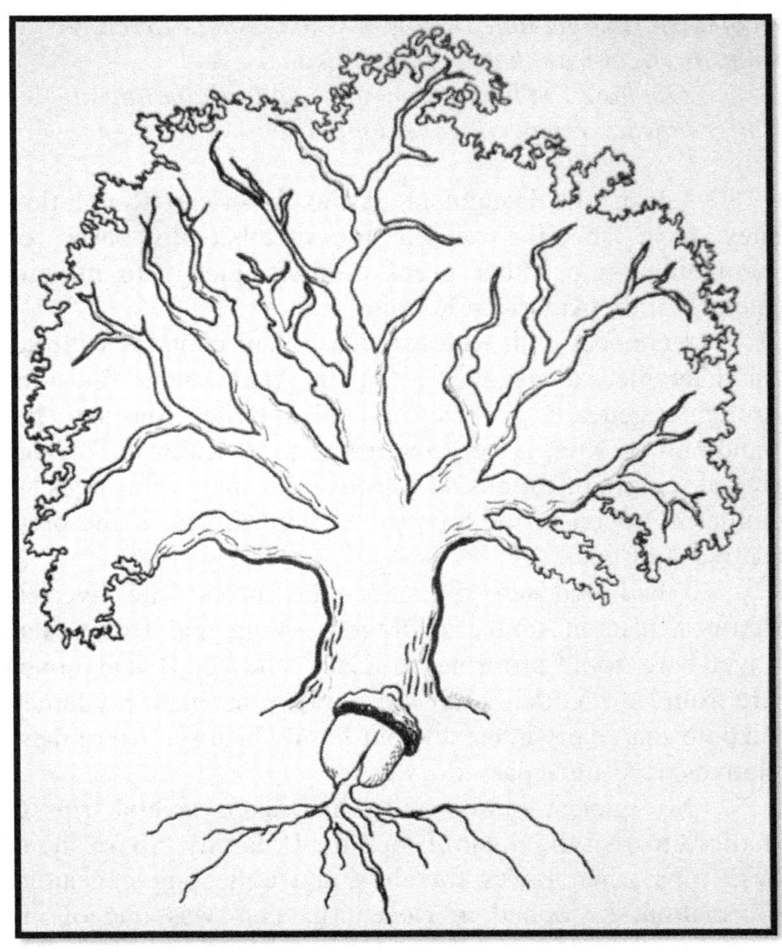

Chapter 22
Rita Simpson
Desperately seeking D.A.R.

An interview with Rita Anith (Witt) Simpson, and her daughter, "Joannie" (a pseudonym). Rita is the wife of my second cousin, one time removed, who is Neel Farrell Simpson. Neel's mother is Minnie Francis Neel.

Oh, how I'm having fun now! Still fascinating no matter how far removed, genealogically.

D.A.R is the Daughters of the American Revolution. They have specific criteria for membership based on documentation or other proof of their lineage to military veterans of the American Revolution.

I connect with Rita through e-mail contacts with her granddaughter, a teenager living in Alaska who finds me through a genealogy website on the Internet. She says her grandmother, Rita, is very interested in genealogy. Through several communications, I discovered that Rita lives in southern Oregon in the town of Roseburg, near some other relatives of mine.

I had two sets of aunts and uncles who lived in Medford, also in southern Oregon. Vera and Bill S. had moved here from California, and Sarah and Ted B. had moved here from New York. Sarah and Vera are sisters of my father, and both shared my interest in our family history. All of these relatives have since passed away.

My nuclear family and I had taken several trips to Medford to visit the S. family and the B. family. So on one of these trips when I was traveling and collecting genealogy information, I stopped in Roseburg. This was one of my genealogy adventures where I went alone, as the other members of my household do not share my enthusiasm for this sport.

When I arrive I find that Rita's daughter, Joannie, lived there also. Joannie looked at me with a look like: "Who are you? How are we related? What are you trying to sell us?" In the end, she seemed to accept me, and it was a very sweet trip.

Trip to Medford and Roseburg, Oregon

5/18 to 5/21/2001

I take two vacation days off from work to get a 4-day weekend to make a trip to Oregon to visit relatives and to meet Rita. This is a transcription of a dictation about the trip below into a tape recorder. Apologies for the less-than-perfect English:

"Hello, this is Todd William Neel. It's Sunday night, May 20, 2001, about 10 pm. I'm on the highway, I think it's Interstate 5, heading south from Roseburg, Oregon to Medford, Oregon after spending a day with Rita Simpson and her daughter, Joannie.

"I drove north to Roseburg today after arriving Friday, May 18 by airplane to spend a four day weekend to be with my aunt Babe and uncle Bill doing genealogy research. So I'm going to talk here about my day with Rita and Joannie.

"I got to Roseburg about 20 minutes late after getting caught up in business, finding gas, getting a tripod for the camera, making copies at Kinkos (for Rita's genealogy questions) in Medford before I left, etc. When I got to Rita's house, she came out to the front of her house and met me in her yard, smiled, shook my hand, invited me inside, and was very nice. She introduced me to her daughter Joannie. I hadn't expected anyone else to be there, and Joannie said: "She didn't tell you she lived with her daughter?" To which I responded: "No, she didn't. Well, I guess we're family too."

"We sat down at the kitchen table, and Rita started showing me pieces of paper and started talking about what our interests were and tried to explain to Joannie how we were

related. Joannie seemed a little skeptical, asking again: "Wait, how are we related?"

"I share stories about my family and Joannie starts telling me stories about her children. Her son Todd died at eight years of age in a logging accident when he was riding on a Caterpillar with his Dad, and their family still has difficulty with that after some thirty years later.

"We went out to lunch at a restaurant and when I was in the bathroom washing up I looked in the mirror and almost started crying because I was so excited because of thoughts of "This is IT!", (meaning) finally making this trip and meeting relatives I had never met before, asking questions and hearing stories first hand. After lunch, I asked if they could show me where Rita's husband, Neel Farrel Simpson, had his business. He had a machine shop and welding business that was written about in the Betty Thorson book, and it had been burned down and rebuilt. So we drove the scenic tour through town and drove to his old place of business. They told stories about it, about the fire, about how it started with a gasoline truck exploding, and about how Neel was the only one really injured, burned, and his hip, foot, and leg were injured in the accident. Next to the old business is some property that Rita still owns and she collects lease money from them. Then we drove around and looked at the countryside, up the beautiful Umqua River, and where it collides with another river meeting head-on at 180 degrees." (This is the end of the dictation into a tape recorder).

It was very sweet and meaningful to meet this family. It impacted me to see my first and last name spelled correctly in their documents, which was about their family members who shared my names and not about me. There was children's artwork on the wall, with "Neel" spelled out in crayon.

As I re-read this chapter, I notice that I am not reflecting the desperation that Rita had to find specific documentation that the Daughters of the American Revolution required proving her relationship with those who fought in the American Civil War from 1861 – 1865. I later had phone calls with Rita after she had moved out of her home, and I was unable to help her find what she needed before she passed away. There was a sweet sadness in her desperation to prove her connection with family in our country's history.

Photo of Rita (Witt) Simpson (left), and myself, Todd Neel (right) on the day of my visit to their home in Roseburg, Oregon on 5/20/2001. (With apologies, as I was unable to locate Joannie for her permission, so I cropped her out of this photo. Rita is deceased.)

Chapter 23
McCools are cool!
(or "Compost, Ashes, and Lagoons")

On a Friday in early August 2003, I leave Coeur d'Alene after work with my boys, Nathan and Joshua, and head for Chehalis, Washington. The event was the annual McCool Family Picnic at the Rosecrest Farm of Gary and Sharon McCool. I was invited by Gary's brother, Larry McCool, who found me on the Internet through my Family Tree Maker website. We have been exchanging e-mails and communicating through social media about our common ancestors since then.

(NOTE: Thanks to the McCools for inviting me to your gatherings, and thank you to those living persons named here for permission to use your names. Other family members are named here but have since been deceased. Rest in peace.)

I have the McCools in my family lineage because my Dad's mother was Agusta Estella "Stella" (McCool) Neel. There were six girls and two boys in my grandmother's family, and her brother, Emmett Robert McCool, was the grandfather of Larry and Gary McCool. Our common ancestor, therefore (for the three of us in the photograph on the next page), are our great-grandparents are William Andrew McCool and Sara Ellen (Garber) McCool.

The children of this marriage between our great-grandparents were Minette "Nette" Margaret Elizabeth McCool, Emmett Robert McCool (the grandfather of Larry and Gary McCool), Agusta Estelle "Stella" McCool (my grandmother), Lydia Susan McCool, Gladys Alma McCool, Harry Paul McCool, Jessie Helen McCool, and Catherine Mona Fay McCool. (All of these people are deceased.)

I had posted on my website a photograph of this family, which caught the attention of Larry McCool and helped him find me. Gary McCool had this photograph on his dining room wall at his Rosecrest Farm. Apparently, there are several copies of this photo going around, and it makes me think about family photographs of me and all of us (alive today) that will be around long after we are gone, and whether our relatives will be standing around talking about it like we did here in this photograph.

My sons, Nathan and Josh (who were ages 9 and 11 at the time), and I didn't make the entire drive on Friday night on the way to the reunion. Instead, we stopped beside Interstate 90 somewhere in central Washington and camped on a frontage road amidst the sagebrush. My boys thought it was cool that we camped in the "desert." Then on Saturday, we drove south of Ellensburg, through Yakima, over White Pass and down to Chehalis, Washington. I was nervous driving as we got closer to the farm to meet a bunch of people I had never met before.

Above is a photo of Todd Neel, Larry McCool, and Gary McCool (from left to right) *with the famous McCool family photograph on the wall of Gary McCool's home at the time of this McCool Family Reunion.*

When we arrived at the Rosecrest Farm, there they were! A bunch of strangers, looking at me, this stranger to them, in this big camper crashing their party. But after I parked, they started walking up to me and introducing themselves, obviously expecting me. Larry McCool was very warm and friendly - he was the culprit that got me here. Others said they had seen my book (Family Hunger - A Neel and McCool Family History), and said they were impressed by the work I did. I gave away about seven books to interested family members, and they offered to reimburse me for my costs.

Present at the picnic were about 26 family members I had never met before, and a total of 29 with my sons and me (too many to obtain all of their permissions, so I'm sorry not to include their names here).

Shirley Ashburn was there at the picnic with her father. (Shirley would be my second cousin.) She and I had also found each other on the Internet, and we had communicated quite a bit about our family. She found out about this picnic from me through our e-mails, and she found out that her father, Paul Malleck, knew about this event and was planning to attend, so she decided to come with him.

Photo of Paul Malleck and his daughter, Shirley Ashburn. (This is a duplicate photo which shows up elsewhere in this book.)

While I was talking to people, Shirley's Dad introduced himself to me as "Malleck," and said he knew my father and his siblings. He asked if I knew Sarah ("Of course, that was my aunt," I responded), asked if I knew Vera ("Yes, my aunt who lives in Medford," I said), asked if I knew Mac ("Yes, my uncle," I replied), or if I knew Floyd ("No, that was my uncle who died when he was a teenager," I said). Paul Malleck said he knew Floyd pretty well, and he remembered that after he died his family used Floyd's bike to learn how to ride, and when the tires went flat they used garden hose around the wheels because they couldn't afford new tires.

If you're trying to track the branches of my family tree, McCool is my paternal grandmother's maiden name, and two of her sisters married Malleck brothers. Paul Malleck's parents were Paul James Malleck and Jessie Hellen (McCool) Malleck. Jessie was sister to my paternal grandmother, Stella (McCool) Neel. He is my first cousin, one time removed to me.

Paul told me that he remembers his "Aunt Stell" and "Uncle Frank" (my grandparents) from when he was a kid in Nebraska. He used to stay at their house one week every summer, and learned to swim in the Republican River with my uncles Mac and Floyd. He remembers my grandfather Frank (Neel) telling my grandmother Stell "Don't sell the stock!" (I told him I had just read a letter from my grandfather (Frank Neel) to my father (John Neel) about the purchase of Studebaker stock). Paul commented to me on the phone that my grandparents "were stinking rich … they had electricity and running water …." I told him I was going to try to find their house, and he told me it should be easy to find, that it might be "6 blocks west of the lumber yard."

Paul said he left Indianola (Nebraska) in 1935. He told me to say "Hello" to Hazel and Bum Malleck in Indianola. He said Bum is probably going to a nursing home soon. (Hazel was married to Howard Malleck, and I think that Bum and Howard would be first cousins).

Another lady, Ruth Briggs, introduced herself to me. This would be the aunt of Shirley Ashburn and the sister of Paula Kathleen Malleck who was present at the picnic. She said she knew Beth Keyes.

Photo of Ruth Briggs (on the left), along with Randy and Loretta McCool

We put up my big family tree that was printed about a year before, which had about 900 people on it. (I had printed out my current tree with about 1100 people on it, but I hadn't been able to tape it together yet, so I gave it to Larry McCool for him to puzzle together.) This led to much discussion and many questions.

As we were standing around talking, I noticed and commented: "It's really neat standing around a bunch of redheads that are family members." We talked about my sister and I being redheads, but other than finding carrot-top Gladys McCool in Olympia, Washington in 1966, we hadn't found any other redheads for a long time. Gary and Larry had traces of red left on their heads and in their beards (amidst their "sun-bleached blond" and gray hairs), and Randy McCool had red hair also. They identified others in their families with red hair as well.

Recently, Gary and Larry's mother, Dorothy (Edwards) McCool, had moved into Gary and Sharon's home due to health problems. Apparently, the day before I arrived, she had to go to the hospital because of further medical complications. This opened the door to some talk about mortality. I shared the story about spreading my Dad's ashes on the mountain behind his house (in 1994) in the area that my Mom's ashes were scattered (in 1980). There was a videotape made of this, which included someone offering the ashes to my son Nathan to spread, who was then about two years of age. He put some of the ashes in his mouth to taste. Josh was quite upset about this when he heard that "Nathan ate Grandpa!"

My Dad had previously made a request to have his ashes flushed down the toilet, and I'm glad he backed down on that request.

For me, part of my beliefs in the afterlife include looking up the hill above my parents' house, looking at the grasses, moss, and trees that grew in the area where their ashes were scattered. I see deer, and other animals eat the grass and other plant life there, ingesting the nutrients of my parents' ashes and bone chips. I imagine the deer growing up giving birth to other baby deer, and maybe some of those deer get shot by a hunter and fed to their children. I can see that hunter telling family history stories at the dinner table, and teaching morals about killing and feeding your family. With this story, I can see how we carry on to generations beyond our physical time here in these bodies. Do you see how morals and values taught and experiences shared with our families carry down to raising our own children if we have any? The author of that moral or lesson might be lost, but the meaning is passed on.

I have a robust and spiritual bond with my compost pile in our garden. This sounds silly, but I nurture that pile of steaming lawn clippings and kitchen wastes, and it makes beautiful soil for our garden of vegetables and flowers. It is mutual because it also nurtures me. That beautiful dirt is my crop. I feel a strong emotional, spiritual, and therapeutic connection with the soil of the earth. After a stressful day at the office, it is very beneficial for me to get my hands dirty by pulling weeds, trimming flowers or shrubs, or turning over the compost pile. When my wife, Mary, was pregnant with one of our sons I remember digging in the garden and thinking about planting seeds of the next generation and remember telling myself that we are building something more significant than a flower bed now, and I need to get my priorities straight.

While touring the Rosecrest Farm, Gary McCool showed us how cow manure is pushed down a pipe and into a lagoon. It is stirred up, mixed with river water, and pumped onto the fields, so the nutrients grow good grasses and other crops for the cows and the milk they produce. As we were standing by the lagoon, he pointed out a large sprinkler spraying the product onto the fields, as the wind blew mist from it into our faces and hair!

Gary commented at one point during the weekend "I'm ready to go … when I die, just throw me into the lagoon and pump me onto the fields!" I can appreciate that.

This story isn't done, just another chapter in my book of life. Maybe in print, it will last longer than my body does. And perhaps the author will be remembered.

Thank you, McCools. You are all cool! I wouldn't be here without you!

Photo of Larry McCool, and my sons Nathan and Joshua Neel, in front of Gary McCool's barn at Rosecrest Farm. Our camper is in the background mounted on the truck called "The John II," named after my father. The camper and a previous truck was purchased with my inheritance from my father.

Rosecrest Farm coat of arms.

Chapter 24
Migration Paper
By Brandon Styles, BA, MA candidate

Brandon Styles
Geog. 103
Migration Paper
2/13/2009

Writing Assignment #1

In a recent look at the family history of both my parents, I have affirmed a European lineage. The dates of their migration to North America were also unveiled; however, why they came to America is not quite clear. Once living in the "New World," migration within the United States occurred in both families. Montana, the most individualistic state in the union, was where both my grandfathers (Neel & Styles) decided to relocate in the years following World War II.

The Styles family was brought to America on October 1, 1834 by my great, great, great, great grandfather, Robert Styles, of Kent, Old England. "Looking out into the future and seeing the more limited opportunities in the already crowded conditions of England, with the hope of youth in his heart and the blood of health in his veins, he had thus come to the age of nineteen, to develop the plan of his life in the broader field of the New World." (Styles. 1991) After a voyage of five weeks, he arrived in New York.

Between the time he landed in New York and 1849, when he married, there is fifteen years that are undocumented. One can only imagine what a young man would discover in the New World. Once he married Rachel Benedict of Alum Creek, Ohio, his life begins to take shape and so does the documentation of his life. In 1852, Robert and Rachel, being members of the Friends' church, took charge of the Shawnee Indian Mission near Leavenworth, Kansas. Mr. and Mrs. Styles lasted just one year as missionaries. One of their children had become ill and they had no choice but to leave Kansas to seek more effective medical assistance. From Kansas they moved to Indiana, and eventually, in 1867, pioneered to Iowa, where they lived on a farm. Robert was a school teacher for fifty years in New Sharon and was titled veteran school master of Iowa.

Rueben Styles, son of Robert Styles was also a pioneer. In 1886 with a wagon and a team of horses, he set off for South Dakota to settle down on a quarter section of land that he broke up for farming. They survived the historic blizzard of 1888, Native American conflicts, and the fires. Long droughts eventually caused surface wells to be insufficient, and in 1890 they were forced to sell the original claim. Rueben took his money and bought 640 acres - half a mile south of the present city of Brentford, South Dakota. They named the farm "Plainview Farm." To this day Plainview Farm is still in the Styles family and is run by my father's cousin, Bob Styles.

My grandfather, Bernie Styles left the Plainview Farm during WWII to serve his country. After the war he took a job as Commercial Manager for KTVQ-TV in Billings, MT. It was in Billings that he met my grandmother and together they raised their three boys Alan, Ronald and Jay. Today my father, Jay and both his brothers continue to live in MT.

John Neel, an immigrant from Scotland, is nine generations back on my mother's side of the family. He was thought to be an indentured servant but no one is certain of this or when he actually came to America. However it is known that he had three children, all born Stateside. The first of which was born in 1746. In contrast, John Neel came to America approximately 100 years before the Styles. Research theorized a high probability that he was migrating to escape the famine that the Scottish and Irish people where suffering.

By the time the Styles' came to America, the Neel family was settled out in Ohio and Nebraska. John Robinson "Honest John" Neel was Sheriff of Holbrook, Nebraska, and his son Frank Neel owned the Holbrook Lumber company and was father to my grandfather, Capt. John W. Neel (b. Jan.7, 1914). Once of age and readiness my grandfather left Nebraska to attend the Naval Academy. He served through WWII as a Capt. in the Navy and after 33 years, retired. He bought a travel trailer, packed up his wife and four kids, and headed (from N.Y.C.) to Missoula, Montana. Missoula had good schools, beautiful mountains, was close to relatives (Spokane) and far from N.Y.C. and commotion. Settling near Alberton, 30 miles west of Missoula, John and his wife Alice built their mountain dream home, spending the rest of their lives in harmony with Cinderella Mountain.

The Styles and Neel families both participated in the new towns and communities of the "frontier" as the Nation migrated west during the 1800's. Migration motivators seemed to be related to a common notion of socio-economic and quality of life improvements; the European economy simply could not compete with the "green grass" of the New World. My research has found limited knowledge of a lineage traced to those that still reside "across the Pond." The role of WWII in my family's migration to Montana raises my curiosity in the power of place; locale is crucial to overall happiness, which is a key component of healthy living and assessment of the quality of life. Of John Neel and Berwin Styles' descendants, all but one son continue to reside in Montana.

(NOTE: *The above was written by my nephew, Brandon Styles. I am very proud of him as a family member, as a father himself, as a teacher, as a continuing student of life, and as a man.*)

Chapter 25
DNA Search

Through my first ***Y-DNA*** submission in 2009 of a cheek-swab sample sent to ancestry.com, I got 250 names of genetic relatives around the world. The Y chromosome traces the paternal line from my father's side of my family. From these connections, I got some exciting and fascinating stories, but no actual contacts where we figured out who-begat-whom that got us here and who our common ancestors were that I could put in my family tree. That didn't come until later.

I did get my connection with Tom Molly in Ireland through this test. (See the *Chapter 28 – Ireland - Banter and Chat and Laughter Between Cousins – Our Irish Cousin Tom Molloy* later in this book, which I consider a gold mine, and he has a gold mind.) I attempted to make connections with other relatives through this DNA test, but some of these have been frustrating. This way of doing genealogy research can be very technical and overwhelming. I suggest you keep the aspirin nearby if you dig deep on this aspect of genealogy. However, because so many people are interested in submitting their DNA sample, I include the following information here in this book. While it can be frustrating and overwhelming at times, I acknowledge that this path has enriched my genealogy search.

This chapter was tedious to write, and it may be tedious to read, so please, if I lose your interest with this chapter move on! (Or better yet, write your own chapter on the topic and keep me posted on what you find!)

With my first submission of my DNA sample to ancestry.com in 2009, I got a "Guide to Your Ancestry.com DNA Test Results" which gave me steps to follow to explore and understand my results. (From here down through the rest of this chapter, I take many words and phrases from the ancestry.com website, so the wording in this chapter gets a little awkward, and I will place quotes around their words.) It helped me find matches (color coded as to how close the relative connection was), stating comments like "Ancestor Match: Within 6 generations Approx 150 years ago." It provided options to make contact with these other people who submitted their samples if they were willing to be contacted. A "conversation" could begin through the ancestry.com website, and I often provided my e-mail address so we could communicate more directly. Many interesting "conversations" began this way, and because of the large number, I had to find a way to keep track of my contacts and conversations.

You can also view their "Full Report" which provides "results, certificate, map, story, and scientific explanation" of their tests. It provides "your ancient ancestral map, (the) likely story of ancient origin, and your haplogroup designation" (which is the "scientific term for this kind of genetic profile"). It displays a map of the world that "shows the likely migration pathways of (my) ancient ancestors." My group is called The Artisans, haplogroup R1b. It says my "ancestors may have been responsible for the first cave paintings, and probably lived in present-day England, France, Spain or Portugal."

Their explanation says my unique values of specific genetic marker sites "don't tell you (or us!) anything about your hair color or other personal characteristics. The way we use DNA is very different from what you may have seen on TV or heard about in the past. If you're interested in learning more about the science behind this test, read Part II of this packet, Digging Deeper."

My recommendation is that if you want to get deep into this DNA stuff, read books by Brian Sykes like <u>The Seven Daughters of Eve – The Science That Reveals Our Genetic Ancestry</u>, (2001), and <u>Saxons, Vikings, and Celts – The Genetic Roots of Britain and Ireland</u>, (2006). Also recommended is <u>Trace Your Roots with DNA – Using Genetic Tests to Explore Your Family Tree</u> (2004) by Megan Smolenyak Smolenyak and Ann Turner. (Saying or writing Megan's last name twice is not an error, as she married a man with the same last name. Her story is interesting as she used

DNA to make sure she had not married her cousin.)

I can "View DNA" and observe the raw data of the 43 genetic markers of my results for this test, and attach it to the family tree that I have posted in ancestry.com in hopes of others finding me if I "invite" them (or you) to view my tree. As they describe, "the numbers that make up your test results may not mean much to you. It's a lot like looking at the whorls on the pad of your fingertip, or the intricate pattern of a snowflake under a microscope." So I tend to trust what the lab is telling me without fully understanding the scientific explanations of this.

I can also "visit" and "join" groups for more opportunities to share research and connect with others. Some connections are made "instantly," and "other connections are made later as the ancestry.com database grows."

The "Most Recent Common Ancestor" (MRCA) suggests through the DNA lab results how many generations my ancestor and another person's ancestor goes back before we can call this MRCA (ancestor) our "grandfather."

I can examine the geographic distribution of my potential relations on a map of the world, with the individual people who are color-coded as to how close our matches are. With a slider control on their website, I can zoom in and see where these other people live all over the world! (It's kind of scary, actually. I haven't been able to look into anyone's bathroom window, yet, but maybe they're looking into mine! That's a joke! Privacy is a serious issue this day and age.)

In 2010 I also submitted the results of my Y-DNA test results from ancestry.com to another company called Family Tree DNA. The information I submitted was:

-Last Name: Neel
-Haplogroup: R1b
-Variant Spellings: Neill, Niall, Neil, Neal, Niel, McNeil, McNeal
-Tested with ancestry.com
-Most distant known paternal ancestor on the direct male line:
John Neel (1716 - 1770)
-City, County, County of origin: Kilwinning, Ayrshire, Scotland
-Genetic profile with the value of the 43 markers of my test results

I attempted a couple of times to upload a Gedcom file (the 3848 persons I had in my family tree at the time) - but it failed with an error in uploading the file. This is a common practice so others who are searching for their relatives can see if we have any common ancestors. "Living relatives" have their names removed for privacy.

I also found neelfamily.org, and exchanged DNA information with the webmaster. We weren't successful in finding common ancestors, but we are still looking.

mtDNA submission for my nephew, Jeff

As I had fun with my Y-DNA submission and the results (if you want to call it that fun), I invited my nephew, Jeff, for a search with his DNA. For him, we did the mtDNA search which uses mitochondrial DNA from the female side of the family. I chose Jeff because he would provide information from my side of the family through his mother (my sister), but also information from his father (who does not share my DNA). This was in 2013.

After I finally got the spit out of Jeff, I found that the current state-of-the-art-and-science changes very quickly as his mtDNA report from ancestry.com was very different from my Y-DNA report through the same company. His results show an "Ethnicity Estimate" from "thousands of years ago" with a heritage of 50% from Great Britain, 20% from Europe West, 20% from Europe East, and 7% from Scandinavia. It also showed a "Low Confidence Region" of 1% Ireland, 1% Finland, and less than 1% Italy/Greece. These results also showed Other Regions Tested with 0% for the Iberian Peninsula, European Jewish, Native American, Melanesia, Polynesia, West Asia, the Caucasus, and the Middle East.

Jeff's results also show "Genetic Communities" from "hundreds of years ago" from Early Settlers of the Ohio River Valley, Indiana, Illinois, and Iowa" with a "Connection: Possible." It said that "some Genetic Communities trace their roots back to groups of people who were isolated geographically. Mountains, rivers, lack of roads, or other barriers made it likely that each new generation would marry someone who lived close to home. Others have their roots in groups who typically married others of the same religion or ethnic group. In each case, these groups came to share a significant amount of DNA. Modern-day descendants who inherited some of that DNA make up Genetic Communities." Their website says that you can "browse more than 300 Genetic Communities (that) are available today. Don't see what you're interested in? Check back later. More will be added in coming months," they say.

My own Y-DNA test did not come back with such results from specific areas of the world or the U.S. This is interesting!

Jeff's test results also showed "DNA Matches" and "DNA Circles" with Strong Confidence of a connection with the William Andrew McCool DNA Circle – 2nd Great Grandfather" with 12 members. <u>It's a hit! It's Grandpa!</u> (Actually he's my great-grandfather, who is Jeff's 2nd great-grandfather.)

It said "When William Andrew McCool was born on March 7, 1856, in Le Claire, Iowa, his father, William, was 47 and his mother, Lydia, was 41. He (Wm. A. McCool) married Sarah Ellen Garber and they had five children together. He (Wm. A. McCool) then married Sarah Mc Cool and they had eight children together. He died on March 17, 1926, in Indianola, Nebraska, at the age of 70, and was buried there." This all matches the information I had in my tree on him! (Except Sarah McCool is the same Sarah E. Garber, and they had a total of eight children together, not five.)

This showed him (Wm. A. McCool) and his father, William McCool, and his mother, Lydia (Jack) McCool, which was also information I had in my tree.

Also, for Jeff, it showed a "strong" Circle connection confidence for 3 DNA matches with djhedges57, with gengen01FamilyGroup (which had two members: gengen01 and K.W.), and with K.S.D. Family Group (which had eight members). Does this make you feel all warm and fuzzy and make you want to get to know these people? It does for me! (I received some people's full names, and for this book, I am just using their initials for privacy if they are living.)

I sent a request for connection to prawnstar195 (3rd cousin of Jeff, 2nd cousin of mine) through ancestry.com, and I also sent her an e-mail and asked her to respond. I have to check my documentation, but I think I am still waiting for more correspondence from her. Lineage for them shows that they are connected with William Andrew McCool and Sara Ellen Garber, to Lydia Susan McCool, to William Fred Derrick, to Karen Sue Derrick (all deceased), and to prawnstar195.

23andMe

In early July of 2018, I submitted a sample of my saliva to another company, 23andMe. Within two weeks I received the results with 995 relatives to chase down. Plus, this service provided me with DNA health information.

Tom Molloy (my DNA cousin in Ireland that I discovered through my first submission to ancestry.com) claimed lineage to Niall of Nine Hostages. Ancestry.com did not link me directly to Grandpa Niall, but 23 And Me does connect me to directly to Niall of Nine Hostages through my DNA sample.

I have a lot of work to do in following up and digesting my 23andMe data. Stay tuned!

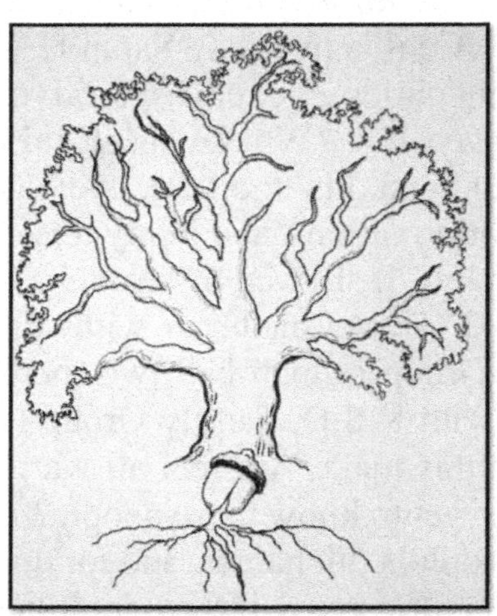

Chapter 26
Neel Family Goes To Europe! - 2010

Travel Blog - I am editing this down for the purpose of this book publication, but originally shared it in a Blog while we were traveling.

This sort of story might (or might not) be of interest to non-family readers of this book. It is an example of some of the writings that might be treasured in future generations for your own family (your story about your family, not mine).

One month until we leave

5/18/2010, Tuesday

Today, on the 30 year anniversary of the eruption of Mt. St. Helens, is one month before we leave on our trip to Europe planned for 6/18/2010. Being that there have just been some disruptions to air travel to Europe from volcanic eruptions in Iceland recently, we hope these don't occur again.

I'm just setting up this Blog and have much to do, so more later …

One week before we leave

6/11/2010, Friday

It is now one week before we leave for our trip to Europe. I feel like our dog, chasing her tail … Much preparation done, with still much preparation to do with a deadline to get everything done in a VERY short period of time.

In one week, on Friday 6/18/2010, about 5 am, we will be picking up a friend, Patricia, in Spokane who will be driving us to the airport to drop us off for our flight at 7 am to Minneapolis, then JFK airport in New York, then to Pisa, Italy for the first leg of our trip. (Thank you Patricia!)

Today is a furlough day (office closure) for my state job, but I have much work to do today because I'll be gone for 3 weeks.

I hope to keep these posts interesting and brief so as to not lose your attention. Later …

We're Outa Here!

6/18/2010, Friday

After an incredible amount of work to cut the ties to "normal" daily living (and especially work obligations), we are in the air! (I'm writing this paragraph here from the plane between Spokane and Minneapolis.) We get up at 3 am this morning, get on the road (late) about 4:30 am, pick up our friend Patricia on the south hill of Spokane (late) about 5:10 am, and get to the Spokane airport for a 7:10 am flight (on time!). Patricia and Marty will save us parking fees for 3 weeks, and they'll pick us up at the airport when we return on 7/10. (Good friends are wonderful! Chosen family!)

Heading to Minneapolis, then JFK airport (in New York, where I haven't been since 1966), and then our long flight to Pisa, Italy!

This second paragraph is being written from the JFK airport. There is a 3 hour difference in time zones from when we got up this morning, and my body is already a little confused. We will get on the plane here at JFK airport @ 8:45 pm eastern time (three hours time difference from Idaho this morning), and we will fly to Pisa, Italy, arriving there tomorrow, Saturday @ 11:40 am (I think that's about 8 or 9 hours difference from Pacific/Idaho time).

Bonjour!

We're In Italy!

6/19/2010, Saturday

We had a very rough night on the plane during the 8 hour flight from New York to Pisa, Italy. Nathan didn't sleep at all, and Mary thinks she may have slept an hour, or maybe none at all. Josh and I may have each slept a few hours, but it was hard to tell. It was very uncomfortable, as the seats didn't recline very far back (on a Boeing 767), and space was tight in the cattle compartment in back. (Actually it was a very large plane, with 7 seats across and 2 aisles in the back of the plane where we were).

We arrived in Pisa on time, a little before noon, but it is raining so hard the pilots pass by on the first landing attempt and fly out over the ocean again to wait for the storm to lighten up. We finally land a little after noon, local time, and with a 9 hour time difference between here and home in Idaho that would be about 3 am for our body's time. We are wasted.

We take a taxi to our Hotel Bologna, check in, and we have a spacious, high ceiling room with two baths (one toilet), and three beds. We're on the second floor where the windows open up to a narrow street – it has a feel like New Orleans, or pictures of that town since I have never been there that I remember. Which came first, New Orleans or European architecture? Our windows have shutters that open up across a narrow one-way street.

After showers (for all) and naps (for some), we walk through narrow streets, looking in shops and bookstores that are all in the Italian language. For dinner Mary and Nathan got tortellini and Josh and I got real Italian pizza – it's really different than Dominos!

Then we walk around more and get handmade Italian ice cream (called Gelato).

It's about 8:30 pm local time here now (11:30 am Pacific/Idaho time), and our body-clocks are still a little screwed up.

I'll try to post some pictures on this Blog.

Arrivederci!

Walking the streets at night ...

6/20/2010 Sunday

Ciao! (My intention to mean "Hello," but I'm not sure I've got it right).

It's now about 2 am Monday, local time in Pisa, and Josh and I weren't sleeping well, so I invite him downstairs with me to the lobby of our Hotel Bologna (like I did the night before by myself).

So now, Monday 6/21, I write about that night, Saturday night to Sunday morning, when I couldn't sleep and I came downstairs to write.

Then I step out into what I had previously dreamed of ... walking the streets of a foreign country by myself in the middle of the night! (This time line is confusing as I'm going back and forth in time travel – hope I don't lose you as a reader.)

When I step outside and smell the night air, I listen to the night sounds. There is one man who looks like a local Italian, walking quietly and keeping to himself. A few minutes later another man walks by, who looks possibly like an American or English man. He walks quietly with an umbrella until he used it to test some loose stucco off the side of a building – it is not so quiet anymore, which causes some feelings of anxiety and fear in myself. I think: "That umbrella may be in case of rain, but it is also an assault weapon!" I find a container of umbrellas just inside the motel door for what appears to be for guests to use, so I borrow one.

I leave the motel that night about 3 am, walk toward the river and do a circuit. I take about an hour with my assault umbrella to boost my confidence. It is very quiet, with occasional people walking around, and very few cars and motorcycles disturbing my quiet stride. Not interacting but observing the people leaves me to imagine what they are doing. Some appeared to have been partying, like the young man who peed off the bridge into the river. Some are in lively conversation, some are quiet leaving me to wonder about their lives and I fill in the gaps with my imagination …

About 3 to 4 am, with less stimulation of daily city sounds, and with my anxiety aroused in me by being out alone at night (with my very own assault umbrella), my senses are heightened and I can hear echoes of the slightest sounds. I smell wonderful breads baking from imagined bakers in their shops before the market opens. I can smell olive oil and other spices in their recipes …

The river is separated from the streets by a high and very thick, very old brick wall (about 4 ft. by 4 ft.), making the river inaccessible to this pedestrian. (I ache to walk on the shore of rivers.) I walk past a very old church along the river, which has amazing stone carvings. I cross over the river by a very old, arched bridge, then walk upstream about 400 yards (how many meters is that?) to another old, arched bridge. I walked past the city hall, which looked centuries old. I try some alleys, looking at the local cars that were parked (Fiats, Citroens, Alpha Romeos, and even some Fords).

An alley cat spooks me.

After returning "home" and replacing my assault umbrella in its place, I return to bed and sleep well.

More later about yesterday, Sunday, which was Father's Day in the U.S. (but not here in Italy) when Josh and I go to Florence, and Mary and Nate stay in Pisa.

The Arno River in Pisa, Italy – Walking the streets at night!

Florence vs. Pisa

6/21/2010 Monday

I'm writing about the trip that Josh and I took to Florence yesterday, Sunday 6/20. It still gets confusing to me about this time tripping thing, so some reference to days may not always match up – I guess that's what vacations are about.

With some stress in the family between Mary and I about separating, Josh and I take the train from Pisa to Florence, and leave half the family behind. (It's Fathers Day, so I get my way.)

We find ourselves on the train sitting across from a couple from Australia, and since they can speak English it's good to compare notes about travel through conversation, and to do reality checks. We have to pay attention to the stops that the train makes to make sure we get off at the right station in Florence (population about 300,000). When we arrive, we are bothered that we have to pay to use the public toilets. I guess they are not so "public".

Exiting the train station into a large open area, we see many old buildings, lots of people, and know that we can't hardly scratch the surface of how much there is to see, especially with the famous art, and the famous lines you have to stand in to see the popular exhibits.

We decide to get on a tour bus of Florence, Italy for a quick orientation. We ride in the top level of the bus, which has open sides with a soft top, and put in ear buds to plug in to hear the recorded tour guide with selectable channels for different languages. We hear about Michelangelo, Galileo, and many other famous and not-so-famous people and places.

It starts to rain hard, and it gets cold and wet, even under the cover of the roof of the bus. After the one-hour tour, we feel somewhat oriented to the town and places we want to try to see on foot, but we have the need for the bathroom, and don't want to pay for toilets again, so there is a familiar sight – McDonalds! And yes, free toilets! After taking care of business, Josh and I get cappuccinos at McDonalds, and wait for the rain to lighten up.

Then we walk for a while, trying to find a famous building we are searching for. We walk by poor people who are just pathetic in their condition - a woman in a dress in a yoga Child's Pose, kneeling in the dirty water running in the gutter of the cobblestone street. She is wet and muddy from the rain, curled up on her knees with her head down, hands out palm up and trembling as if having a seizure. (Is this for real, or good drama for a cash donation from the tourists?)

We attempt to enter a beautiful church, and are turned away with our camera but they are allowing local people in for what appears to be services (this is understandable). Another woman is begging outside the church, and Josh gives her a coin, but in her Italian that we don't understand, she gestures to try to tell us it wasn't enough for her "cinque bambinos" (five children?). We wave her off, and she later tries to take another run at us, as if she didn't remember us from the first time.

Josh and street lady in Florence, Italy.

We tour a museum of photographs (which was expensive and disappointing). We walk more, and duck out of the rain for another bathroom stop at a local restaurant, which is crowded with local people watching the World Cup soccer match (Italy vs. New Zealand).

We finally surrender, glad we saw parts of this famous city, but disappointed it was too big and too crowded and too much to see for such a short time. We get back on the train to Pisa, get a quick dinner, and get back to the hotel before the agreed-on time, and find that Mary and Nathan attempted, unsuccessfully, to climb the Leaning Tower of Pisa. They got lost and scared trying to find hotel again. (I'll let Mary tell that story.)

We Travel to Vernazza

6/22/2010 Tuesday

My laptop tells me it's 5 am Tuesday, but other than that, I wouldn't know. My body woke me up about 4 am today (which is much better than it has been – I think yesterday I woke 1:30 am in Pisa, and didn't sleep again – I took another great walk in the night on the streets along the river, this time with camera and monopod as my defensive weapon, which I didn't need, and I watched the sun rise and got some great shots).

Check out time in Pisa was 11 am at the Hotel Bologna. As Josh and I hadn't gotten a chance to see the Leaning Tower of Pisa, all four of us hired the hotel shuttle driver to take us over to the Leaning Tower for a quick eyes-on and photo shoot. This is NOT the way you're supposed to do it - so American! Because of the time crunch, we had the driver wait about 10 minutes for us and then went back to the hotel to get our bags.

Mary was feeling very ill, and then Josh started getting sick. Time was very pressing now, as we had to catch our train, which was about a 15 minute walk away with our bags. At the last minute, we hired the hotel shuttle again instead of walking as Mary and Josh were taking turns running to the bathroom. The train station was a little easier to negotiate for Josh and me since we were here the day before when we went to Florence, but it was all new to Mary and Nathan. Our two "sickies" had to stay close to the bathrooms. We were expecting the train to NOT have a "WC" (or water closet – that's European for bathroom), so it was NOT fun.

We did make the train on time, cramming into a small elevator and going underground to another train platform. This train took us from Pisa to LaSpezia, Italy to buy tickets and catch the next train to the Cinque Terra.

We found a McDonalds (arrrrgggh!) to get some drink and food. I got train tickets for the next ride, and hurriedly got to the next train out of LaSpezia.

The train enters the Cinque Terra through tunnels in the mountain rock (at sea level!), and comes out into the light only at the five towns with beautiful views of the Italian Rivera (the Mediterranean Sea).

Ours is the fourth of five villages - Vernazza. To quote Rick Steves' Europe Through the Back Door: "*The Cinque Terra (CHINK-weh TAY-reh), is a remote chunk of the Italian Riviera ... not a museum in sight ... God's great gift to tourism ... for a home base choose among five (cinque) villages, each of which fills a ravine with a lazy hive of human activity ... the chunk of coast was first described in medieval times ... this land was watched over by castles. Tiny communities grew in their protective shadows, ready to run at the first hint of a Turkish Saracen pirate raid. Marauding pirates from North Africa were a problem until about 1400 AD ....*" Rick Steves is well known for his travel information – I encourage you to look him up and buy one of his books if you plan to travel, and/or watch him on television. (Well, enough homework for the moment … I'm on vacation.)

Arriving in Vernazza, communication with the Italians for us is difficult. With a printed copy of our Itinerary, we were somewhat able to communicate with the train clerk behind the counter, and he called the manager of our apartment, Francesca, who spoke very little English. We pulled out our index cards (that my co-worker Lorissa had prepared for us – Thanks, Lorissa!) We made attempts to flip through them to communicate the length of our stay, at the same time while negotiating stairs, crowded walk ways, and lugging our bags trying to keep up with our guide.

Vernazza, Cinque Terra, Italy – view from our apartment window.

Our apartment is incredible. Certainly not fancy, but adequate in space with a small room for the boys with 2 beds, and a room for Mary and me, with windows that open up to the town square of a very colorful village and the bay.

After settling a little, looking out over the community center at a very old church, Nathan want to explore and go visit the church. He and I left while Mary and Josh rested from being sick.

I did some catching up on writing while here, but as the Internet is not accessible in our room, and we have to pay for WiFi in the village. I'm going to stop writing for a while.

Ciao!

Life in Vernazza

6/24/2010 Thursday

Travel is amazing! The people, the richness of the variety of Life! The town of Vernazza, Italy was so sweet - it has been here since medieval times and 600 people still live here. There was a very old church right on the edge of the Mediterranean Sea built in the 1300's I think.

My son, Nathan, and I are looking inside this old church, and a man came inside and starts setting stuff up on the altar. He then came and sat down in the pews near us and he started chanting in Italian with Rosary beads in his hand. Then little old Italian ladies, one after the another, came into the church and joined him in call-and-response until there were about 20 ladies all around us, saying the Rosary call-and-response in Italian to this man. (Why only this one man, who appeared to be a priest in civilian clothes or a lay person, and all of these old women? Where were the other men of the village?)

The next day in Vernazza (which is the first whole day in the Cinque Terra), I get up early to see the sun rise and had coffee at the Blue Marlin café while the family slept in. Later in the day the family takes a train to Monterosso (the fifth of five communities in the Cinque Terra), and we take a boat back to Vernazza after walking along the water front of this resort community on the Italian Rivera.

On the second whole day in the Cinque Terra, I didn't sleep well again and got up at 2:30 am. I take a walk, and take the 6:30 am train to Riomaggiore (the first of five communities in the Cinque Terra). I am by myself, and am unsuccessful in finding any coffee. I returned to Vernazza on the 7:30 am train but the family was still asleep until 8 am. I took a nap until 9:30 am while the family had breakfast without me at the il Pirate restaurant, ran by twin brothers who were very entertaining. Mary made reservations for dinner there that night. I rented Internet time (thirty minutes for 3 Euros). The whole family then takes the train back to Riomaggiore for a nice lunch and a boat ride back to Vernazza. The famous trails between towns were too steep for this tired family. On this boat ride some of us get too hot, dehydrated, and sea sick, so I take another 90 minute nap. (Is this a siesta in Italy?) Then we swim in the Italian Rivera before dinner.

Mary, Josh, Nate, and Todd in Monterosso, Italy.

On our last full day in Vernazza, we hear the church bells sounding differently than usual, and we go down to the village center and find all these local people gathering in front of the church. Then they started walking behind a vehicle with something like "Social Services" (in Italian) on the side, with a casket inside the vehicle. The gathering procession followed the vehicle and casket up and out of the village.

Later that night, in the dark, I find the cemetery high up on the mountain above the village - very, very beautiful that brings me to tears. I could feel the life, the history, the people, the spirits there.

It's so beautiful.

Upon return to Vernazza by boat from Monterosso, Italy.

Vernazza at night from above.

Nice is nice, but this isn't where we planned to be tonight
Thur. 6/24/2010

We're staying, unplanned, in a nice motel in Nice, France (pun intended). There were rumors in Vernazza, Italy that Italian trains were going to strike on Friday, the day we planned to leave Vernazza. As that is a big travel day for us out of Italy and we have to catch a train in Nice, France to Paris, we decided to leave Italy a day early to avoid the risk of not being able to get out at all.

But then we run into another problem. By avoiding the train strike in Italy on Friday, we find out there is a train strike in France on Thursday! We don't know this until we get to the last town in Italy (Ventimiglia) before crossing the border into France. We discover this standing in line in Ventimiglia to get tickets to Nice when another customer tells us that on this day, Thursday, the French trains are on strike! And so we can't get out of Italy by train on the French trains to Nice. There were other travelers we talked with who helped us understand logistics. We need to go about 90 km to Nice, and so we plan on sharing a taxi to France with a man who can translate for us. But the taxis won't take more than four people, so we have to abandon our translator and our family ends up taking a taxi to Nice by ourselves (which is expensive).

The taxi driver, Pierre, is French. He speaks fairly good English. He lives in Nice, but his taxi business in his modern, small Mercedes is out of Monaco. He has many interesting stories about his other rich clients – not us! He helped us find a motel room in Nice near the train station. Motels are crowded because of conventions and the Ironman triathlon competition in Nice this weekend. This is the same weekend that Ironman is also in Coeur d'Alene, Idaho, our home town.

Ah, but it's nice here in Nice. (Be sure to pronounce that properly.) Mary and the boys waded in the French Rivera, we had a good dinner, two deserts, and were entertained by great street artists.

Goodbye to Nice, Bonjour to Paris!
Traveling from Nice to Paris
Friday 6/25/2010

So, we had printed e-mail confirmations of e-tickets from Nice, France to Paris. We let the boys sleep in late in this comfortable motel (with 2 rooms), and after the boys get up, Mary stays behind while I walked to the train station and try to get the actual tickets. I am unsuccessful this time as I stand in lines, try e-machines that won't work with my credit card, and give up after about an hour. I run back to the hotel as I am running out of time.

I am hot and tired, but we drag the family and our bags to the train station. I stand in the ticket line again while Josh sits with the bags while Mary and Nate go across the street for take-out Chinese food for the trip.

The clerk at the ticket window tells me there had been rain water over tracks somewhere, and the scheduled 7 minutes between trains wasn't enough time to change trains in Toulon, France. So we are able to go on another train an hour earlier hoping all our connections will be right. On the train, clerks tell us to not get off the train in Toulon, but instead go on to Marcelles. (Someone is watching out for us!) This makes us very anxious, but they were right, AND we barely had time to transfer from the Nice-Marselles train to the high-speed Marcelles-Paris train. (More blessings in disguise). I believe if we had kept to the original plan of doing the whole trip from Vernazza, Italy to Genoa, Italy to Ventimiglia, Italy to Nice, France, to Paris, France on Friday, we wouldn't have made it. Turns out we were exhausted when we arrived in Paris, anyway.

I am now writing while on a high speed TGV train, advertised in the magazine on board as going 320 kmh. It was posted in our e-mail when we bought these tickets on-line as going 185 mph. It doesn't feel that fast, but it is very modern, moving smooth and fast, and when I can see a distant highway (like one of our Interstate highways), we are certainly moving well-faster than the fastest vehicles.

I'm looking out the window, traveling north from Marseille, France to Paris, France, through Avignon and other towns (and making very few stops since this is a high-speed train).

We fly past ancient looking churches in the countryside, past electricity-generating windmills, past nuclear power plants … what a time-warp! When trains fly! When pigs fly!

PARIS!

Saturday 6/26/2010

So, it's now 11 am, Saturday, and I'm sitting in the comfortable, old lobby of our Hotel de la Bourdonnais in Paris. We get free a WiFi Internet connection, so communication is easier from my laptop, although a secure connection to our bank to check balances is uncomfortable because I'm a little concerned about someone seeing our passwords and account numbers.

We got here to the hotel about 11 pm last night after arriving in Paris on the high speed train from Nice, France about 9 pm.

High speed TGV train after arrival in Paris, France.

I'm sitting in the lobby with a gentleman named Steve who currently lives in Portland, and we visit. He works with lasers in Portland, and since he's a scientific guy I asked about the kph translation to mph. He says 320 kph would be about 192 mph. It was amazingly fast watching things go by, but it was very smooth (there were glasses and dinner on the table in front of us on the high-speed train, and nothing fell off until the water bottle was empty, and then it fell off).

Further visiting with Steve here in the lobby of our hotel in Paris, he tells me he grew up in Missoula, Montana, where I grew up from 1966 until 1984. We both went to Rattlesnake Grade School, and to Hellgate High School. I graduated from high school in 1973, and he graduated high school in 1981. So far we haven't been able to connect any more common names that both he knew and I knew. He lived on Aspen Drive up the Rattlesnake, which is the road where some of my good childhood friends lived, like Allen J. and Ken W., but he didn't know them.

So now we have 5 days and 6 nights in Paris before we get on a plane to London.

Josh is going crazy, because the rock band, Green Day, is playing a concert tonight, and he really wants to go. More later on that ...

Check In from Paris - Happy Birthday to Tim!

Tuesday 6/29/2010 (e-mail to my brother)
HAPPY BIRTHDAY, TIM!!!
I'd sing you a song, but you don't have Skype!
What are you going to do today?
We're sending you a package from Paris, so it will be late.
Sorry about that.
It's Tuesday morning. Mary and I are awake downstairs in the motel lobby having breakfast and coffee while the boys are sleeping in, again. Last night we took a cruise on the River Seine, starting near the Eiffel Tower, and cruising upriver for about 1/2 hour, passing Notre Dame, then turning around and getting off the boat just before the lights on the Eiffel Tower turned on. We're saving the elevator ride up the Eiffel Tower for Wednesday, Nathan's 18th birthday, which is tomorrow night. We want to be up in the tower in the dark to see the lights of Paris from up there. It's only a few blocks

from our motel.
The day after we arrived, Josh was going crazy wanting us to check and see if tickets were available to the Green Day rock concert that night. They were, and we did. It took us two trips across Paris in the Metro (subway) to get the tickets, get back to the hotel and have dinner, and then get back across town for the concert at 6 pm. The four of us saw opening acts Billy Talent, Paramore, and then Green Day. The concert went from 6 pm to almost 11 pm, with Green Day on almost 3 hours! Billy Joe Armstrong, Tre' Cool, and Mike Dirnt, along with their support musicians (another guitar, and keyboard/sax player) put on an amazing show, really engaging the audience, a huge French crowd who seemed to know the songs by heart, and sang along with all of Green Day's songs in English. Very entertaining. In Paris!
We've been taking bus tours to get oriented to the city, and to have English piped into our ear buds so we have a better idea of what we are looking at. There is a LOT of history here. Hitler was here! Napoleon was here! Kings, Queens, Joan of Arc and many others were executed here. We visited the Louvre yesterday (a huge museum), that was way more than we could handle.
It has been very hot here. Josh has been getting sick from dehydration and the heat, making it very difficult for the rest of us. We're going to try to go see Notre Dame today.
You take care of yourself today, Tim, and have a Happy Birthday!
Love,
Todd and family

Check In from Paris - Happy 18th Birthday Nathan!
Wednesday 6/30/2010

Today is Nathan's 18th birthday, and he gets served breakfast in bed, and gets the remote control for the TV at the same time. (French television is not much fun for me, as I don't understand it).

The family went to Notre Dame Cathedral yesterday, and the Arch de Triumph. It was hot and we were really on “survival mode,” trying to maintain liquid intake, heat, nutrition, energy, patience, communication, respect, karma … Travel like this as a family can magnify our strengths and weaknesses in challenging environments.

Notre Dame Cathedral is very crowded as we tour the inside of this historical, beautiful chapel. We consider climbing 400 steps up to the towers of the cathedral, but while eating ice cream and figuring the time standing and waiting in line in the sun, we didn't figure it was worth it. (More on Notre Dame later when I make the trip back to it by myself.)

We make our way back from Notre Dame in the open-air, double-decker tour bus, plugged in our English translating headphones again, and make our way towards the Arch de Triumph, which has only 284 steps to the top.

The French started to build the 165 foot tall Arc de Triumph in 1809 to celebrate Napoleon as the emperor of a "New Rome." It was not finished before his death, but "*it was finished in time for his posthumous homecoming in 1840. Nineteen years after he died in exile on St Helena, his remains were carried in a grand parade underneath his grand arch*". (from Rick Steves' book, Europe through the Back Door). It has a beautiful view of the Champs-d'Elysees and all of Paris, and I take a series of panoramic photos all around.

It's hard to get around Paris, and the heat and lack of air conditioning in public places make it difficult.

We see the Pere La Chaise Cemetery where many famous people are buried and we find many headstones, among them Oscar Wilde, Gertrude Stein, and Jim Morrison (from the Doors). We do not find Fredrick Chopin's marker. At Oscar Wilde's marker, there is a brief resume for him on the back, and there are lipstick marks all over it as he was a "writer and martyr to homosexuality who is mourned by outcast men and by wearers of heavy lipstick …" There is a class tour of high school age kids there at the time, and girls are posing for their photo by friends while kissing the marker, leaving their own lipstick.

After the cemetery, we can only get reservations at 3 pm to go up the elevator in the Eiffel Tower, at Nathan's request. (We want to go up after dark to see the lights, but there are no openings at that time.) It is very cool! Interesting that it is more windy on the ground, while the air was very calm on the top, just under the 1,063 ft. peak. This was built in 1889 for the World's Fair there by Gustav Eiffel. He had an apartment at the top where he entertained guests, and this had a model displayed at the top posing Gustav with his daughter and Thomas Edison, who had visited there.

This is our last full day in Paris, as we get on a plane tomorrow afternoon for London.

Last day in Paris - Bus #69 to Notre Dame, and then some: Report on last day in Paris

Thursday 7/1/2010

I get up early Thursday morning at 4 am, and I take a city bus ride by myself on route 69 from our neighborhood near the Eiffel Tower to the Notre Dame Cathedral and other places. This bus route was made famous to us by Rick Steves' travel books as one of the more local, "back door" ways of seeing this part of Europe. I get across town fairly quickly on the bus, and I start to recognize places we had seen on previous days on the tour bus. So I believe I can get off and back on the bus fairly quickly without getting lost, and see locations that were now more quiet and cooler, it being about 7 am, and many other tourists are still in bed or getting ready to amass on the cobblestones again soon.

I get off near Notre Dame, walk a few blocks to it, and walk quietly and peacefully among the local Parisians, workers, homeless people, pigeons, etc. I snap a bunch of pictures, and remember that being behind the camera is another way of being removed from really being there.

I admire the beautiful stone work, towers, gargoyles, and other beauty that made this creation famous. I am reading information signs in front of the opening and notice people starting to gather around me. A worker from inside the Cathedral came out, talks to some of the individuals as if they knew one another, and she opens the gate.

Being that the gathering group of people are going inside, and I am one of them just by my physical presence, I go inside with the flow. Besides being able to see the beauty from the inside again, there is a Catholic mass scheduled, which I join with my own mixed emotions.

It seems that all of the other people are local French people, or French travelers as some of them were wearing heavy backpacks. The language spoken was in French so I don't understand the content, but it is emotional for me because it was so beautiful and it brought me to tears at times. When the priest starts doing the ritual of the sacrament (the wine and wafers to symbolize the blood and body of Christ), I get uncomfortable and I leave at that time. But I feel something powerful and I can't quite put words to my feelings.

Some of the feelings I can recognize are about my internal conflict because of my own belief systems about spirituality and my High Power, and my judgments about the Catholic church, their history, etc. I am a social worker with child protection services, and I had read about John Knox in Scotland telling off Mary, Queen of Scots to have her church elders to stop molesting the children. I leave trying to sort out what my head and heart were telling me.

I work my way back across the River Seine to the bus, and get back on again, soaking it in. Pedestrian, car, motorcycle and bike traffic is picking up, and the bus starts going into parts of Paris that I don't recognize. It stops and parks suddenly. All the people get off, and the bus driver indicates (not in English) that I also needed to get off. I stand on the sidewalk trying to sort out the bus schedule, and then notice that another bus, and then another, and then another bus, all with #69 on their fronts, pulled up, stop, drivers get out, and four of them were left empty! Rick Steves didn't tell me about this! This was like a bad movie!

Thinking about this strange foreign city, with Mary and the boys back at the motel and not having cell phones and not having experience using local phones, I start to worry a little, balanced out with trusting the process. Eventually another driver gets on one of the #69 buses. Other passengers get on and I follow them. We start moving through the route again. I trust it will circle back to the Eiffel

Tower and the neighborhood we are staying at.

Eiffel Tower through the Peace Monument.

I don't know if you have any experience traveling on the streets of large cities in Europe or not, but it can be scary! Some places in Europe they drive on the wrong side of the road (like the U.K.), and the streets are very narrow, and they hardly ever go straight. Bus Route #69 ended for me this morning with the driver stopping, getting out, and looking at his huge bus just inches away from a parked Volvo, waving traffic to back up, and trying to back up himself. I got off the bus and sauntered away, as I recognized the streets and knew I could walk back to the motel from here.

Later that morning we checked out of the Paris motel, juggling luggage, boys, currency (this is the last place for us to use our Euros). We grab the shuttle to the Paris airport with the driver who spoke very little English. The shuttle picked up two other passengers from Scotland, which was very interesting to talk to them as they knew information about our future travels.

We caught the plane from the Paris Charles de Gaulle Airport to the London Heathrow Airport, quite an experience itself. We took a train from the airport to a London station (the Paddington Station), then hired a classic English taxi for ride to our motel in the Victoria neighborhood and check into The Elizabeth. We walk to dinner at the Ebury Pub for fish and chips!

Writing From The Elizabeth Hotel in London about Paris
7/2/2010 Friday

We arrived in London last night. Paris had been very hot, and transportation around that huge city was complicated, so that slowed us down. We got to see a lot, but you could spend a life time there (and some people do!).

Josh read something that if you spent 5 minutes at every exhibit at the Louve it would take 7 years. We did visit The Louve museum, but it was so huge we only saw a small portion. We tried to get in an English speaking tour group, but they were all full. We can say we were there, but we didn't really appreciate what we were seeing, not knowing what we were looking at. We recognized some classic pieces, but I think I would want to start reading history books about the artists and the times they lived in.

We saw the Mona Lisa, and it was packed with crowds around it and was difficult to get close to, so it was kind of disappointing. The public was kept about 30 ft. away from the Mona Lisa, and we read that at one time an employee had stolen it and kept it rolled up under his bed for 3 years. (I wonder what they did with that guy when they caught him. I wonder where he is now?)

We rode up the elevator of the Eiffel Tower on Nathan's 18th birthday at his request. We heard that when Hitler was in Paris that the elevator malfunctioned so he had to climb up the tower to the top. And after he left an employee figured out what was wrong and fixed it with a simple screwdriver. Poor Adolf.

There was a lot of bloodshed in Paris. Nathan thinks our American soldiers fought in Paris, but someone said the Germans left here before we arrived. We'll have to get out the history books (or look it up on Wikipedia).

I'll keep this brief, and post more later.

Josh, Nathan, and Mary at The Louve Museum, Paris.

London
7/2/2010 Friday

Our motel (The Elizabeth) is in an old, and expensive, neighborhood. Our room is very small, in the basement, and we do have a daylight window, but the air conditioner requires the window to be opened about 6 inches (by about 5 ft. wide), so it is only marginally effective. Mary didn't sleep well last night because of the heat.

I didn't write that at the Notre Dame Cathedral in Paris, there was a statue of Joan of Arc who was executed at age 19 for being a witch and a heretic, and then later a decision was made at Notre Dame to save her reputation and she was then made a Saint. (I started to look Joan of Arc up on Wikepedia – check it out, or read a book!).

Learning a lot on this trip.

On this date, we took an open air, double-decker bus tour of London ("Original Tour"). We went to Picadilly Circus, had lunch, and walked around. Back in our neighborhood, we had a bad Japanese dinner "walk-away" (or take-out, as we call it in the U.S.).

London – busy blur …
Saturday 7/3/2010 - Tuesday 7/6/2010

On Saturday, 7/3, we saw the changing of the Guard at Buckingham Palace, had lunch at the Hard Rock Café &

The Vault (rock & roll museum that was part of the London Hard Rock Cafe - which was the first Hard Rock in the world). We walked through Green Park & St. James Park, visited the Churchill Museum & War Room, rode on the London Eye (which is a giant ferris wheel built for the Millennium on the Thames river), and had dinner at the Shakespeare Pub.

Josh, Nathan, and Mary with a classic English taxi.

On Sunday, 7/4, we went to the Tower of London, and visited the British Museum.

On Monday, 7/5, we went to Westminster Abbey, St. Paul's Cathedral, had dinner at Garfunkel's (I had a traditional British Breakfast for dinner, otherwise known as "heart attack on a plate" – it wasn't very good). This was an ambitious day, as we ended the day with a live musical play at the Dominion Theatre called "We Will Rock You" with the music of Queen with a great, live rock band.

A little more on the Westminster Abbey, which was right next to Big Ben and the British Parliament on the River Thames. There was a lot of history in the Westminster Abbey, as Kings and Queens have been coronated and buried there, and many other famous people buried there, including Charles Darwin, Isaac Newton, Keats, William Shakespeare, Charles Dickens, Laurence Olivier, and George Fredrick Handel, among many others. (My mom sang Handel's Messiah with the Pensacola (Florida) Choir and we have a LP record of this.) After the Westminster Abbey, we went to

St. Paul's Cathedral that survived the aerial bombings of Britain by Germany during World War II.

The London Eye ferris wheel.

We leave London by train on Tuesday, 7/6 for Edinburgh, Scotland, so we are able to see the countryside during the 4 ½ hour train ride. There's a lot of history there that I want to see and experience, and my family history comes from there, as far as I know.

During the train ride from London to Edinburgh, we passed countryside that looks like the mid-west U.S., around Missouri that we have seen, with rolling hills, agricultural land, and older farm houses and villages. We also passed clusters of modern wind turbines and also what looked like many nuclear power plants (about a half-dozen sites with clusters of 4 to 7 cooling towers, the shapes of what look like our nuclear plants).

Edinburgh, Scotland

Tuesday 7/6/2010 - Saturday 7/10/2010.

In Edinburgh, we stayed at the Princes Street Suite, and this was by far our best accommodations with 2 separate bedrooms, a large living room/dining room combination, full kitchen with dishes, and laundry in the apartment! (None of our previous housing situations had laundry, and we had been washing our clothes in the sink and hanging them to dry in the humid European climate, as when we asked where Laundromats were, we were referred to dry cleaners who would do a shirt for 4 pounds or $6, as one pound was about $1.50). Each bedroom had a small flat screen television, and there was a large, flat screen TV in the living room (and the TV shows were in English!, including many American TV shows and movies). They also provided an iPod docking station, which the boys really liked.

We started out the visit in Edinburgh with a guided, double-decker tour bus of Old Town and New Town, to get oriented to the city and get a narration from a guide about things to see. (Sometimes we got very entertaining guides, and sometimes they were very dry and flat in their presentations.) We could hop on and off the bus, so we got off at the Edinburgh Castle to tour that, walking through the marching area where the famous Military Tattoo is held the full month of August every year, which is a bag pipes and drums competition - I suggest you hit YouTube and look up videos of these talented musicians. There was endless shopping to be done, and we supported their economy with our small donations (but I did not buy a kilt – too expensive).

The famous Edinburgh Castle, which was built on the rock of an extinct volcanic plug for visibility and protection, was at one end of the "Royal Mile." At the other end of the Royal Mile was the British Royal Palace and the Scottish Parliament. The original Parliament of Scotland for the Kingdom of Scotland during the 13th century was ended for 300 years by the "Acts of Union" of 1707, and England ruled Scotland from the Parliament of the United Kingdom in London until just recently, when in 1999 the Scottish Parliament began again. The Queen of England still visits here regularly, and she was overdue for her spring visit this year.

Edinburgh seemed older than London, and/or what it could be was the presentation and maintenance of the buildings, or maybe the origin of the stones (granite vs. sandstone). The old stones of Edinburgh seem to have been allowed to age more naturally, as they were very dark and rough, while the stonework of London was lighter in color, and they were very clean and smooth.

On Thursday 7/8/2010, we rode for 12 hours on a

tour bus to the mountainous Highlands north of Edinburgh to Inverness and back. We saw beautiful countryside, and if there are such things as genetic or “DNA memories,” I can see why my father and mother choose to live in western Montana as their final home after retirement. The land of the Scottish Highlands is a lot like the mountains of western Montana and in Idaho, where I currently live.

We stopped and visited the ruined Urquhart Castle on the shores of the famous Loch Ness (“Loch” means “lake). We took a boat ride from this castle to the end of the lake, where the tour bus picked us up again, drove through Inverness, and then back to Edinburgh. (Of course, we saw Nessie, the Loch Ness Monster, but my camera wasn’t working for some reason).

Edinburgh is in the "lowlands" (rolling hills), and up north is the "highlands" (with steeper peaks). Mountain peaks up there are not that high, the highest being Ben Nevis at 4409 ft. above sea level, and we would have seen this highest peak in the United Kingdom except for cloud cover on the day of this trip. We drove past ski areas, which closed about 3 weeks before we were there (but I did not see large enough snow fields to ski on at that time). We saw where the Campbells attacked and killed hundreds of the MacDonalds in their sleep. (How does that saying go? “Never trust a Campbell”?) We saw where portions of the Harry Potter movies were made. It was beautiful country, again, looking like what you might find in western Montana and places in Idaho.

Loch Ness is connected by a chain of lakes and man-made canals and locks, which connects the Firth of Lorn and the Sea of Herbides and the Atlantic Ocean near Northern Ireland on the west coast of Scotland to the North Sea on the east coast of Scotland.

Scotland was beautiful, and it really tugged at my heartstrings. (See the next *Chapter 27 - The Dream of Standing in the Homelands of My Ancestors*).

Chapter 27
Scotland – The Dream of Standing in the Homeland of my Ancestors

I began this chapter at home in Idaho before this trip to Europe with just a title and a dream - sort of a "dream of a dream" because it was a daydream, wanting to be inspired by a visit in the night from some ancestral ghosts that never came. Some of this chapter was also written during the trip to Europe, and now I finish it back home in Coeur d'Alene, Idaho, about a week after our return. So this is kind of a "Back to the Future"/"Back from the Past" journey. Did you see those "Back to the Future" movies?

Flash back: Here, now, I sit about 1:45 am, Saturday 7/10/2010 in Edinburgh, Scotland, the homeland of my ancestors. I push a button on my Timex digital wristwatch, and I can see that it is 5:45 pm, Friday 7/9/2010 in our home town of Coeur d'Alene where we will be by 2 pm this afternoon, crossing nine time zones to get there, flying about ten hours in the air.

We are up early this morning to catch our flight to Spokane, Washington and then for the drive home to Coeur d'Alene, Idaho, after three weeks of "holiday" in Europe. This family vacation that I had previously never before dreamed of as possible for me is from the gracious generosity of my wife, Mary, and her decision to take our family to Europe on vacation with her inheritance from her parents. It was about a year ago, on July 11, 2009 (one year from tomorrow), that her mother, Phyllis, died. It has been from Mary's parents' choices in careers, investments, and lifestyle choices which has allowed us to live for three weeks like royalty in Europe! What a blessing this has been!

We vacation like royalty here in Europe. I choose the word "royalty" with a small "r" for a reason, as we have enjoyed four nights here at the Princes Street Suites here in Edinburgh, the capitol of Scotland. We are literally across the railroad tracks from the Queens' Palace and the Scottish Parliament at the end of the Royal Mile, which runs from Edinburgh Castle to Holyrood Palace. There have been many beheadings of Royalty throughout history that we have heard about on our trip, and I don't want to be a part of any of that Royalty.

Flash forward: Here, now, I sit about 6:45 am, Saturday 7/17/2010 in Coeur d'Alene, Idaho. Back home again.

Reflections: Part of this trip has been a pilgrimage for me. This pilgrimage has been a search in Scotland, the homeland of my ancestors, for traces, for some record, some sign of my ancestors that came before me. My questions: Who were they? What were their lives like? What caused them to leave Scotland in the 1700's? What did they dream about? Were they good people? What legacy did they leave behind?

This trip and the record of it is a legacy that I will leave behind for family and friends on an Internet Blog and my self-published book Family Hunger. I wonder: Will my descendants come looking for traces of me someday? Will they find these words? Will they have an interest in our collective heritage, will they have a "family hunger"? These words you are reading are evidence of my physical body, which bears traces of my ancestors. The DNA from my ancestors that I carry through to the present day is in my body is in these fingers that I move to type on this keyboard, and in the neurons of my brain that play with these words. We are living legacies. We are miracles!

Will my descendants have questions about me someday, like: Who was this guy? What was his life like? What caused him to go to Scotland in 2010? What did he dream about? Was he a good guy?

Now, in case you didn't know this about me, I'm kind of pre-occupied with our family's genealogy. I was hoping that while in Scotland I would have found the gemstone of information that would be the key to my search to where I came from. But, alas, no gemstone. In Edinburgh, I did visit the Calton Cemetery right next to our hotel, and I did find the gravestone for John William Neill (an architect, d.o.b. 7/22/1781, and d.o.d. 1/28/1827) and other members of his family. But is this my family?

Now, this next paragraph may be "TMI" or "too much information" for those not interested in genealogy, so you can skip to the end this chapter if you wish: I did find the location of the national Scotland Registry of families (also known as Scotland's People Centre and available over the Internet), and I visited the building where it is housed. I found on their computers the same document that I had already found on the Internet through ancestry.com. That document is a scanned, digital copy of a parish record of John Neil, immigrant from Scotland: d.o.b. 12/8/1716 from Kilwinning, Ayrshire, Scotland, and his parents John Neil and Margaret Johnstoun. The staff at Scotlands People told me they have the original document, but they would not let me see it because of the age and the condition of that document. But is this my family? I made this John Neil as a family member by adding this information in my data base to "John Neel – Immigrant from Scotland," the first Neel who immigrated to America that I found in the "Neel Genealogy" books by Doris Neel Groves and Betty Thorson. But I didn't find proof of it. They didn't keep very good written records of family history in the 1700's.

On the last day of our stay in Edinburgh, I found The Scottish Genealogy Society Family History Center and Library, but it was closed! I have been communicating with them by e-mail since we returned home, but I haven't found proof of my lineage through their documentation.

I have submitted my own DNA sample through ancestry.com and I found one genetic relative in Ireland, three genetic relatives in Scotland, and eleven genetic relatives in England. Some of these people have responded over the Internet, but I have not been able to meet any of them face-to-face yet.

So, you have read about my dream here. I did stand in the home land of my ancestors, and I have come to appreciate some of the hardships they may have gone through and the blessings of the beauty of their homeland as I walked the streets of Edinburgh, toured the Highlands by bus, and soaked up some of the history of Scotland and the United Kingdom. But the reality is that I did not get any real "hits," in genealogy terms. Not yet anyway. I do believe in miracles! I'm still looking!

A note on these photos of the Highlands of Scotland: As you might also see here, I notice a similarity of these lands with Montana landscape where I spent a good many years growing up. Was my father drawn to retire and lay his body down in western Montana in similar landscape that his ancestors came from? Did he have some deep genetic longing to live in the mountains? His final home in Alberton, Montana looks somewhat like these photos.

The Highlands of Scotland.

Chapter 28
Ireland
“Banter and Chat and Laughter Between Cousins”
Our Irish DNA Cousin – Tom Molloy

By Todd Neel and Tom Molloy

Through my Y-DNA submission of a cheek-swab sample to ancestry.com I got 250 names of genetic relatives around the world, as stated previously in the chapter on *DNA Search*. Finding Tom Molloy through this was a real find, and he has agreed to allow me to use his writings that he has shared with me in this book.

Ancestry.com says that Tom and I are both in Haplogroup R1b, and that we are genetically related. It says “Ancestor Match: Within 14 generations, approximately 350 years ago.”

Tom claims lineage to Niall of Nine Hostages (also known as Niall Noígíallach), the man who kidnapped Patrick from England at age 14, in the 5th Century, and took him to Ireland where Patrick was a slave until about age 21 when he escaped and later became St. Patrick. (Check out Niall of Nine Hostages on Wikipedia.com, or maybe read an actual history book.)

This growing chapter is a bit long (64 pages in this 6” by 9” book in November 2018). It is rich with very humorous e-mail interchanges between my DNA cousin, Tom Molloy in Ireland, and myself. I think it is well worth the read.

NOTE: Tom’s comments are left-justified, while mine are right-justified.

4/14/2010
From: Tom Molloy
To: Todd Neel
Subject: Would like to connect with you as a result of using Ancestry.com's DNA service
hello todd,
good day to you, and i am sorry for not replying earlier. if i can be of any help in finding a family connection i will certainly provide you with any information i have.
my family name molloy is a very old irish name, we can trace our name back to niall of the nine hostages, who it is said brought st patrick to ireland as a slave.
the name molloy in irish is "maolmhuaidgh," meaning great leader the family motto is "gearraigh agus dogh buaidh" which means
cut and burn to victory, so as you can see we are not a friendly lot, what with slave trading and wanting to cut and burn to victory maybe you might want to disconnect rather than connect
our families.
only joking,
so todd any questions i can answer i will and any information i can provide i will
take care
tom (slave trader) molloy

Note from Todd: I wrote back to Tom telling him that if he, and his family, are over that (cutting and burning and hostage taking), that I would like to keep talking).

From: Thomas Joseph "Tom" Molloy
Paternal Test: Y-46
Paternal Haplogroup: R1b
Group Membership: O'Molloy Clan Association
Number of members: 16
Our surname of interest is O'Molloy Clan Association. We are looking for additional participants. Individuals interested in collaborating on family history and using genetic testing

to assist our research efforts are encouraged to join. If you are a male with one of the included surnames and are interested in researching your direct paternal line further, you can participate. This project study is using the DNA test that looks at a portion of the DNA called the Y chromosome. The Y chromosome is unique to males and can be used to identify one's direct paternal line. For this reason, females cannot contribute directly, but can find a male relative (father, brother, cousin, etc) to be tested as a representative of her line. Females can also participate by acting as a Project Coordinator or in other administrative capacities.

4/14/2010

Hi Tom,

Thanks for writing back so quickly. When I wrote you previously, at that time I was so overwhelmed with messages from ancestry.com it was hard for me to sort out which messages to respond to (I had just gotten my DNA results, and I got 250 names). I do remember your story, though, about Niall of the Nine Hostages, and it lead me to do more research about him and St. Patrick (who at the time I hadn't realized had been taken hostage).

And I do remember your translation of the Molloy family motto being "cut and burn to victory."

Are you and your clan done with that tradition?

Well, of course, it would be great if we could help each other with genealogy research and figure out how our families are connected. Since I got the DNA information, I have yet to make actual linkages with those DNA relatives with my known family. I can share my own database with you if you're interested (I currently have 3800+ persons). I also have a book I generated on my home computer using Family Tree Maker software. (The book is a bit expensive to print, but you're welcome to an electronic version of it at no cost - my intention is to make family connections, not to make any money).

But this work is not just about gathering numbers. For me it's also about adding color to my family tree, with interesting stories like yours. I would like to hear more about your story,

and about your family's history.
Can you tell me more about yourself?
And, my family is coming to Europe very soon (my wife, Mary, and our 2 sons Nathan, who is age 17, and we'll celebrate his 18th birthday in Paris, and Josh, who is age 16). We have plane tickets, but we have to work out more details, like hotels, ground travel, and other logistics. There were so many places we want to go, and we have to set some limits because of time and money restrictions. (I also have to be respectful of my wife's wishes, also, because this trip is being paid for with her inheritance - her mother died last summer, and we consider this as a gift from them, our children's grandparents). This is possibly a "once in a lifetime" sort of trip, as I had never imagined going to Europe, but then again maybe this will just be opening doors for future trips there.
So, Tom, how can we help each other? Are you willing to share information about your family?
And what would you like from me?
Thanks,
Todd

3/6/2011
hello todd,
good to hear from you, i hope you and your family are doing fine and are as healthy as a butcher's dog.
we are fine over here except for a small debt of 150 billion yoyos
we owe the imf (International Monetary Fund) and european bank,
i've taken on extra work to help pay this debt, but have been told making hooch is still illegal, but we find great enjoyment from it and days seem to blend into each other unlike our pooteen.
staying drunk is good as we never suffer hangovers, and we smile constantly. we maybe poor but we are happy.
sorry you can't make our rally this year, and if i keep making poteen i won't be at it either,
take care of yourself and your family

keep in touch visit me in prison
tom
Note from Todd: "pooteen" is alcohol, as Tom explains later.

3/28/2011

Hi Tom,

Good to hear from you. Hope you're not in prison when you receive this. You're a funny guy.

We're actually not "healthy as a butcher's dog," as my wife and I joined "The Biggest Losers" competition at our health club, trying to lose weight. (I don't know if you get that TV show, but I actually hate the show). I've lost about 10 lbs. so far, and I'm feeling better.

Yes, the Irish financial situation sounds pretty bad. Does it make daily living bad? We've been in financial hard times here for a while, but not like you've got there. In my family, we've got 2 parents working full time (me and my wife), and our 2 boys are almost done with high school, so hopefully soon they will be working and moving towards independence someday soon, freeing up some family finances. But then there's the potential for grandchildren. I hear they can cost some money out-of-pocket also.

So, funny guy, what is "pooteen"? I actually don't drink anymore because I'm a recovering alcoholic. I almost killed myself in a car accident in 1973 when I ran into a tree, and I still have a metal plate and 8 screws on my thigh bone, but that didn't stop me drinking then. I kept at it until 1981 when I finally got treatment, and I've now been sober for 30 years. Don't let that scare you, as sometimes when people seem to back off when I tell them I'm sober. Seems like they might think it's contagious.

I don't want to lose my only known living relative in Ireland, as you're my only connection to Niall of Nine Hostages. And I might be able to make it to my Irish homeland someday, and I might need some directions in how to find the bathroom or a headstone or something.

Regarding good old Niall of Nine Hostages, you think you can find some time away from your hooch to send some more information on your family lineage before you go to prison, or you are under one of those headstones? I'd really like to keep this line of communication open and share more information on our family. Maybe in case you're having a hard time focusing on this, I can start with some specific questions, like, can you tell me about your own living family? Your wife and kids? Your parents? You have any brothers and sisters?

(I do intend the tone of my e-mail here to be funny here, and I hope you take it that way!)

Cheers! From your cousin,

Todd Neel from Idaho (or "Spudhead Todd")

3/29/2011

hello todd,

good day to you, and thanks for the irish humour and the fact that we can laugh and fine no offence in our banter.

a bit of my history, born 08/08/56 one of 9 children and it was a case of "first up best dressed" after that it was various degrees of nudity till all the rags were gone.

berries and nuts were our staple diet we always had hunger pangs but we were regular.

my father sold furniture for a living, unfortunately it was ours, we were so poor our mother would send us out with a shopping list to chase the garbage truck, we went to kfc to lick other people's fingers,

i asked for a yoyo one christmas, my parents could only afford a yo,

we lived on the poorer side of town, toilet paper was all you would see hanging from clotheslines,

our house was so small if we got a large pizza we had to go outside to eat it.

i am the father of two daughters 19 and 16 years old, my wife of 25 years is celine

we live in geashill co offaly, about 20 miles from moneygall, the homeland obama's ancestors hailed from, and is due to visit in may of this year.

so todd if i have,nt put you sleep with my long and winding tales of hardship and poverty i will finish with a take care of yourself

and your family
tom
two wrongs don't make a right, but three lefts do

3/29/2011

Hi Tom,

Do you also currently live in the poverty you were raised in, as it appears you (or your Dad) sold the Caps key on your computer. Laughing to keep from crying seems to be your case. You could be a writer, except for the Caps key. (Although there was a poet who didn't use Caps either, I think ...) So you had a KFC in your home town where you grew up? What town?

I also have 2 kids, boys age 17 and 18 (Joshua is a Junior and Nathan is a Senior in high school now). This is spring break, and I'm taking a vacation day today to go skiing with them, then back to work tomorrow. My wife, Mary, and I have been married since 8/1989, so that makes it 21 years for us, although we have been friends since college since about 1978.

Looks like you are about one year younger than me, as I was born on 7/25/55. I am the second youngest of 4 kids, with our oldest brother having been adopted into our family, and he has had a very troubled life (we're out of touch with him, and not sure if he's still alive).

I wasn't raised in poverty, as we were pretty middle class. My dad was in the Navy for 32 years, which provided stability for us. He was at the bombing of Pearl Harbor on 12/7/1941 (his ship was the Shaw, a Destroyer in dry dock, and Dad was home mowing the lawn on that Sunday morning when the "funny looking" Japanese planes flew overhead).

What do you do for a living? Still gathering nuts and berries? Would you like me to send you a fresh roll of American toilet paper?

4/1/2011

Hello Todd,
In Tullamore town a lad named Tom
use of cap keys he frowned upon

till his cousin todd in amerikay
begged and pleaded use the keys (i'm no oscar wilde)
now i use them i've changed my ways
all long the days, all long the days
now that is epic, pure epic poetry
i paint and decorate with my brother and we are artistic OR should that be auspicious, i do hope it's one or the other. we are not doing much AT the moment, things are very quite. But it will IMPROVE,
My home town is Tullamore Co Offaly but i live in Geashill about 8 miles away. Geashill is a very small village as is the natives.
I worked in London Heathrow for 17 years with Aer Lingus or air fungus as we would call it, but returned to Ireland in 2011, since then myself and my younger brother Micheal have painted and sometimes decorated our way through life. We lead a very colourful and bohemian expensive sorry that should be existence not expensive (just in case revenue is watching)
well todd enough of my waffle,
take care, tom

4/8/2011

Greetings, Tom,

I hope you're writing all this down, because, yes, you do write epic poetry! (Wait, I guess you are writing this down!) And thanks for responding with CAPS. I'm so glad you've still got that option. You don't have to use it, as it's not a NEED of mine, just a concern that it wasn't stolen or sold out from under you by your father.

Now, is that artistic, auspicious, or autistic? And Bohemian - isn't that a brand of beer?

Are you into music? I have done hand drumming for a number of years, and in the last 6 months or so I have been playing with some friends (almost) every Monday night playing Celtic music (currently called the ID-WA Celtic Fiddlers, because Idaho musicians sometimes get together with Washington musicians playing Scottish and Irish music).

I ask the fiddlers the difference between Irish and Scottish music, and they have an answer, but I couldn't repeat it.
I'm curious – so you can move back and forth between Ireland and England and work in both countries? You live in the Republic of Ireland (as opposed to Northern Ireland, correct?)
I'm a social worker by profession, working for the state of Idaho for the past 21 years. I also am a volunteer ski patroller and do other stuff as well.
When am I going to get to hear more from you about your/our connection with niall of nine hostages?
Your cousin in Amerikay, Spudhead Todd

4/11/2011

Good afternoon Todd,
I hope you are well and also your family, we paddy's are doing ok.
Music, yes you know why bagpipers walk when they play? to get away from the noise.
My kind of music is very varied from Van Morrison, Rod McKuen, Don Williams, Elvis Presley, my favourite Irish balladeer is a guy called Frank Harte, look him up on Google to me he is a legend. I love a good rousing rebel song, Clancy Brothers, Dubliners, Paddy Reilly and one of the greatest, Christy Moore.
i'm really impressed that you are involved in Celtic music, nice one Todd.
Irish nationals have always had free movement between UK and Ireland and British people also have the same freedom. I think we have the best of both worlds and our past history maybe a bit dodgy but all in all we do well as neighbours.
Now Todd about this unspeakable Niall of Nine, what would you like to know, we Irish don't like to speak ill of the dead, and maybe after what knowledge you gain you may decide to disown myself and the entire clan Molloy.
What's the difference between a banjo and a Harley Davidson? you can tune a Harley Davidson
TaKE Good care
your cousin in irroland, Tom

4/16/2011

Hello Tom,

Elvis, really? Did you know he has left the building? I'm looking up Frank Harte now as I'm writing this. Thanks for turning me on to him. I just watched a YouTube video of him singing Valentine O'Hara, and in the introduction it says he sings it in English. (I take it he sings in Gaelic or some other tongue also?) I heard him in another recording introducing the song Spanish Lady, and I have to adjust my ear to make out his accent. (Do you have an accent? I don't).

By the way, I saw Van Morrison play a concert with Bob Dylan and Joni Mitchell at The Gorge, in Washington in 2008. Van the Man is one of my favorites also.

Well, Tom, I hope I'm not waking you up, as I woke up early this morning (4 am). One of those nights. And while I was drinking my second cup of coffee, I started exploring the Internet for Frank Harte, Niall Noígíallach (our great-great-great-etc. grandpa), and other things.

I've wanted to get the lyrics to one particular song that really touches me and almost brings me to tears by David Wilcox, one of my favorite musicians. The song is called Ireland. I'll paste it at the end of this e-mail.

It's now time for me to shower up, get breakfast, and get out the door to do my ski patrol duties.

4/17/2011

Hi Tom,

I did my day of skiing yesterday (wet spring conditions, heavy snow, rained much of the day). Glad the season is almost over. Just one more duty day to take care of my responsibilities.

While at the top patrol shack of Silver Mountain, I brought my Zune (music player) and speakers, and played Martin Hayes (Irish fiddler often with Tom Cahill, on guitar), which was appealing to the ears of my friends. Have you heard his music? (he's on YouTube)

This morning I was listening to a YouTube mix of Frank Harte again, and it took me to a lot of other Irish music. One song about Joe McDonnell, Bobby Sands and a lot of men who were killed, apparently in the conflict with Northern Ireland, the IRA, etc.

Now I'm downloading music of others that you suggested (Christy Moore, Clancy Brothers, Dubliners).

Is this the kind of e-mail that bores you? Don't want to do that, so I'll keep this short.

Your DNA Cousin,

Todd

4/17/2011

Subject: Grandpa Niall

Hi Tom,

So, on the Internet, I can look up lots on Niall Noígíallach (some of which I have difficulty pronouncing):

"Niall is placed in the traditional list of High Kings of Ireland. His reign dated to the late 4th and early 5th centuries. The Annals of the Four Masters dates his accession to 378 and death to 405.[2] The chronology of Keating's Foras Feasa ar Éirinn broadly agrees, dating his reign from 368-395, and associating his raiding activities in Britain with the kidnapping of Saint Patrick (ca. 390-461).[3] However, the traditional roll of kings and its chronology is now recognised as artificial. The High Kingship did not become a reality until the 9th century, and Niall's legendary status has been inflated in line with the political importance of the dynasty he founded. Based on Uí Néill genealogies and the dates given

for his supposed sons and grandsons, modern historians believe he is likely to have lived some 50 years later than the traditional dates, dying circa 450."

And then there's his early difficulties:

"A legendary account of Niall's birth and early life is given in the 11th century saga Echtra mac nEchach Muimedóin ("The adventure of the sons of Eochaid Mugmedón"). In it, Eochaid Mugmedón, the High King of Ireland, has five sons, four, Brión, Ailill, Fiachrae and Fergus, by his first wife Mongfind, sister of the king of Munster, Crimthann mac Fidaig, and a fifth, Niall, by his second wife Cairenn

Chasdub, daughter of Sachell Balb, king of the Saxons. While Cairenn is pregnant with Niall, the jealous Mongfind forces her to do heavy work, hoping to make her miscarry. She gives birth as she is drawing water, but out of fear of Mongfind, she leaves the child on the ground, exposed to the birds. The baby is rescued and brought up by a poet called Torna. When Niall grows up he returns to Tara and rescues his mother from her labour."

So we can go on VOLUMES on what is publicly known (or unknown as much history was not written back then). What is your take on Niall?

Todd

P.S. I hope it's not disrespectful to call him "Grandpa"

4/21/2011

Good day Todd,

How are you? hopefully in good health. Myself, I'm fine.

This Niall, sometimes I ask myself, do we want to be associated with this character of low morals and debauched activities, whose standards are far below what is expected of a clan of our proud heritage.

Without any hesitation I bellow to the very heavens, Yes!!, Yes!!, by God let us rejoice, Hossana, and as Martin Luther King said " I have a dream"

Who would want an upright, full of good intentions and asskissin relative, not me. Let us build a temple to this false God and sacrifice fatted goats and even fatter calves and enormous turkeys, let every day be Thanksgiving Day " I have a dream".

Frank Harte is a great balladeer and was never fully appreciated as a great voice of Irish songs and ballads. I have some great albums of his and love his interpretation of songs we don't hear any more, and that need to be kept safe for a new generation. It's the same as old photos keep them safe, our children need to know about the past.

About whether or not I have accent, yes I do, what is known as a broad midland of Ireland accent. Just a monotone that neither rises or fall except when drink is consumed in very large quantities and a fight start or a song needs to be sung

and Brendan Behan is alive and well, and we stare at the stars and howl for a past long gone, a song unsung, to clasp a hand and dance with maidens until cock crow.
Well Todd,
Take care
Tom

4/21/2011

Hi Tom,

I was listening to Christy Moore (love his music!), and I was reading about him and saw he played with a band called Planxty, so I downloaded some of their music also, and I am now listen to them as I write this. And as this is going on, at your suggestion I searched for Brendan Behan, and I'm downloading an album from him as well. (This is not the same as preserving that old music through albums like you were talking about Frank Harte - but I do have a ton of old records saved, but I don't use the turntable much anymore. My sons are curious about the records sometimes, and we spin a disc sometimes).

Your writing about grandpa Niall seems like a cautious embrace of the darker side of humanity, of family. We might sometimes want to be careful about holding in high esteem the darker behaviors, as others might fear us as being the same dark side. But there is a fine line between the murders and rapists who are in prison who acted out their darker side, and those of us who might have those same murderous passions and didn't act on it (or didn't get caught doing it! Joking …). Our civilized society tries to distance our civilized culture from those criminals by locking them away. But there's a lot we can learn from them.

I agree, we shouldn't act on some of our passions (we shouldn't crap on the carpet!), and we should have morals that keep us from murdering, raping, kidnapping, and crapping in the wrong places. But that potential is in all of us. Many of us just deny it.

Someday I'll tell you of my adopted brother who was in prison.

More later ... I need to get another cup of coffee, and have to go take a crap ... (or maybe we shouldn't talk about that darker side?)

Your Cousin, Todd

5/3/2011

Hello Todd,

Sorry I haven't replied sooner, lots of celebrating and family gatherings, bank holidays, school holidays and great weather.

Dolores Keane, now that woman is the voice of Irish ballads, Mary Black another great sound. Look up The Johnsons, Margaret Barry, Peeker Dunne, Sarah Makem, Paddy Tunney, Joe Heaney, Sean MacDonnchadha, John Reilly, John Lyons, The McPeake Family from Belfast, Tom Lenihan, Len Graham and groups like Four Men and a Dog, Patrick Street, The Ludlows, Emmet

Spiceland, Sweeneys Men, Diarmuid O' Leary and the Bards, Barleycorn, The Dublin City Ramblers, The Black Family and The Fureys and Davy Arthur, The Hughes Band, Goats Don't Shave and The Pogues. More and more, lots and lots from this great nation of ours that was scarred and torn by famine and war, losing our young to far off shores on coffin ships, and others transported to lands in desolated places to slave

"Oh the shot them in pairs coming down the stair in the valley of Knockanure".

Keep the Tricolour flying

Tom

5/4/2011

Subject: Music

Hi Tom,

Thanks for sharing all of these suggestions for music. I have been listening a lot to Christy Moore, and I'm especially loving his album "Live at the Point." I am downloading Dolores Keane now, and I found a lot of albums by Mary Black, but they're not available through the music service I use (Zune

Marketplace). I can find some of the artists you suggested, some I can't. One problem I'm having is my hard drive is getting full, and I
have to erase stuff.
Where do you get your music? Radio? Music stores? Online?
Wow, you used Capitol Letters!
How's your family?
Todd

5/5/2011
Subject: Diaspora
Hi Tom,
Do you have any affection, or disdain, for Scotland? I may have told you that I was going "gun ho" for studying up on Ireland, hoping to visit there last summer when my family was planning our trip to Europe. But as I was losing out on visiting Ireland (in the debate with my wife), and saw we were going to Scotland instead, I studied up on Scotland (and still am). (I have family roots in Ireland, Scotland, and England).
One of my friends who I play music with travels to Scotland often, so she sends me information on it. She recently sent me a link to the following quote and I'm wondering if there aren't similar issues with Ireland about Irish "diaspora," those who left the homeland and the feelings about it:
"There are three Scotlands: (1) the never-never land of Brigadoon, where kilted Rockettes dance in the moonlight on heather hills, and men, having greeted the dawn with a quaich of Scotch, sally forth to shoot a deer or two for breakfast;
(2) the Scottish Homeland, an area of just over thirty thousand square miles inhabited by five or six million people on the northern part of the island we call Britain;
and (3) the Scottish Diaspora, consisting of the vast millions of people of Scottish birth or ancestry dispersed throughout the world (in the United States alone an estimated five times as many as in the Homeland) who look to the Homeland with that deep affection and occasional exasperation that people never bestow on anyone but their mother" (from Geddes

MacGregor, Scotland: An Intimate Portrait, Boston: Houghton Mifflin Company, 1980)

When I look up "disapora" on Wikipedia, it says "A diaspora (from Greek διασπορά, "scattering, dispersion") [1] is "the movement, migration, or scattering of people away from an established or ancestral homeland," [2] or "people dispersed by whatever cause to more than one location," [3] or "people settled far from their ancestral homelands."

Your cousin,
Todd

5/7/2011

Hello Todd,

My music is obtained from the traditional section in music shops, but then again we have a bigger range of local/traditional music to call upon. Radio stations still play a range of "Irish" music over here and we hear it every day. It hasn't got a vast audience but a few old "traddies" like myself still like the lure of it.

A lot of people I mentioned to you are well known names over here but may not be so well known outside of Ireland.

Scots and Irish, now that's a monkey puzzle of an issue. We have a lot in common, Celtic blood, Celtic language, a history of occupation, of fighting for independence, but yet we don't share a great love for each other.

We as a nation of Irish people have suffered a great deal and a million pages have been written on this issue, yet we have come out of this hard past with our wit, language, song, poetry, a "fighting Irish" mentality.

The Scots are seen as a dour lot, who whine a lot and speak of independence, but are afraid to do much about it. We Irish have been there, and done it and have done well for ourselves as a small nation on the edge of Europe.

Take care of yourself and your family.

Tom "the Cap king"

5/8/2011

Subject: Irish language and stuff

Beannachtaí, Tom,

(Did that come out properly? I mean to say "Greetings" in Irish. I looked it up on Google)

I'm reading a book "Ireland - A Short History" by Joseph Coohill. It says "Irish" is a more accurate term for the language because "Gaelic" covers a family of languages. And that "Irish" became the official first language of the Republic of Ireland in 1937, and is taught in schools. I'm open to a brief exposure to your native tongue, but the possibility of learning to speak "Irish" is not likely for me because there is no one here that I can regularly practice with.

My friend here, Jan, (that I play music with) does speak some Scottish words and terms, and it's really baffling to me.

I'm listening on my headphones as I write this an album called "Martin Hayes" that I wrote to you about previously. YouTube says he is Irish fiddler who often plays with Tom Cahill, on guitar. And the next book on my list to read is "How the Irish Saved Civilization" by Thomas Cahill. I wonder if this guitarist and book writer are one and the same?

Do you listen to AM or FM radio stations? How do you get the news or do you just ignore it? Is there still talk of Obama coming over there this month of May?

I'm still digesting/listening to the music suggestions you gave me. Yes, you do like a lot of the old traditional stuff, don't you?

Regarding the Scots and Irish "monkey puzzle," I guess I've got both in my blood, so this monkey is puzzled. Ancestry.com says there are 2 Scots and 1 Irish person (you) that I'm related to genetically that's in their data base. (I'm having the most interesting conversations with you!) The one Scot person that responded to me (Adam Smith) didn't seem to want to exchange too much information through e-mail, so I thank you for these on-going exchanges, Tom.

There is some value in thinking about "us" and "them" - there's a reason for national borders and differentiation - and

sometimes it creates divisions and wars and deaths.
Can't we just all sing together?
Now I've got Mrs. Sarah Makem, Ulster Ballad Singer in my ears, and it's hard to write while I've got her words in my ears, so I sign off now.
Great job on the Caps!
Todd

5/11/2011

Tom,

Was that you that invited me to the O'Molloy Clan group DNA site? I posted a photo of me and my son there, posted a couple of discussion comments (including mentioning you and Niall of Nine Hostages, and asking you to comment in the discussion group). I also uploaded my family tree there. Did you say you have lineage back to 300 - 400 AD from you back to Niall of Nine Hostages? Are you able to tell me more about that?

Thanks,
Todd

P.S. We're leaving for Europe very soon. We will be in England and Scotland, but didn't fit Ireland into our trip (a big disappointment).

5/12/2011

good morning todd,
welcome to the omolloy association.
we don't engage in secret handshakes or blindfolded
one trouser-leg rolled up initiation rite. we do on occasion
sacrifice the odd goat, well at least the goat finds it odd
but not for long!!!
i will look up the info i have on our slave trading relative
niall and will forward some info soon.
take care todd,
tom
ps. i saw the photo on omolloy association of your goodself
and your son. really nice, we do look alot alike grey hair,
glasses and a big smile

5/13/2011
Subject: Irish language and stuff
Topofthemornin' Todd,
Garlic!!, don't talk to me about Gaelic, beaten not bestowed on us as children.
Nuns with large canes and they slapping the bejesus out of us as young children to speak the Garlic,
no fond memories there.
Taught in schools you say, we thought we were in school but more like a torture chamber, it still sends a shiver down my spine when i see a penguin. I don't care much for my native tongue after years of slapcrazy nuns.
As for Obama, it's so well security closed we natives won't see much of our famous son. He will be surrounded by nasty men with large dark glasses and even larger guns, so no thanks. I hope nothing bad happens as he has so many groups baying for his blood and like any other country we have lots of nutters, some even became nuns!.
I'm glad you have had a chance to listen to some good and great Irish singers and musicians, we produce them like bunny rabbits, we could pack them like sardines and export them on coffin ships to far flung corners of this outpost in space. oops!! we might have done so already.
So Todd me auld comrade and bosum buddy I've you given enough blarney to pack into sardine tins and export!! good God I can't stop, as Sigmund Freud said about the Irish "This is one race of people for whom psychoanalysis is of no use whatsoever" and remember God invented alcohol to stop the Irish from ruling the world.
Take care
Tom

5/21/2011
Hi Tom,
Sorry I'm slow in responding to you here. I love getting your e-mails from the other side of the world.
At the risk of offending you (but I doubt I will), my friend who travels to Scotland said to ask you what they do with pee in the UK? (The risk being the last time I wrote about

body functioning, i.e. "crapping on the carpet ..." you didn't respond for a while, but I think that was because you had a family gathering. Or maybe talking about crap offended you?)

Did you have your Molloy/O'Molloy Clan Association gathering?

Todd

5/24/2011

Subject: Pee and Obama

Topofthemountain to you, Tom.

Yes, the topic is pee. I asked my music friend who travels to Scotland about this joke, and she claims it's no joke, and she sent me this link:

http://entertainment.stv.tv/tv/209469-life-of-pee-sally-magnusson-writes-a-book-about-urine/

On this page it says:

“And yet within living memory in Britain there were horses and carts going round people’s houses and people were handing out buckets of urine to be taken back to fool the cloth. I didn’t know that and I don’t think that people do.”

And it has links to some of this information in it:

Wee whisky

“James Gilpin collects his diabetic granny Patricia's pee, boils it, cleans the sugar crystals which are left and then adds them to rain, malt and water to create the alcoholic drink. He came up with the unusual brewing idea after reading that sufferers of diabetes have a lot of sugar in their urine because of their high blood sugar levels. James - who is studying at the London Royal College of Art - said: "The urine produces a very nice drink." He has also used the wee from a number of volunteers and he puts their names and ages on the labels of his Gilpin Family Whisky, however, he insists he has no plans to sell his odd liquor."

I was watching Obama on TV last night speaking to a crowd in Dublin, talking about being in Moneygall. Did you hear anything about it?

Your cousin,

Todd

5/25/2011

Subject: Pee and Obama

Todd me auld pal,

On the subject of pee, we have in this fair country of ours, politicians actively engaged in taking the piss out of the people all of the time, and these so called politicians are getting well paid for pisstaking, and I do believe that diuretics are been given to us in our foods and also been told to drink more fluids!!

oh my God!! what is happening to us, we are been used by super intellectually superior beings to produce pee for the drinks industry. So what we drink we pee and what we pee we drink.

Is this what flower power and free love and San Francisco with Janis Joplin and that hippy Sob Dylan done to us, made us pee producers, my mother did say no good would come of all that poncho and beads. Woe! Woe! Whoa.

Obama made us feel good about ourselves, we did need that and now all we Irish need is money, cos we is broke, we haven't got what would jingle on a tombstone, but we are happy because we can now consume large volumes of our own piss.

Todd remember, Honesty is the fear of being caught

So I must retire, time to lay a grey head onto a pillow and dream of hope and song and days long gone and absent friends and silly kamikaze pilots who wear helmits!!

WHY

Take care, Tom

5/26/2011

Subject: Re: Pee and Obama, moving on to St. Patrick

Mornin', Tom.

Hope that last subject didn't piss you off. Hope this one doesn't either.

In spite of, or because of our Grandpa Niall's kidnapping of the Patrick who became the St. Patrick (let's forgive Grandpa, since that's just what they did in those days - no moral judgment on his soul or our DNA), tell me what you think of this man, Patrick. I don't know if Patrick had any offspring or not, but his actions did affect those abusive Penguins who fed you the Garlic!

Todd

6/2/2011

Subject: link to brief video of our Celtic music group

Hi Tom,

You can see me drumming (mildly) with our music group last weekend here:

(link sent in separate e-mail)

How's it going with you?

Todd

6/4/2011

Subject: Re: link to brief video of our Celtic music group

Hello Todd,

Great music from you and your pals, very nice tone and tune, it had my feet tapping and I enjoyed it. All of you should be proud to be keeping traditional celtic music alive and well. We "O'Molloy clan" are still putting together our clan rally progmamme for August, lots of last minutes details and we hope to have a great weekend of "ceol agus craic"

We have a great group of people and we work well together. Now Todd I must away and busy myself Bee like with my nose to my shoulder and my grindstone to my wheel, keep up the music and song and enjoy all of it.

Take care

Tom

6/7/2011

Subject: Re: link to brief video of our Celtic music group

Hi Tom,

Good to hear from you.

Thanks for the compliments about our music. We were scheduled to play for one hour last Sunday night at a "Ceilidh Benefit For Spokane Highland Games." We had 12 musicians from Spokane and Coeur d'Alene show up, but there was a 7 member rock band outdoors who moved up

their timing because of threatening rain,
so we only got to play for 1/2 hour.
This weekend we're expecting family from Montana for my son, Nathan's, high school graduation this weekend.
Lots to do to get ready for that.
Good luck with your O'Molloy Clan gathering! (I tried to translate ceol agus craic through the computer but couldn't figure it out. What does that mean?)
Be careful with which body part you put against that grindstone!
Peace, Todd

6/8/2011
Subject: Re: link to brief video of our Celtic music group
Hello me auld buddy,
How is life treating you?, I hope gentle and kind.
Our weather here at the moment is in par with monsoon type, lots of "feckin" rain, more like what you would encounter in October, moisty and misty.
"ceol agus craic" is translated as music and chat (ceol "keol" /agus as in august without the t/ craic "krack") but craic has come to mean jokes, banter, jibes, and having a good time, people you meet would say "how is the craic" rather than "how are you." Sometimes "ceol, craic agus ol" which is translated as music, chat and drink, ol meaning drink, "ole" without the e, so thats todays lesson in speaking gaelic.
I hope you and yours enjoy Nathan's big day and have plenty of ceol, craic agus ol, family time is very important as is family, and if you do feel the urge to sing, sing an Irish song
"step it out Mary my fine daughter
step it out Mary if you can
step it out Mary my fine daughter
show your legs to the country man"
remember this "never tell a man with a chainsaw he has bad breath"
and so with those words of wisdomism, I will arise and go now
and go to inisfree to a bee loud glade.
Take care and enjoy your son's day and life, Tom

6/21/2011

Subject: can't sleep

Top o'the Monsoon to you, Tom,

How are you doing? Been a little while since I chatted with you. It's early right now where I am (about 3 am), as I drank too much water when we played music last night with the Id-Wa Fiddlers practice. A young man (Junior in high school) joined us with his mandolin (making 5 players total) last night, and it added new energy to the jam. He was wearing a t-shirt with the band "Blood or Whiskey" on it, so I found and I'm downloading and am now listening to an album by them on the headphones this morning. They're great! He also suggested the Dread Naughts, and The Pouges, but I can't find these on my Zune Marketplace.

Nathan's graduation and our family gathering was great. My sister and brother, and their families came over (total of 9 added to our family of 4 made a crowded house).

I shared some of your e-mails, which helped thaw out the glacier.

I think I've written to you before about this book I'm reading called "How the Irish Saved Civilization" by Thomas Cahill. On one page it states words about the Irish slavery business, and how our grandpa Niall captured and sold Patrick who became St. Patrick. Have you read this, Tom? What do you think about this story?

I've got a joke for you:

A Texan walks into a pub in Ireland and clears his voice to the crowd of drinkers. He says, "I hear you Irish are a bunch of hard drinkers. I'll give $500 American dollars to anybody in here who can drink 10 pints of Guinness back-to-back." The room is quiet and no one takes up the Texan's offer. One man even leaves. Thirty minutes later the same gentleman who left shows back up and taps the Texan on the shoulder. "Is your bet still good?," asks the Irishman. The Texan says "yes" and asks the bartender to line up 10 pints of Guinness. Immediately the Irishman tears into all 10 of the pint glasses drinking them all back-to-back. The other pub patrons cheer as the Texan sits in amazement. The Texan gives the Irishman the $500 and says, "If ya don't mind me askin', where did you go for that 30 minutes you were gone?" The Irishman replies, "Oh...I had to go to the pub down the street to see if I could do it first."

Peace, Tom, and sleep well!
Your cousin,
Todd

6/21/2011

Subject: can't sleep
Halo Todd my little angel,
How are things at your end of the tunnel?, at my end a faint light has appeared, it either the bright majestic lights of heaven or a spark from a mega fire of hellish proportion, now where did I leave my crystal ball.
I'm glad (your family gathering for Nathan) had a (good) meet up and hopefully things will get better, and I am really glad you all had a good time. Family time is important and we all need it.
I am pleased to hear my emails went down well, humour is very good medicine and if taken in very large doses can heal a host of ailments, but not halitosis.
Patrick was a nice sort of a lad, full of good cheer and going mad to convert Irishmen. He was at it morning noon and night, never stopped it was said, couldn't get enough of telling us about purgatory, hell and sins of all sorts, genuflecting and crying for forgiveness,
sure we didn't know whether we were coming or going, and Niall called him aside one day and just to have a quiet word saying " go easy on them Paddy, next thing you know that lot will take to the drink" and no sooner had he said that when we was off drinking and dancing and fighting, curseing and swearing and we haven't stopped since.
That my good friend is what that boyo Patrick did for us, begeeus if I could only get me paws around his drinkless neck I'd murder the bum.
Is it the Pogues that you were looking for, a great group of musicians led by Shane McGowan what fantastic lyrics he has written, a musical Brendan Behan or Patrick Kavagnagh, he truly is a great song writer, all hail Shane McGowan.

night Mary Ellen, John Boy sleep well
Take care
Tom

6/22/2011

Subject: can't sleep, again!

Good Morning, Tom!

It's 3:50 am now, as my bladder called for me again at 2:30, and again, my brain wouldn't let me go back to sleep. I checked my e-mail on my phone (which is next to my bed as my alarm clock), and I found your e-mail reply.

Thank you very much! Very sweet!

We are all angels, or have them watching over us, if we acknowledge them watching over us. (I guess we have choices about something from hell just being over the other shoulder also, if we wish).

After reading your e-mail, I tried listening to quiet music to put me back to sleep, but that didn't work. I was listening to a Scottish musician, Duncan Chisholm, from his album Door of the Saints, and it starts with this song: "Chro Chinn t-saile" No words in the tune, just very melodic, repetitive, quiet. Do you know the translation?

I first heard of the light at the end of the tunnel joke when I was in inpatient treatment for my alcoholism in 1981. The light was described either as something spiritual, a locomotive chasing me down, or Sister Anita, my addictions counselor. I hope you are not preparing to leave this physical world. How is your health?

I really do appreciate our exchanges and connections we are making. I cherish your words of humor (English) /humour (Irish), and support.

I had dinner with my friend, George, last night. He is my age (55) and he is preparing to visit his father in Las Vegas (speaking of hell) who is going into surgery and facing end-of-life mortality issues. So lots of deep thoughts for us ...

As I say elsewhere in my book, Family Hunger:

"Again, I say - hug your family - those you can reach. Love your family, those you can find (including your ancestors). If it wasn't for them, we wouldn't be here. They are the people who brought us into this world, and they are the ones who will lay us in (or on) the ground in the end."

Peace, and love to you Tom (in a Man-ly sort of way),

Todd

6/27/2011

Good Day to you Todd,

I hope all is well at castle Neel and all subjects are behaving as subjects should, we sons of slave traders have to keep control or all hell will break loose, I've just unshackled a couple of slaves to clean my car and tidy the garden, plus a few minor jobs which need doing. It's hard to give up old habits of our past.

"Chro Chinn t-Saile must be scottish gaelic, which is different from our gaelic in lots of ways but t-Saile can mean ease or comfort this side of our common language, I must give a listen to Mr Chisholm.

My health is not bad apart from a bad back, flat feet, dodgy heart beat, blood pressure at it's peak, corns, my hearing is more or less null and void, my memory is buggered, insomnia is a worry and can keep me awake all night, my teeth have started to fall out and as a result I get it hard to chew and have resorted to sucking my food through a straw, ingrown toenails make it hard for me to walk upright and now have a stoop to contend with, but you will never hear me complain, oh and by the way some good news I'm going to have a disease named after me.

Todd I know at this stage you must be ready to slash your wrists with all my bulls##t flowing like "Old Man River" it just keeps rolling along, but before I go did you know the worst time to have a heart attack is during a game of charades, just a sliver of advice me old bud.

Take good care of yourself and all you hold dear

Tom

ps. I hope dad of George is ok as is George,

xra nice words on " Family Hunger"

7/2/2011

Hi Tom,

The Castle Neel is doing fine. How's the Molloy castle? Did your slaves do your bidding? Need to do any flogging? Which of your body parts is diseased that they are they going to name after you? Is your health a result of the state of healthcare in Ireland (vs. the U.S.), your genetics, lifestyle, or other stuff? (I hope that's not too personal or political of a question). I'll turn age 56 later this month (I thought you were younger than me?) and I don't have these health issues you have. Of course, I quit drinking 30 years ago, too. Do you smoke? I'm feeling pretty healthy and fit when you list your health issues (I don't mean to be bragging here, just very grateful!)

My 17 yr. old son, Josh, and I are leaving today for The Gorge, a natural amphitheater along the Columbia River outside of George, Washington (about a 2 hr. drive from here towards Seattle). We're going to watch a concert by the rock band "Rush." Have you heard of them?

Information was passed around our fiddle circle that there will be a weekend "Bitterroot Scottish Irish Festival" for a 3 day weekend at the end of August that I hope to go to. If you like, check out the website http://www.bitterrootscottishirishfestival.org/ If you hit the "Entertainment" link there, you'll see that an Irish-rock band name Potcheen is playing. On the web site it says "Potcheen (Poitin') means "the Illegal Moonshine Whiskey" and it sometimes contains impurities and off flavors. On rare occasions, it may contain dangerous levels of toxic alcohols just like the Colorado Celtic Pirates that have scorched the throats of crowds from New York to San Francisco with one helluva kick." Seems you and I have talked/written back and forth about this before.

I hope your health is well (or getting better).

We're having a 3 day holiday weekend here for the 4th of July. Happy 4th!

Todd

7/12/2011

Subject: Re: can't sleep, again!
Hello Todd,
How the devil are you and yours? super I hope
and on top of the World.
Things are really busy with our clan, and with just over a month to go to our rally it's all hands on deck and deck is ok with that, he moaned a bit at first but a gag is a wonderful item, now it's less of a moan more of a whimper. We have lots to do as a group or should that be grope?, if we include deck, it can get complicated at times.
We hope to have a spit roast pig at our rally finale on Saturday night, the 13th of August, the pig got a wee bit upset but we promised to be gentle and he spoke about Animal Farm and all that and we listened and that seemed to comfort him, now he can't wait and promised to get good and plump for our night and wished us well,
two legs good, four legs bad.
We will be putting together a small booklet about our clan and we have lots of material to include, things like slave trading, drunken marauding piracy, cattle rustling, some pilage and rebellion, loads of blarney and swear words, it will be a best seller and Steven Spielberg is eyeing it up for a major movie of biblical propotion. We need a title for the book, any ideas?
I hope you and Josh enjoyed Rush and were not in a hurry
I'll finish now Todd before you get sick of my banter
Take care
Tom
ps. my health is like myself full of s##t

7/14 /2011

Subject: did sleep last night!
Good morning, Tom!
Good to hear from you. I did sleep well last night, and what a difference it makes! (The day before I was up since 3:30 am due to work stressors, etc.)
I've been getting ready to drum with my musician friends, practicing for a gig this Saturday when we get to play Celtic

music on a stage for 40 minutes at a church music and arts festival.

What all are you going to do at your clan rally besides group gropes, making deck(s) moan(s), and spitting on pigs? If it's not just your blarney, could I get a copy of your booklet about your clan?

I don't know if you're interested, or if you will be fast enough, but if you want to see my family web page paste the following in your web browser:

(I'll send you a link in a separate e-mail)

Keep me posted on your clan gathering developments there in Ireland!

7/26/2011

Good afternoon me auld bud,

How are all in the Neel mansion?, healthy, wealthy and wise I hope.

Things here are ok, IMF are still on our case and we are just about keeping our heads above the murky waters of default, and that just our house!!

Our clan of slavetraders are having a press launch this Thursday to advertise our upcoming rally, we hope all goes well and rosary beads are rattling and eyes are looking towards heaven for a sign of hope and salvation "Rock of ages, cleft for me" and all that.

Did I mention to you that I have relatives in Chicago, My granduncle's grandchildren, we keep in contact through the internet and hope to visit them in the near future. They are good people and we exchange lots of family photos and information. The story of our separate branches of the same family is long and typical of Irish history, full of hardship, hunger and high seas, with tears and fears, and lashings of riches to rags tales.

Some day I'll write it all down and bore my children to sleep with my yapping and tear filled story of my family.

Now Todd before I put you to sleep with boredom,

Take care of thyself

Tom

7/26/2011

Good morning Tom

Healthy, wealthy and wise are relative terms. Compared to your description of the Molloy mansion in Ireland, I supposed we would be all of that, what with your previous description of your health, and your current descriptions of the IMF after your house. Good luck to you on that.

I look forward to your press launch of your upcoming rally! Wish I could be there!

No, you did not mention you had relatives in Chicago. If you are really considering going there to visit, maybe with enough notice I could come see you there in Chicago?

I woke up early again this morning stressed about work.

Good luck with your rally and your future travels to Chicago, if you go.

Peace to you and your family!

Todd

P.S. Wish me Happy Birthday. I turned 56 yesterday.

7/26/2011

Mornin' Todd,

I'm really sorry to hear about what is happening in your workplace and hope the hurt goes away, life can stink sometimes and I don't have answers, but you are a good person and you have a good family and that will get you through.

"I am tired of planning and toiling
in the crowded hives of men;
Heart-weary of building and spoiling
and spoiling and building again.
And I long for the dear old river,
where I dreamed my youth away;
For a dreamer lives forever,
and a toiler dies in a day."

Take care Todd
and dream
Tom

7/26/2011

Thank you, Tom. You're a beautiful man. And you have a song (or a poem?) for me!

I woke up early again this morning (3:40 am), and this habit of early wakening has got to stop! But I'm not tired, and am not exhausted at the end of the day. I wonder if my body is changing and so don't need as much sleep.

In the dark this morning in my bare feet I stepped in cold, wet cat sh##. Kind of a metaphor of life ... maybe a song right there ...

"Cat sh## in the dark
Feels just like work
Maybe I should put some shoes on
Or just get a new line of work"

No, I don't think I can get a job as a poet or song writer. Guess I gotta keep being a social worker for a while ...

I read and re-read your poem/song you sent me, and that really is quite beautiful. (Where did it come from?) I'm going to print it out and put it on my door at the office. (My boys and I are going to Montana this weekend to visit family and get on a river, so it is very appropriate!)

You have a very good day, Tom. Thank you for your very kind response! It's perfect! You do have answers! -Todd

7/27/2011

Subject: newspaper article on my wife, Mary

Hi Tom,

Here is a link to a newspaper article on my wife, Mary, who has been a social worker at Hospice for 24 years or so. Very nice article on a very nice lady. (Sorry about you having to look at advertisements for the local newspaper with this link, but if you scroll down to "Mary Neel: No kind deed too small" you will see her picture and the article on her.

http://www.cdapress.com/lifestyles/article_dd778206-83cb-507c-a089-d45e6f90ece5.html

Peace, Todd

7/27/2011

Evening Todd,

I read the article you mentioned about your good wife, she is a good and kind woman and you must be very proud of her. Tell Mary I said hello and well done. It is a hard job and she deserves praise for the help she gives to people.

The poem I forwarded to you is by John Boyle O'Reilly 1844-1890 and the poem is "The cry of the dreamer," I gave you just the first verse, google John Boyle O'Reilly and read about this great Irishman. The poem is one of his most read and it gives all of us something to think about.

Well Todd take care of your good wife and family and get back to sleeping a full night for when we sleep we dream.

8/6/2011

Hi Tom,

We (Nathan and Josh and I) went to Montana last weekend and had a great time with family. Spent Friday night and Sat. at my nephew's (Jeff) helping him fix a roof, mowed his lawn, and got to ride on his new tractor). Then Sat. afternoon and evening went into Missoula to my brother's home for a BBQ, and there happened to be the Missoula Celtic Festival for free downtown concert by the river, and we got to watch an outdoor concert by The Young Dubliners - they were great! And then on Sunday we got on the Blackfoot River for some hot summer white water river running - 8 people in 8 boats (canoes and kayaks), and had 3 sets of brothers (myself and my brother Tim, my 2 sons Nathan and Josh, and my 2 nephews Jeff and Brandon), plus 2 wives.

Had great family time!

I found out my nephew, Jeff, had 3 copies of my self-published family history book "Family Hunger: A Neel-McCool Family History." So I got 2 copies back (they didn't need all 3!), and I would like to send you a copy. It has stories, pictures, family data. I printed this edition in 2004, and had about 1000 people in my family tree data base then. (I have about 4000 in my tree data base now - I'd like to figure out how to put you and your family into it - including Grandpa Niall). If you'd like me to send you a copy, please

send me your mailing address and I'll send it on.
How's your Molloy Clan gathering going?
I am now in Missouri for the start of a one week vacation at my brother-in-law's home, where my wife Mary grew up as a child. We flew here today with family (myself, Mary, Nathan, and Joshua).
How's it going with you?
Peace,
Todd

9/2/2011
Well Todd me ould jewel,
What is going on?
are you on the run or is it the gypsy soul in you?
Idaho, Montana, changing email accounts!!!. Good God man stand still, stop moving around,
I get dizzy with all this shennanigans.
I have been busy of late and I am way behind on replying to emails and texts and sometimes even the call of nature has to wait awhile, my legs are crossed as I fumble on the keyboard at this very moment in time.
Our rally went really well, lots of great times and grand people to "blarney" with, we are on youtube "2011 O'Molloy clan rally." We also have a new Chieftain John P. Malloy of Chicago, our first chief outside of the forty shades of green.
Todd, I will go now as I have things to do, people to see, and miles to go
before I sleep.
Take care and stand still,
Tom
ps I would appreciate a copy of "Family Hunger"
and I will forward you a copy of our rally 2011 booklet.

9/17/2011
Hi Tom, me old cousin from the 40 Shades of Green Island!
I have been here the whole time! Just busy, like you have. I have been moving around, but keep returning home.
I went to the Bitterroot Irish Scottish Festival in Hamilton, Montana at the end of August, watched a Celtic rock band

called Potcheen, watched other marching pipe and drum band competitions, and looked at other things like art booths and family clans.

That same weekend in Montana I floated on the Clark Fork River going down the Alberton Gorge (class 3 & 4 whitewater). There was a professional photographer trying to make money taking our photos, then he posts them on the web to try to get us to buy them. I am in "The Canoe Group" at http://www.montanariverphoto.com/canoe-alberton-gorge-20110828 (you might be able to paste that address in your web browser). If you can see these photos, I am in the last 10 photos, in the red canoe with the yellow spray skirt, and I'm wearing a yellow helmet. (The other canoers are my nephews and friends).

I watched the 2011 O'Molloy Clan videos on YouTube, and the 2008 video also. Are you in these pictures? How far away did people come from for this? Further than Chicago? I wish I had been there. Maybe someday ...

I got a couple of e-mails from another genetic relative in Belfast, Northern Ireland, and his name is Niall McSperrin. Ancestry.com showed a map that said that he was in Germany, but he says Belfast. He does not get on his home computer very much, so our exchanges are not as frequent as you and I.

Could you send me your address so I can send you a copy of my "Family Hunger" book? I will type in my address so you can send me your rally 2011 booklet.

Go take a pee, man!

Peas,

Todd

9/18/2011

Well hello Todd me auld blood relative
and fellow slave trader,

How are all in Idaho? hoping all is good at the ranch and that the only rustling going on is leaves falling from the trees this Autumnal season.

We is good over here and getting by on what crumbs Master Europe lets fall from the table of austerity, but come the

revolution brother Che, come the revolution.
I will send by post or pigeon our book of lies and fables that is "O'Molloys of Firceall"
Take care Todd
Tom.
ps If you are looking for me on our youtube excerpt, I'm the one with the red face and white hair, but time was when it was red hair and white face in times gone by.

9/19/2011

Hi Tom,
I got out a copy of "Family Hunger," and I'll mail it out to you at the following address:
Tom Molloy
(address deleted from the book for privacy reasons)
(Your address is so simple – No zip code? No street address?)
OK, I looked again at the YouTube video "2011 O'Molloy clan rally," and there's a lot of gentlemen that fit the description "the one with the red face and white hair …," and who used to be a red head. In the interest of self-disclosure, I am attaching a photo of myself and my wife, Mary, that looks it was taken in the 1980's, when I definitely had red hair (maybe I'm about age 30 here, before we got married). I looked through my photos on my hard drive for a recent picture of me with my white hair, and I'm having difficulty finding a recent one, but I'll keep looking, or maybe I'll have a family member take a current photo of me to send to you. Can you send me a photo of you?
I look forward to seeing your "O"Molloys of Firceall," from
Todd

9/20/2011

Howdy partner,
How are all in Idaho? good and wholesome
I would venture a guess
We is all doing ok here living off the crumbs falling from the table of European austerity measures, but come the revolution Che, come the revolution.

I posted off the booklet to your good self, and you should have it on your doorstep asapupsdhl.
I saw the photo of that handsome woman called Mary and some bloke was standing behind her all gooey, mushy and doe eyed in love, Cupid was grinning from ear to ear, "and they call it puppy love" Donny Osmond crooning in the background, those were the days, Sob Dylan, Pelvis, Simple and Garfunkle, Krisp Krisstoffeson, and who can forget "Mr. Ed" the talking horse.
If you want to scare the bejasus out of folk, have a look at my mugshot.
Take care
Tom

9/26/2011

Tom,

You do scare the bejasus out of me. So since you're into disguises, here is a picture of me behind my camera. And here is a photo of our family. No disguises, just ugly faces. That's me, Mary, Nathan, and Joshua, from left to right on the Eiffel Tower in Paris last summer on Nathan's birthday.

Todd

Neel Family: Todd, Mary, Nathan, Joshua (Eiffel Tower, Paris, France 6/30/2010 on Nathan's 18th birthday)

9/20/2011

Hello Cousin Todd,
The photo was really me, I really do sport a fine moustache that has enthralled people, all my brothers grow fungus on our upper lips, it a tradition that goes back to our seafaring days on the high seas, playing the squeezebox and singing shanties, port side and oars and all that pegleg parrot on the shoulders routine, oh arr Jim lad,
Now where did I bury that treasure!
Take care Todd lad
Tom

Tom Molloy

9/28/2011

Tom,
OK, what did you do this time? How did you get yourself AND your family locked up?
How can you ever reap the harvest of European austerity measures if you keep doing this stuff? Is this what you mean by the revolution Che, not approved of by Authority (those with the bigger sticks)?
Behave yourself!
Todd
P.S. I did receive the O'Molloy Clan Association flyers and the booklet "O'Molloys of Firceal." Very nice, and a lot to read. Thank you very much. Let me know when you get my book.

9/30/2011
Subject: Re: book in the mail, and photo attached
Hi Todd,
Just got your book, and can I just say WOW!!, what a great achievement. You have done yourself proud, really well done and something to hand down to your sons to cherish and pass on to the next generation of Neels.
I can't even imagine all the long hours spent on this great and historic book, but midnight oil was well spent and Thanks for giving me a copy, I shall look after it and keep it safe.
In your letter you asked if you could use the Emails we send to each other, no problem Todd, use them as you wish, after all it is just banter and chat and laughter between cousins.
I have decided to come out of disguise and send you a photo of myself, my good wife Celine and my daughters Rachel, (red hair) and Aoife. It was taken at Rachel's 18th birthday party, two years ago now and since then my moustache has gone white!
Take care and again thank you for your gift,
Tom

Tom Molloy, daughter Rachel, wife Celine, and daughter Aoife.

10/2/2011

Hey, me auld Cousin from the auld country!

Thank you, Tom, for the very nice compliment. With the Internet snowballing the size/quantity of family members (my tree has grown from 1000 in 2004 when I printed the last edition to over 4000 members now). Plus another distant cousin in Florida sent me her data base with over 5000 more names to fit it. I still value the colorful, quality stories and contacts with individuals over the masses of cold data (like the exchanges that you and I have have).

How can you make a connection with 9000 people? How can you remember them? I don't remember them all (that's why we write them down), but I do remember the ones that take the time to exchange meaningful communications.

Maybe someday, some distant relative will take the time to read what you and I exchanged, and it will make a difference in their lives.

Now I have 2 photos of you (very handsome family you have there!) Can I include your photos with our e-mails in the next edition of Family Hunger? (Do you like the title?) Thanks for permission to include our "banter and chat and laughter between cousins" - That's a good chapter title right there!

Hey, if you send me a plane ticket to Ireland, I could write a really colorful story of my visit to your home!

Peace,

Todd

10/6/2011

Hello to me old matey from Idaho,

Good day to you and yours from my lot here on the shamrock shore and may you have a full moon on a dark night and the road downhill to your door.

Thanks for the compliment on my family and you have my permission to use anything we send back and forth to each other and that includes my email address, and also my "banter and chat etc" heading.

I was listening to Liam Clancy last night and on an album called " The Dutchman" and a song on it titled " Farewell to Tarwathie," the song is beautiful and is about a sailor who

journeys to Greenland to hunt the whale and seeing how bleak and cold the lands were in this snow filled landscape, remembers his native green and lush birthplace and its birdsong and compares it with cold seas around Greenland "tho the birds here sing sweetly o'er the mountain and dale, there is no bird in Greenland to sing to the whale," what about that then, it hit me like a kayak paddle, what lovely lines of poetry.
Todd, take good care,
Tom,
ps. good luck on your new chapter of "Family Hunger"

10/12/2011
Subject: music
Dear Tom,
Thanks for your permission to use our "banter and chat," e-mail address, etc. in the next edition of Family Hunger. Can I post your bank account numbers also?
Thanks for turning me on to Liam Clancy. I searched my music subscription service and I'm downloading "The Dutchman" and "Two for the Early Dew" now. (There are 22 albums related to him, and I'll start with these).
Speaking of music, our Celtic music group is getting ready for a gig in November at the Spokane Fall Folk Festival. Attached to this e-mail is our set list is a Word document (I don't know if you can open and read this file, or if you care to – no worries if you're not interested). Do you recognize any of these tunes? (Were considering calling our group "The Nine Pint Coggies").
Todd

10/12/2011
Subject: dark, dead humor
Tom,
As I think you know, my wife, Mary, works at Hospice (do they have that in Ireland?). To cope with the sometimes heaviness of that work, they sing songs like this to one another on their birthdays:
"Happy Birthday

Happy Birthday
Sickness, sorrow, and despair
People dying everywhere
Happy Birthday
One more day till you're dead!"
Peace, and enjoy the light!
Todd

10/15/2011

Good morning, evening, night Todd,
I am glad you enjoyed Liam Clancy, and what a great voice he had and his interpretation of songs is very unique. He is sadly missed as is the Clancy Brothers, we have very few up and coming singers as good as our Liam, RIP.
My bank account you can have and God bless you Todd if you find funds in it, what you will find in it is a threatening letter from my bank manager and a gun!!
I have to wear disguise when I visit town, hence the large white moustache, my friends no longer speak to me as I owe most of them money, and now a contract is out on my head "bring me the head of Tom Molloy" is the chorus of the day, but hell Todd sometimes we have to live close to the edge, and we Molloys are made of strong stuff but just in case I wear a bulletproof vest and only go out at night.
What is a "nine pint coggie"? forgive my ignorance, and some of the tunes you have listed I have heard, you really are into your music and seem to enjoy it so much, it must be the Oirish blood running through your veins, we Irish are a strange lot, somebody once said "Irish people are the nation God made mad for their wars are happy and their songs are sad."
Now Todd it is getting dark and its time for me to lift the lid of my coffin and make for town in my rather large white moustache, if you hear a shot and a lot of shouting you will know they have the head of Tom Molloy and my remains will be put on display to warn others to pay your debts until then me old pal say a prayer for one who lived on the edge and was pushed, shhhs quietly now. Take care and sing a song for me and let it be

"The Parting Glass"
Tom (the head of) Molloy

10/29/2011
Hi Tom,
I don't know what to say, except, send me a plane ticket quick before your banker or "friends" shoot you.
A "coggie" is a container, so a "nine pint coggie" is either a 9 pint container to put whatever you put in such a thing (like fermented urine), or a song, or a band.
Do you celebrate Halloween there?
Todd

10/30/2011
Subject: Re: photo of home in Idaho
Hello Todd,
Good afternoon buddy, I hope this email finds you all hale and hearty, we, your poor cousins in far off Paddyland are doing ok.
Thanks for the photo of your Autumnal abode, the dog looks very happy, and ready to chew on a bone or the rear end of a passerby. We used to have a canine pal, we named him "Blacksmith" because every time we opened the door, he'd make a bolt for it, good God Molloy stop with the old jokes.
Halloween is celebrated in Ireland as much as anywhere, I love to dress up as something nasty and evil, frightening people and making them shake in fear and cry out for mercy, so I dress up as an IMF official, that usually put the fear of God into them. All trick no treat.
We in Ireland don't have seasons, it either rains or not, mostly it rains, sometime the rain is warm, we call that Summer, when the rain is cold we know it must be close to Christmas or New Year, we don't buy swimwear we buy wet gear, we don't have the song from crickets but the creaks from rickets, I could go on but my eyes are welling up and tears are close, so with that sad refrain
Todd, me auld shoulder to cry on, I'll sniffle a sad Take care.
Tom

11/16/2011

Hi Tom,

I don't think I replied to your last e-mail on 10/30. Sorry about my delay.

I hope you and your family are healthy and happy.

What happened to your dog, Blacksmith? Bolted and never seen again? Our dog's name is Bonnie - How's that for an Irish, or a Scottish name? We love our Golden Retriever!

Our music group was practicing heavily (twice per week) up until last weekend when we had a gig at the Fall Folk Festival in Spokane, Wash. Sometimes our old name of ID/WA Celtic Fiddlers sticks to us like glue, and sometimes our new name of Nine Pint Coggies comes out.

Here is a link to photos of several performers at the college cafeteria (scroll down to the 9th photo which is our band - you can't see me very well - I'm the head wearing a black cap just over the left shoulder of the gentleman guitarist, Dirk. That is not my white shirt. We sometimes play with Ebb and Flow, which is the band in the 3rd photo).

http://spokanefolklore.org/FFF2011/caf.html

Here is a link to photos of several performers at the college cafeteria (scroll down to the 9th photo which is our band - you can't see me very well - I'm the head wearing a black cap just over the left shoulder of the gentleman guitarist, Dirk. That is not my white shirt. We sometimes play with Ebb and Flow, which is the band in the 3rd photo).

We also got on YouTube, and I'll forward you that link in a separate e-mail.

Do you celebrate Thanksgiving there in Ireland? Our family will get together for turkey and all the trimmings next Thursday.

Take care, Tom.

Todd

Bonnie Neel, Spud Dog from Idaho

11/24/2011
Hello Todd,
I watched your performance at the Spokane festival and it is very good lots of toetapping craic and again I admire your interest in Irish/Celt music, keep it up Todd, and I know you enjoy it so much. Say hello to the other Coggies, and well done to them also.
I hope all at your villa "El Neel" enjoy the Thanksgiving holiday and all it entails, and it is also a time for a family to meet up and have fun and enjoy each other's' company.
Not a lot happening here, all is quiet and an errie calmness is all about, rumours about a large male securing entrance to houses through the chimney in the near future abound, and he is believed to be dressed all in red, with a team of reindeer as cohorts, one of the reindeer has a glowing nose, sounds like he likes the juice of the Barley a bit much, he is the lookout guy. The crime scene is awash with evidence, from reindeer crap next to chimney pots to soot stains on roof tiles,
Todd be careful, and just on another note are Turkeys putting on the pounds or what? strange, very strange.
Take care and keep an eye on the roof, James Taylor "up on the roof."
Tom "grassy knoll" Molloy

11/24/2011

Hi Tom,

Happy Thanksgiving! My bladder woke me up at 3 am, and my brain wouldn't let me go back to sleep, so it gave me a chance to work on cleaning up my e-mails and hard drive on my laptop.

What's a craic?

It's great fun being part of a talented group of musicians that read and play beautiful music that speaks to my roots. Sometimes I want to (and do) just stop and listen. And they haven't figured out yet that I'm just faking in – I can't read a lick of a note on a piece of paper. I've got just 3 notes – base, tone, slap. Hard to mess that up! They haven't kicked me out yet! The fourteen 9 Pint Coggies are feeling pretty good about themselves right now. Thanks.

I'll pass on your Irish compliments!

Our villa "El Neel" is doing well. We'll pack up this Thanksgiving morning and drive to Montana to my sister's home (about 2 hours away) to have a traditional Amerikan turkey dinner.

My nephew, Jeff, has asked for help in cutting and splitting firewood, so that should bring us together, except my sister-in-law, wants to get home to Missoula (30 miles away) before dark after our scheduled 3 pm dinner (it gets dark now about 4 pm).

My nephew, Jeff, lives close to his parents. His workshop burned down this fall due to a faulty electrical box (Jeff is a talented cabinet maker, and it was a real loss as he just finished re-building his shop this summer).

We attend Unity Church here (a Christian church where we honor all Churches). Last night, 11/23/2011, we celebrated "Taize" with music, readings, and prayer. At this celebration we honored religions of Native American Indians, Buddhist, Islam, Hindu, Jewish, and Christian. The theme this year is "Peace Around the World" with an emphasis on 6 major religions. Readers will talk for 3 minutes about how their assigned religion reflects on Peace. I volunteered to speak for 3 minutes on the Native American spiritual path, and here is what I read:

"I am Caucasian of European descent, and most of my ancestors are the Immigrants here in America. My ancestors are the Invaders of this land.

"Are there any Native Americans or First Peoples here tonight of any percentage of Indian blood? Thank you for your Gift to us and what you continue to give to us.

I want to read you a story from <u>Seven Arrows</u> by Hyemeyohsts Storm (and so I read from the story of The Pipe in this book) …

Peace.

Happy Thanksgiving!

(That's the end of my talk, Tom)

Peace to you and your family, Tom!

Your cousin, Todd

<u>11/30/2011</u>

Good morning Todd,
It is Wednesday 30th of Nov., at 09.33 and all is quiet here in Ballydownan
Kids in school and college and my wife has gone to work, I'm having a coffee and contemplating life and looking out my sitting room window at Winter and wondering should I put on a warmer Geansai, decisions,decisions.
Craic is a gaelic word meaning, chat, banter and has comes to mean good company good music and chat, so we use the term "great craic" to say we had a great time good company, music and chat ("craic" pronounced as crack), Geansai is also a gaelic word, "gansee" and means Jumper or cardigan.
I hope all went well on Thanksgiving and all behaved themselves and enjoyed the family occasion, always nice to have family around and maybe Christmas and Thanksgiving were put there to achieve that.
The words you spoke at your church were good and there is a lot of meaning in them and makes us stop and think, sometimes in the hectic world we live in with its deadlines and timetables, we seldom have time to sit back and gaze at this wonderful world and all the simple pleasures that surround us, family, friends and what we see, hear and smell.
Well Todd, I have to be away now and can no longer tarry, the morning mist has lifted and my warmer Geansai awaits,

things to do, people to see and miles to go before I sleep
Hello to all and take care
Tom
" a real friend is one who walks in
when the rest of the world walks out"

12/8/2011

Hi Tom,
Here's some more thoughts to make you Thoughtful:
Be Thankful
Be thankful that you don't already have everything you desire;
If you did, what would there be to look forward to?
Be thankful when you don't know something;
For it gives you the opportunity to learn.
Be thankful for the difficult times;
During those times you grow.
Be thankful for your limitations;
Because they give you opportunities for improvement.
Be thankful for each new challenge;
Because it will build your strength and character.
Be thankful for your mistakes;
They will teach you valuable lessons.
Be thankful when you're tired and weary;
Because it means you've made a difference.
.........author unknown

I'm flying to Utah tomorrow for work. We'll have a Family Group Decision Making meeting to help one of our families find a permanent placement for 3 children, currently living with grandparents and aunt & uncle. The parents in another state don't seem to be interested in acting like parents (they've only talked to their children twice in the last 2 months). Do you have much knowledge about child protection services in Ireland?

12/12/2011

Hello Todd,
Good day to you sir, and I hope this email finds you and yours in good health,

for surely health is wealth beyond measure.
All is fine here, the natives are smoking the pipes of peace with our "friends" in Europe and we are allowed to loosen the shackles of servitude to our master in Europe a little, but the fight will go on, as we gather to sing "we shall overcome" and perhaps dream of freedom in the cold night of austerity, we may be in the gutter
but we are looking at the stars.
Now excuse me while I take my medication and lie down in a dark room for a few moments.
You spoke of parents and how they treat their children, well it happens here to, my brother and his wife do fostering and some of the tales of abandoned children are horrendous, and social services are getting new cases every day, 200 kids on the waiting list for fostering and that is just in two counties, we have a further 24 counties and God knows how many are on their waiting lists. God help us.
Well Todd it is time for more of the medication and sleep and that will make it go away, all the cares and woes, John O'Dreams will come and make it all go away, go away, go away, nitetynite Jimbob, Peggysue, Ricky Nelson, she wore blue velvet, nite
Tom

NOTE: There was a long period of time when our communications stopped, but we have renewed contact again. I found out that Tom's wife, Celine, had passed away, and he is deeply grieving for the loss of his beautiful wife.

I got plane tickets to Dublin, Ireland to meet and stay with Tom in November 2017. He picked me up at the airport and we had a wonderful week together. He gave me a personal tour of his beautiful country. (Maybe there's another book about this trip!)

POST NOTE: As I was preparing this book for e-publication, I communicated with the Molloy family, and they said they would like updated photographs, and so below are photos of Tom and his wife, Celine, and their daughters, Rachael and Aoife. These photos are in color in the electronic version of this book (e-book), but the printed book only has black and white photos in greyscale in the paperback version.

Chapter 29
– My ~~Obituary~~/Eulogy –
In Case You Didn't Get It

By Todd William Neel
(d.o.b. 7/25/1955 – d.o.d. x/x/20xx, A.D.)

Now that I have your undivided attention, in case you didn't have time to read my book, copies are for sale in the lobby! I hope you're not too late for an autographed copy.

While this chapter started as an Obituary, upon doing more research, I found out that "Obits" are supposed to be short, like the ones that go in a newspaper. Since this was getting too long for that, I decided to rename it as *My Eulogy*. Or, if you have read this far and you still don't get me, this ought to explain me fairly thoroughly, just in case you didn't understand who I was by the time you have read this far in my Book of Life.

Basically, this chapter is about things that matter to me. If my family (blood, legal, or chosen) are looking for words to use at my Celebration of Life after this body has quit, there's plenty of thoughts to choose from here.

I recommend you write your own eulogy or obituary while you still have the chance.

If you want more data on me, see "About the Author" at the end of this book. (But you may have heard way more than enough by now.)

The Ralphie Question

What's it all about, Ralphie? (There is a similar sounding question from a famous song and movie.) What has my life been about? I want to have lived my life like it made a positive difference. Like I had a purpose. Like I had reason to get up in the morning and that I had made a contribution to the world. I don't want to be just a consumer that leaves more waste behind than I created. I want to produce something of value to others, and not just make widgets or other worthless things that are going to be discarded for landfill. I want to be good compost!

There is something hypocritical about this, as I also want to walk a path through life with humility, to leave a small footprint, not take credit for what is not mine. But "living a life that makes a difference" almost shouts "Look at me!" and "I made my mark!" Ah, but I guess if we're going to walk a path, our own way, then we're going to leave footprints, aren't we? Maybe it's about being conscious about what kind of footprints we leave behind.

Kindness and love in relationships, that's what it's all about. Not just to acquire things and to exist.

NOTE: In our men's group we play with this theme as we have a member named Ralph. Thanks, Ralphie! With apologies to the owners of the copyright of the original song and movie title. To the reader, I encourage you to search your brain, or a friend's better brain, to look for the movie and listen to the song. (It's good to have friends with better brains than our own!) That song is a good one!

Things That Matter

It's been useful for me to remember these things that matter, in no particular order. (I suggest you write your own list of what matters to you):

- Leave the world a better place than I found it. Take personal responsibility for this, and be a role model for others in this practice. Pick up that piece of trash on the ground that someone else dropped, as I have probably done more than my own share of littering. Work on my resentments about picking up cigarette butts. Work on this metaphor!

- Do no harm, and if I do, then try to make it right.

- As I pay attention to the things that matter, let go of the small stuff but be respectful of the things I don't think are important because they might matter to someone else.

- Build bridges, not walls. Don't burn my bridges, as I may need a way back.

- Don't kill the goose that laid the golden egg. Remember my source.

- Live by the Golden Rule – treat others the way I wish to be treated. Be kind to them first – don't wait for them to start it! Pay it forward!

- There is a proper time and place for everything, including a good cliché! Appropriateness is inappropriate. Political correctness does not have to be dishonest or hurtful. Be tactful. Use my inside voice when indoors. Flatulence is a natural, organic function that all people experience (or should), and in some families there are rules that you don't need to apologize for natural processes. (I think it was it Shrek that said: "Better out than in.") However, that is not the rule in my family. Don't fart in people's faces! Be civilized!

- Take responsibility for my own thoughts, feelings, and actions. Pay my debts. Pay it back. Be debt free if possible.

- Make conscious choices about my relationships, and notice that I prefer others that desire to take responsibility for themselves.

- Do my own personal work, work out my issues. Consciousness is preferred over unconsciousness and blindly motivated actions.

- Notice that I chose relationships where there is a return on my investments. Ponder this: What about those who don't invest in me? (This is an issue for me that I'm still working on. Stay tuned to this channel.)

- Be assertive in speaking my truth, not aggressive and disrespectful of others, and not passive in my words and behaviors. Don't be a doormat for others to wipe their shoes on. Don't be passive-aggressive, especially. Be clear about what I need. Know that what I want may be very different from what I need.

- Sometimes it's useful to be gentle and forgiving of others, letting go of old stuff, and this may appear passive sometimes. Patience is the rule.

- Attachments are the source of all pain, yet, if it doesn't hurt, why bother?

- Powdermilk Biscuits, and other good nutrition, give us the strength to get up and do what needs to be done! (Thank you for this, Garrison Keillor, from the Prairie Home Companion radio show.) Take care of the "machine," our bodies. Eat, sleep, exercise well, stay hydrated. We only get one physical body in this lifetime, and it has limited mileage and no warranty. We might be able to get replacement parts, but is our insurance paid up? Remember to check the oil, other fluid levels, the tire pressure, and do regular maintenance as we do for our other vehicles. What kinds of miles do we want to put on our machine: on rough roads experiencing high adventure, or stay on the pavement, always smooth going? Our body is the vehicle that was gifted to us to make miracles happen!

- There are lions, tigers, and bears out there, and sometimes a skunk still stinks, or worse. A tiger can't change its stripes, and a shark will still bite because that is who he is. (Thanks for this life lesson, "Bob.")

- Seek the Inner Life, with a balance between action with knowledge, and repose with passivity of mind for some periods of time. "*Know that there is inner justice which is working beyond the worldly justice, and when (one) does not observe that inner law of justice, it is because at that time he is intoxicated, his eyes are closed, and he really does not know the law of life.*" (From The Inner Life by Hazrat Inayat Khan, © 1997. Reprinted by arrangement with Shambhala Publications, Inc., Boulder, Colorado. www.shambhala.com.) My good friend, George, says he learned in law school that it is a long way between what is legal and what is justice on the continuum.

- Ask myself "Am I done with that, yet?," and after a moment ask "Are they done with that, yet?" Has everything been said that needs to be said? Pass the Talking Stick on, as I need to hear what you have to say.

Heaven and Hell

I believe in Heaven, and I accept that there is Hell, but I do not necessarily believe that these exist in the afterlife as I don't have proof of that, yet. Through our choices and our perceptions, we can be living in Heaven on earth. Or we could be living in Hell on earth, right here and now. Knowing that I will burn if I cross that line can keep me from crossing that line! I can live my life to make choices that keep my butt out of the fire, or I can make choices that lead me towards the light.

Afterward, when this physical body stops breathing, and this physical heart stops beating, I don't know what happens. Compost, maybe. Good crops from the seeds we planted, I hope. I see evidence of Karma and reincarnation in compost and recycling. Our bodies will be plant life before we become animal life again. We will become energy before we become matter again - that's the Golden Rule. We harvest what we reap. Love is all you need. Imagine what John Lennon was trying to tell us, as he says it's easy if you try.

Our bodies will, most likely, be plant life before we become animal life again, unless we're eaten by the bear!

When I get to the other side, I'll send you a message if I can. Will you listen? Will you hear it? Can you hear me now?

While I am here in this physical body and I still have the ability, I can make snow angels or ice sculptures, but they will melt someday as the seasons change.

Boy Scouts

Remember the Boy Scout Oath ("On my honor I will do my best, to do my duty …"), and the Scout Law ("A Scout is trustworthy, loyal, helpful, friendly, courteous, kind, obedient, cheerful, thrifty, brave, clean, and reverent"). Sometimes these can be useful, like a good Scout knife. Use the right blade or the right Law at the right time, but most of the time put it away out of sight, keep it in your pocket, and let it quietly guide you, using the right tool for the need when it comes up. Keep that pocketknife handy, except when going through the metal detector at the airport. Some blades on those knives I never figured out how to use, though. I am still an Eagle Boy Scout, and I appreciate all those experiences I had in Scouts, especially the cold and rainy campouts which stick out more strongly in my memory than the blue-sky days.

Twelve Steps

Remember the Twelve Steps and Twelve Traditions of Twelve Step Recovery Programs (including the principal of anonymity). They have helped me to not only be dry but also to be clean and sober. They can help to deal with so many situations in life and the hereafter. There are lots of invitations in our culture to be intoxicated, by way of more than just with chemicals. I need to be responsible for getting myself out of my dis-ease, and to do the best I can to be clear about my boundaries when it comes to your dis-ease (dis-ease = not at ease). We can do together what I cannot do alone. Being sober does not mean to lose our sense of humor. We can laugh <u>with</u> one another more deeply with true joy than when we laugh <u>at</u> one another.

Remember the Serenity Prayer: "God, grant us the serenity to accept the things we cannot change, the courage to change the things we can, and the wisdom to know the difference." It's beautiful to help us be clear about our boundaries.

Men's Groups

My experiences in men's groups began around 1985 during graduate school. Men together, without women, on a regular basis, can be great community! A wonderful chosen family! Brothers in life! My men's work started when I observed my partner, Mary, and her involvement in women's groups, as I envied her close relationships. I have experienced so many deep and lasting experiences with my men's groups, and my life has been richer because of it. I encourage you to find one for yourself. (Women, I encourage you to find a women's group also!)

Men and women together are also magical!

The Profession of Social Work

As a social worker since 1986, I am current with my license with the state of Idaho as an LCSW (Licensed Clinical Social Worker). I do subscribe to the NASW (National Association of Social Workers) Code of Ethics, which includes the core mission, ethical principles, and ethical standards. Some of these reflect the values of service, social justice, dignity and worth of a person, importance of human relationships, integrity, and competence.

On Toothpaste ...

Remember to squeeze the toothpaste from the bottom of the tube, and after you spin the lids off the bottles, spin them all the way closed when you are done (this rule also goes for the vitamins, catsup, the mayonnaise, etc.). This is important if we are going to live together as family! Then I will be happier, and it will be a better world.

Sooner or Later ...

"Sooner or later a person begins to notice that everything that happens to him is perfect, relates directly to who he is, had to happen, was meant to happen, plays its little role in fulfilling his destiny ... When he encounters difficulty, it no longer occurs to him to complain— he has learned to expect nothing, has learned that loss and frustration are a part of life, and come at their proper time— instead he asks himself, why is this happening? ...by which he means, what can I learn from this, how will it strengthen me, make me more aware? He lets himself be strengthened, lets himself grow, just as he lets himself relax and enjoy (and grow) when life is gentle to him."

(from Das Energi, by Paul Williams)

Church

I do believe in spirituality, but not in a religious fashion that can be too dogmatic. I do believe in Jesus, I do believe in Buddha, and I do believe in an infinite number of the names for God. We all have access to God, and we don't need church authority to interpret God for us. But churches can be useful.

I found an extended family in the community of Unity Church, which helps my spiritual practices and helps give meaning to me in everyday life. These seem to fine tune my nervous system on a daily (or weekly) basis, orient me towards living a better life and relationship with our fellow humans, with our precious world, and with the cosmos. We are all stardust!

Here are Five Basic Principles of Unity:

(1) There is only one presence and power in the Universe (we are all one, it's not "my church is right, and your church is wrong");
(2) There is a divine spark of God in each of us, the Christ-Light, (or Higher Power as you understand him/her, as referred to in the Twelve Step programs);
(3) Prayer and meditation alters our own consciousness of our Oneness and divinity;
(4) The thoughts in our mind are the creators of our life ("thoughts in mind produce likeness in kind"); and
(5) We live our beliefs and practice them daily.

Unity says we honor all churches, which is a challenge for me on some days.

Nature is a huge part of my belief in spirituality and being outdoors renews me deeply. Mother Nature is compost in action! You can see it, feel it, hear it, smell it, touch it! (Thank you, Ernie Hawks, for your book Every Day is a High Holy Day. It is beautiful and should be a classic someday!) Ernie says in his book, in his essay *High Holy Days*: "I often celebrate communion in the Cathedral of the Tamarack, Fir, and Pine ....". Me too!

Regularly doing Dances of Universal Peace and hanging out with Sufis has been a very honorable experience. It is wonderful to sit in the center of a circle of dancers and singers, to feel our energy, to sing and play and dance together, to exchange darshan, to move as a community arm-in-arm, and to learn new languages for love. Participating in the Dances of Universal Peace is like "body prayers" for me. Doing it regularly keeps bringing it home. I can still feel the sounds and movements of the waves of motion of Spirit at the cellular level of my body.

I can't tell you what to believe about spirituality. You have to experience that yourself.

I believe in the circle of life and the interconnectedness of all things, living and non-living. There are modern movies like "Avatar," "Cloud Atlas" and many other good and great films that have shown this on the big screen - some are just good, some are great, but all are valuable if you have the time.

I do believe that we are all compost, that we are dying as we are living, and we are living after we are dead and gone. Compost! Bodies are recycled!

Stories are remembered and may be re-told ... because after my body is gone and my deeds are done, all that's left are stories, pictures, echoes, footprints ... but where did my essence go? And I ask, did my stories, pictures, echoes and footprints make a positive difference or at least a net contribution to this planet and to this universe rather than a gross deficit when the final audit is done?

The Clock is Ticking

A snapshot in time: I am sixty-three years of age at this time as I re-write and re-edit this paragraph now for the umpteenth time in 2018, listening to the tick, tick, tick of the clock on my living room wall, early in the quiet morning when I do my best writing ... I am conscious that my mother died at fifty-nine years of age. I passed her by if the race is measured by years lived.

I was conscious of my mortality and the fragility of life as I was scheduled for surgery at that time on January 9, 2014 (one of several operations I've had in my life when the doctors brought me to the edge of life and death with anesthesia so they could cut me open). I had hoped and prayed that my anesthesiologist remembered the pseudocholinesterase deficiency that I wrote about in my medical records. Thank you for modern medicine, and I'm grateful for alternative medicine! What did our ancestors do without health insurance?

I picked up my thirty-seven-year sobriety chip from my home group just a few months ago, on January 2, 2018, and I am grateful that my terminal disease of alcoholism/ addiction is in remission, today.

On January 7, 2014, on my father's birthday, he would have been one hundred years old if he were alive. He died at eighty years of age. Or, rather, he lived until eighty years of age as he died in 1994. Dad has been gone over twenty years now. Mom has been gone for thirty-eight years now. Thank you for all you did for us, Dad and Mom. You are still giving to us. I love you.

Tick, tick, tick … Can you hear it? Like mileposts on the highway. Will we pass by this way again? (As Tom Molloy joked, two wrongs don't make a right, but three lefts do! Can we make enough turns on our roads of life to double back again?) Is time linear or circular? Compost, and the written record, lives on!

Perceptions and Point of View

The human mind is not a perfect or permanent recorder of history. The human heart helps to remember, but it is indeed not a perfect or permanent record, tainted by emotions of ghosts from our past. Each of us has our own points of view, each from our own positions in the circle, and our own experiences on the path. Our perceptions are only the unique truth for each of us. It is vitally important that if we are going to live together as a community that we try as best we can to listen to others and understand their point of view, their feelings, their wisdom. I need to know what you see, as I have blind spots and I cannot see from your eyes where you are. We can do together what I cannot do alone.

Headstone Marker?

Will there be a headstone marker for me after I'm gone? I don't know, that's more for the living persons remaining behind, not for the dead who could care less. I do, at this time, want to be cremated, and have my ashes scattered around the top of Dominion Peak where I have already spread the remains from our beloved Golden Retriever dog, Bonnie. (See *Chapter 9 - Sojourn Into Montana – Home of My Heart*.) I feel my heart is in Montana, and my ass is in Idaho, where I have settled and called home since 1987. Idaho is where I married my wife, Mary, and we set down roots and made

Coeur d'Alene our home. Idaho is where we raised our children, Nathan and Joshua. Ah, my boys. There's another few chapters or another book there to write. My wife and my children - I wouldn't be here without you! I need your help! I love you, my family! Let's sing! Let's dance!

Celebration

I do want a Celebration of Life, an opportunity for grief for the living after I'm gone, if you have any of your own grief. I don't want a funeral of sad, sad people, but would rather have a room full of joyful tears - that would be great! Tears, sweat, and blood pulsing through our hearts! The Soup of Life! Add the random ingredients and mix it up! Ah, HO!!

Maybe you'd instead rather celebrate my death. If you do, I'm sorry if I have done you harm. I know that I have not always been as patient with others as I wish I would have been. Or patient enough with myself, sometimes, which may have been imposed on you. Or had enough grace and gratitude. If pain is what I left behind, it is not the kind of footprints I wanted to leave with you. I'm sorry for those who may have been hurt by my words or deeds. Let the wind sweep them away! Remember, resentments are anger held onto. Does it still serve you?

Physical Life

At the time of this writing, since these are my physical fingers writing these words, this chapter and my book are incomplete, as I hope my life is incomplete just yet. As this may be (at least part of) my actual eulogy to be read at my requested services for a celebration of my life and of our lives, I have faith that I have tomorrow to continue this work (and next month and next year, I hope, I hope). A traffic accident or a doctor's mistake or other unforeseen events could happen any day for any of us.

Consider this an undeveloped photograph. Don't dip me in lacquer yet (am I repeating myself?) … But if these are my final words, I'm doing the best I can with what I've got.

Use that long-lasting archival ink and pull me down off the shelves once in a while, and tell stories. And don't forget to write and tell your own story.

Torch the Pyre

If this writing is being used in my obituary or eulogy, after my death, then I guess it's time to hit one final "Send." Then go ahead, dip me in lacquer, and light the match and torch the pyre. Any ashes that remain scatter them to the wind on the mountain tops, to nurture the roots of the grasses, bushes, and trees, to feed the critters, to flow to the rivers and the oceans and recycle to the skies.

I hope some descendants and friends want to celebrate not only my life but to celebrate your own lives. Tell and make stories. (It's useful to be able to discern fact from fiction, though. This is a special message to my friend, Tim, from men's group!) Make a good noise! Be seen! Be heard! But also listen! If we're too busy making noise, then we don't hear our brothers and our sisters, and we won't hear other members of God's family. Can you hear the wind in that hawk's feathers? After a time of noise, let there be a time of stillness to listen for that most quiet voice ...

Family

I say … hug your family - those you can reach. Create new family by making friends, and most importantly, be a friend of the kind you need your friends to be for you when you are in need. Love your family, those you can find (including your ancestors). If it weren't for them, family and friends, we wouldn't be here. Family are the people who brought us into this world, and they are the ones who will lay us in (or on) the ground in the end … including new family who may (or may not) be of the same blood. Ah, but have you done your DNA spit test yet? Maybe we are of the same blood!

"***All I want is to be home***." (from Dave Grohl's song "Home" by the Foo Fighters). Home, wherever I am.

What Kahlil Gibran said about Death

And, again, Kahlil Gibran said:

"Then Almitra spoke, saying,
We would ask now of Death.
And he said:
You would know the secret of death.
But how shall you find it unless you seek it
in the heart of life?

"The owl whose night-bound eyes
Are blind unto the day
cannot unveil the mystery of light.
If you would indeed behold the spirit of death,
open your heart wide unto the body of life.
For life and death are one,
even as the river and the sea are one.

"In the depth of your hopes and desires
lies your silent knowledge of the beyond;
And like seeds dreaming beneath the snow
your heart dreams of spring.

"Trust the dreams ...

"For what is it to die but to stand naked in the wind
and to melt into the sun?
And what is it to cease breathing,
but to free the breath from its restless tides,
that it may rise and expand
and seek God
unencumbered?

"Only when you drink from the river of silence
shall you indeed sing.
And when you have reached the mountain top,
then you shall begin to climb.

And when the earth shall claim your limbs,
then shall you truly dance."

(from The Prophet by Kahlil Gibran, 1923)

When does my breath become the wind? When does this same wind become your breath? Where do I end and where do you begin? What happens to the Copyright when I have quoted others so much that I forgot who the original author was?

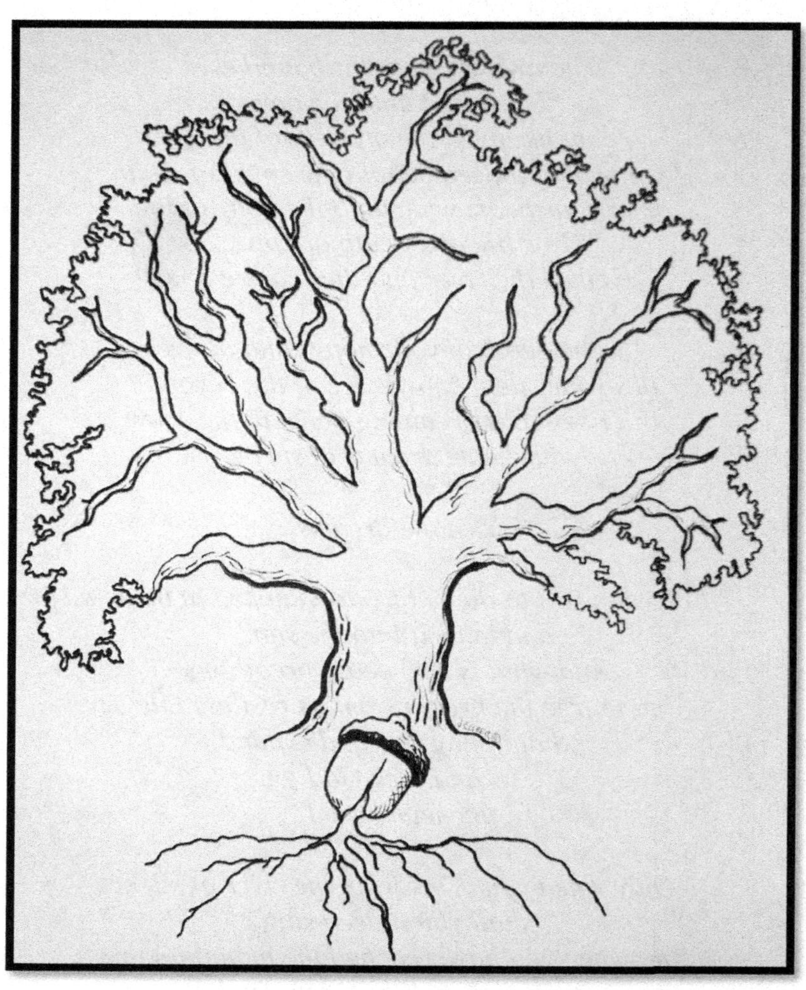

Ingredients for my Celebration of Life: Please read the "Translation of Aramaic version of the Lord's Prayer," which is referenced elsewhere in this book (look for it!) This version of the Lord's Prayer is by Mosheed Samuel L. Lewis (Dances of Universal Peace tradition, and is also from Mark Stanton Welch's CD "*Riding the Sound Current*" – Thank you Mark for all the wonderful times we had at Unity kids' camps, and at your workshops!)

Songs/tunes to play at my funeral/celebration of life, and/or to play for me if ever I am in a coma, or if I have "gone away" with dementia or Alzheimer's or other such disease. (These are listed and printed here, and because of Copyrights I am only sharing song titles and authors under fair use laws):

- "I Would Not Be Here" by John Hartford (version from the album "Me Oh My How the Time Does Fly: A John Hartford Anthology")
- "Old Time River Men" by John Hartford (version from the album "Live at College Station Pennsylvania")
- "Dreaming" written and played by George Conrad (from the album "Reflections")
- "Star Star" by The Frames (from the album "Dance the Devil")
- "Wandering" written and played by George Conrad (from the album "Reflections")
- "Imagine" by John Lennon (from the album "Imagine" by John Lennon)
- "What Happens When the Heart Just Stops?" (by The Frames in their album "Set List")
- "Between The Lines" (from the album "The Steve Goodman Anthology: No Big Surprise")
- "The Family Tree" (from the Steve Goodman album "Live At The Earl of Old Town")
- "Transitions" written and played by George Conrad (from the album "Reflections")

- "Home" by the Foo Fighters (from the album "Echoes, Silence, Patience, and Grace")
- "Wall of Thunder" written and played by Mark Krielkamp (from the album "Rustlin' In My Soul")
- "Ava Maria" sung by Peggy Decker
- "Far Away Waltz" by Peter Jung and played by the 9 Pint Coggies

Musicians requested:

- Mark Krielkamp (guitar)
- Carolyn Rogers (Native American flute)
- Drums of Unity from the Unity Church of North Idaho (a.k.a. Unity Spiritual Center of North Idaho)
- Peggy Decker (chanting with Drums of Unity and singing "Ava Maria")
- "Ancestors" Dances of Universal Peace Ensemble (Bruce Calkins, Beth "Anahita" Barclay, Mark Krielkamp, Beth "Basira" Fergin, Michael Norris)
- George Conrad, piano
- Jan Clizer, fiddle
- 9 Pint Coggies ("Far Away Waltz")

Some inspirational questions, since this book is supposed to motivate you to do your own work:

- Have you thought about end-of-life issues for yourself?
- Have you written a will?
- Have you talked with your significant partner about your end-of-life issues?
- Have you attended a funeral or memorial service lately for someone else?
- Have you thought about who might be at your funeral, and what will be said about you?

Chapter 30
Epilogue

Well, this first book of mine was about my roots, where I come from, and to honor those whose shoulders I stand upon. Their ghosts are in my fingers as I write this as I attempt to reach across space and time to introduce and offer a handshake with future generations.

This is not just a biology experiment, but it is social-psychological-spiritual research. This is about those experiences my immediate family and friends had together in my time here, and about those interactions my ancestors and the compost of the universe had together. This is how lives were touched across the miles, across time, across the cosmos. This is about the chemistry of stardust.

And it is to recognize that I have left footprints, fingerprints, genetic evidence, and stardust behind me.

This is intended to be a message of hope to the future.

A dialogue:

HEY!
DID YOU GET IT?

What? Who said that?

WHO? I CAN'T TELL YOU WHO,
BECAUSE I AM NAMELESS. I HAVE
A THOUSAND, INFINITE NUMBER
OF NAMES. TO TRY TO NAME ME IS
JUST FOLLY, A FUTILE ATTEMPT
TO CAPTURE AND UNDERSTAND
THE MYSTERY OF WHO I AM.

I AM THAT STILL SMALL VOICE
INSIDE YOUR HEAD,
BIGGER THAN YOUR LITTLE EGO.
I AM THE I AM THAT I AM.
THE EVERYTHING OF THE UNIVERSE!
I AM A MYSTERY!
DID YOU MAKE ME UP?

Huh? What are you talking about?

I AM THE COLLECTIVE WISDOM
OF ETERNITY THAT ENABLED
THOSE NEUROTRANSMITTERS
TO JUMP ACROSS THE SYNAPSES
OF YOUR BRAIN CELLS
AND YOUR NERVOUS SYSTEM
THROUGHOUT YOUR BODY,
ALLOWING YOU TO CONSIDER
HITTING THAT "N"
ON YOUR KEYBOARD
WITH YOUR RIGHT INDEX FINGER
OR INSTEAD
WITH YOUR LEFT INDEX FINGER
FOR THE NEXT WORD.
I AM THE COLLECTIVE WISDOM
THAT CREATED
THE FRONTAL LOBE OF YOUR BRAIN
TO CONSIDER YOUR INTENTIONS,
TO HAVE MORALS
AND ETHICAL STANDARDS,
AND TO THINK ABOUT
WHETHER YOU HAVE DELETED
THE NAMES OF
(OR GOTTEN PERMISSION FROM)
ALL YOUR LIVING RELATIVES
FROM YOUIR BOOK
BEFORE YOU SENT IT TO THE PRINTER.

I KNEW YOUR MOM AND DAD.
AND YOUR GRANDPARENTS.
AND THEN SOME ...

Oh, I think I'm catching on.
I think I know who you are.
I'm a little slow sometimes.

TO NAME ME IS TO REDUCE ME.
TO NAME ME IS TO TRY
TO CONTROL ME,
AND THAT'S IMPOSSIBLE.
THINK OF ME AS YOUR
GREAT EDITOR-IN-THE-SKY.

I'LL JUST REPEAT MY QUESTION:
DID YOU GET IT?

Hey, did you know
that when you use CAPS
on the keyboard,
some people consider
that as shouting?
That could be construed as rude.

To answer your question,
I get it that
I am just a small part
of a bigger whole,
and from my small
humble position,
I am grateful
for those who
came before me,
and I appreciate
and truly have hope for
that which will come after me.
And I appreciate
those who are with me now.

Including the germ and cancer bugs
and my immune system.

And, you're blowing me away!

I don't think
my story is finished yet.
Not ended yet.
No! NO! **NO**!
I'm not done yet!

But, do you know
something
that I don't know?
Is there a train coming
for me at the next crossing?

While I'm pretty sure
I got some of it,
I'm also sure
there is some of "it"
that I did not get, yet.

What is it that you think I didn't get?
Why are you asking that question?

Sorry, I didn't mean
to shout at you.
I turned my CAP key off, now.
I just wanted to get your attention.
I know I gave you free will.
I gave you choices.
And I gave choices to all
your brothers and sisters
and those little germ bugs
that you talk about.
Really, I did!
You might be in one of
their cross hairs right now!

What do you think of that?

That makes me kind of nervous.

Are you taking your vitamins?
Did you get enough rest last night?
Did you drink enough water today?
Do you look both ways
before you cross the street?
Do you buckle your seat belt?
Do you do everything you can
to be clean and sober today?
Do you try to leave the world
a better place than you found it?

Well, yes,
I try to remember to do
all those things,
and I try to remember
to live by the Golden Rule.

I try to remember that
I only have to floss the teeth
that I want to keep,
but I do get lazy
and complacent sometimes.

I try to leave good tracks,
small foot prints.

And I know that
some of my descendants
might be looking
for evidence of me someday,
just as I try to look
for my ancestors now.

I try to respect the earth
so it can be a safe and nurturing place

for my children and grandchildren
seven generations from now,
as the Native Americans say.

But there is this guy,
this politician
we have right now,
this devil in disguise …

Now wait a minute.
Don't go blaming others!
Did you get the part about
taking responsibility for yourself?
Did you vote?
Have you considered
running for office yourself?

Oh, yeah. I remember that part.
I voted, and I encourage others to vote also,
even if I don't agree with their politics.
And, no thanks,
I don't want to run for office.

I know I am a social animal,
and I need others for my survival
and I enjoy others to enrich my life.
Even the ones who are a pain in the ass!

I know that we are better together,
that we can do together
what each of us cannot do alone,
that there is
true meaning and purpose
when we find each other,
and when we truly meet.
Especially when we have found
a way to overcome our differences.

And I know not to kill the goose
that laid the golden eggs.

And that engaging
and sustaining relationships
are going to help me
get through the challenges
I have in this life.
And that I need those
with whom I disagree.

Good. And don't forget this:

God, grant me the serenity (deep peace)
to accept the things you cannot change (others),
the courage to change the things you can (yourself),
and the wisdom to know the difference.

Keep working your boundaries ...

You can use that God part if you want ...
It keeps you humble.

How does your story end?

Are you done?

What's next?

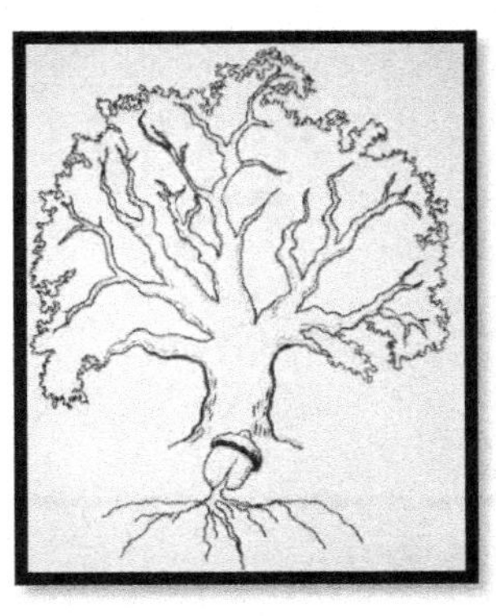

Chapter 31
Questions To Ask Your Family Members

There are some questions from Good Housekeeping magazine (March 1994), and other questions gathered randomly from the Internet and other resources. Because of Copyright they are not included here in this book. If you need help I encourage you to seek them out on your own, or get help from a genealogy buddy or other experts. Contact me if needed.

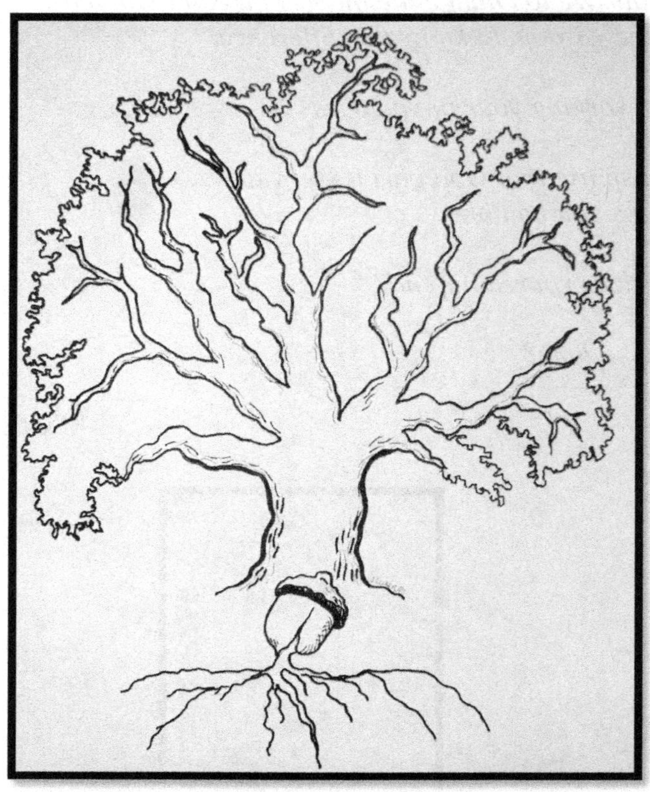

Chapter 32
Bibliography

(Note: Permissions have been obtained by publishers when Copyright protected, unless content is covered under "Fair Use" rules.)

Ainsworth, Mary D. Slater, Blehar, Mary C., Waters, Everett, and Wall, Sally N., Patterns of Attachment: A Psychological Study of the Strange Situation, Psychology Press and Routledge Classic Editions, (2015).

Anonymous author, "Why Men Don't Have Friends, and Why Women Should Care" (Google article on Internet).

Black, Claudia, It Will Never Happen to Me!, M.A.C. Printing and Publications Divisions, 1850 High Street, Denver, CO 80218 (1981).

Bly, Robert, Iron John: A Book about Men, Perseus Book Groups, (1990).

Bowlby, John, A Secure Base: Parent-Child Attachment and Healthy Human Development, Basic Books, A Subsidiary of Perseus Books, LLC, (1988).

Bradshaw, John, Bradshaw On: The Family – A Revolutionary Way of Self-Discovery, Health Communications, Inc., Enterprise Center, 3201 Southwest 15th St., Deerfield Beach, FL 33442, (1988).

Brazelton, T. Berry, M.D., and Cramer, Bertand G., M.D., The Earliest Relationship – Parents, Infants, and the Drama of Early Attachment, A Merloyd Lawrence Book, Addison-Wesley Publishing Company, Inc., (1990).

Brown, Brene', Ph.D., L.M.S.W., The Gifts of Imperfection, Hazeldon, Center City, Minnesota, (2010). hazelden.org

Cahill, Thomas, How the Irish Saved Civilization, First Anchor Books, Division of Random House, Inc., New York, (1995).

Carter, Betty and McGoldrick, Monica (authors and editors), The Changing Family Life Cycle - A Framework for Family Therapy, Gardner Press, Inc, Gardner Press Distribution, 540 Barnum Avenue, Bridgeport, CT 06608 (1988).

Carter, Betty and McGoldrick, Monica (editors), The Expanded Family Life Cycle – Individual, Family, and Social Perspectives, Third Edition, by Betty Carter and Monica McGoldrick (authors and editors), Allyn & Bacon, A Pearson Education Company, 160 Gould Street, Needham Heights, MA 02494 (1989, 1999).

Cassidy, Jude and Shaver, Phillip, Editors, Handbook on Attachment, Theory, Research, and Clinical Applications, published by The Guilford Press, New York and London, (1999).

Coohill, Joseph, Ireland - A Short History, Oneworld Publications, 185 Banbury Road, Oxford OX2 7AR, England, (2008).

Gibran, Kahlil, The Prophet, Borzoi Books, published by Alfred A. Knopf, Inc., New York, (1923).

Goleman, Daniel, Emotional Intelligence – Why It Can Matter More Than IQ, Bantam Dell, A Division of Random House, Inc., New York, (2005).

Goode, Erica E., quote from poster on siblings in "*Chapter 6 - A Brother's Story*".

Harris, Thomas, MD, I'm OK, You're OK, Avon Books, The Hearst Corporation, 959 Eighth Avenue, New York, New York 10019, (1969).

Hawks, Ernie, Every Day is a High Holy Day, MichalHawks Publishing, (2014).

Karen, Robert, Becoming Attached – Unfolding the Mystery of the Infant-Mother Bond and Its Impact on Later Life, Warner Books, Inc., A Time Warner Company, (1994).

Khan, Hazrat Inayat, The Inner Life, Boston: Shambhala Publications, Inc., (1997).

King, Stephen, On Writing – A Memoir of the Craft, Scribner, A Division of Simon & Schuster, Inc., 1230 Avenue of the Americas, New York, NY 10020, (2000).

Kubler-Ross, Elisabeth, Death, The Final Stage of Growth, Prentice-Hall, Englewood Cliffs, New Jersey, (1975).

Ladinsky, Daniel, Love Poems From God, ("*With Passion*") Penguin Compass, Penguin Group, 375 Hudson Street, New York, NY 10014, (2002). (From the Penguin Publication, *Love Poems From God: Twelve Sacred Voices of the East and West* by Daniel Ladinsky, copyright 2002, and used with permission).

McLaren, Karla, The Language of Emotions– What Your Feelings Are Trying to Tell You, Sounds True, Inc., Boulder, CO, (© 2010) karlamclaren.com Excerpted with permission of publisher, Sounds True, Inc.

Minuchin, Salvador, Families and Family Therapy, Harvard University Press, Cambridge, MA, (1974).

Minuchin, Salvador & Fishman, H. Charles, Family Therapy Techniques, Harvard University Press, Cambridge, MA, (1981).

Peck, Scott, MD, People of the Lie – The Hope for Healing Human Evil, Simon and Schuster, New York, (1983).

Perry, Bruce and Szalavitz, Maia, The Boy Who Was Raised As A Dog, Basic Books, Pereus Books Group, 387 Park Ave. South, New York, NY 10016-8810, (2010).

Pirsig, Robert M., Zen and the Art of Motorcycle Maintenance – An Inquiry Into Values, A Bantam Book, published by arrangement with William Morrow and Company, Inc., 105 Madison Avenue, New York, N.Y. 10016 (1974).

Richman, Talia (Baltimore Sun), in article "*Woman details alleged torment by suspect in newsroom shooting*", The Spokesman-Review, p. A8, 136th Vol., Issue 23, Rights & Permissions, The Spokesman-Review, P.O. Box 2160, Spokane, Washington 99210, (7/3/2018).

Rogers, Carl, On Becoming A Person, Houghton Mifflin Company, Boston, MA, (1961).

Rosenberg, Marshall B., PhD, Nonviolent Communication – A Language of Life, (2nd Edition), PuddleDancer Press, Encinitas, CA, (2005). Also NVC: A Language of Life, (3rd Edition) by Dr. Marshall B. Rosenberg, (2015). www.nonviolentcommunication.com

Sagan, Carl, Cosmos, A Ballantine Book, The Random House Publishing Group, New York, (1980). Copyright © 1980 by Druyan-Sagan Associates, Inc. formerly known as Carl Sagan Productions, Inc. Originally published by Random House. Preprinted with permission of Druyan-Sagan Associates, Inc. This material cannot be further circulated without written permission of Druyan-Sagan Associates, Inc. All rights reserved.

Satir, Virginia, Peoplemaking, Science & Behavior Books, Inc., Palo Alto, CA, (1972).

Siegel, Daniel and Hartzell, Mary, Parenting From The Inside Out, Jeremy P. Tarcher/Putnam, a member of Penguin Putnam, Inc., 375 Hudson Street, New York, NY 10014, (2003). www.penguinputnam.com

Simmons, Jane, You Can't Sleep Through Your Awakening, The Q Effect Publishing, LLC (2017). www.theqeffect.com

Smolenyak Smolenyak, Megan and Turner, Ann, Trace Your Roots with DNA – Using Genetic Tests to Explore Your Family Tree , Rodale, Inc., distributed by Holtzbrinck Publishers, (2004).

Steves, Rick, Europe Through the Back Door, Avalon Travel, a member of the Perseus Books Group, 1700 Fourth Street, Berkeley, CA 94710 (2008).

Storm, Hyemeyohsts, Seven Arrows, Ballantine Books, a division of Random House, Inc., New York, (1972).

Strunk, William, and E.B. White, The Elements of Style, Second Edition, Macmillan Publishing Co., Inc., 866 Third Avenue, New York 10022, (1972).

Styles, Brandon, B.A., Migration Paper (college paper for Geography 103, University of Montana), (2009).

Sykes, Brian, The Seven Daughters of Eve – The Science That Reveals Our Genetic Ancestry, W.W. Norton & Company, Inc., 500 5th Ave., New York, NY 10110, (2001). www.wwnorton.com

Sykes, Brian, Saxons, Vikings, and Celts – The Genetic Roots of Britain and Ireland, W.W. Norton & Company, Inc., 500 5th Ave., New York, NY 10110, (2006). www.wwnorton.com

Welch, Mark Stanton – "Translation of Aramaic version of the Lord's Prayer by Mosheed Samuel L. Lewis" – (Dances of

Universal Peace tradition) - transcribed from Mark Stanton Welch's CD "Riding the Sound Current"

Williams, Paul, Das Energi, Entwhistle Books, Box 232517, Encinitas, CA 92023, (1973). www.paulwilliams.com

Williamson, Marianne, Return to Love – Reflections on the Principles of A COURSE IN MIRACLES, Harper Collins Publishers, 195 Broadway, New York, NY 10007, (1992).

Dedication

Again, another year, and I'm still not done with this project. (Unless you happen to have a copy of this book in your hand that doesn't say "Proof" draft in its back cover. Is it real? Is it done? Am I still alive?) Even if you have this finished book, just wait until my next planned book with a working title Chasing Headstones - it will be a blockbuster! It's a process, process, process … Got … to … get … it … done! (I know, Jeni, I know …)

This book is dedicated to everyone, starting with those whose lives had to have happened or I wouldn't be here (Mom, Dad, Grandparents, Great-Grandparents, etc.). Also, this is a deep appreciation for those who are blood-related to me who weren't essential for my existence, but were critical for the development of my character (my children, siblings, cousins, aunts and uncles, chosen family and friends, etc.). This is gratitude for those related to me by marriage (my wife and her side of the family), to those legally related to me by adoption (oh, what a mystery that is), and to those I have a relationship with by shared daily or once-in-a-lifetime experiences (and everything in between). In addition, a shout-out to those whose lives genetically didn't matter in my being here but had direct or indirect interactions with and influence on my parents, grandparents, great-grandparents, etc. Our choices cause us to bump into others and affect our paths, even if we didn't meet one another face-to-face. We are stardust randomly crashing into one another in the Soup of Life! Every one of you is essential (though maybe not vital to my existence)!

We may be in individual orbits with different little wobbles around our star we call the sun and the universe beyond, but we do affect one another. I dedicate this to our Network of Humanity, the Soup of Life! Not meaning to discount all the little germs and plant lives that have also been important to bringing me to this point! They have also been important, but I don't want to get carried away (not yet, anyway). I hope there are no hard feelings in leaving the germs out of my expression of gratitude here in the first few paragraphs of this Dedication. But disease and dis-ease are part of who I am today - I acknowledge that.

I reflect on the story of my father's first wife, Beth, diagnosed with cancer in Honolulu, Hawaii. She was sent stateside because it was the start of World War II. If she hadn't died, my Dad wouldn't have met and married my Mom, and I wouldn't have been born. Did Beth matter to me? Yes! She is a part of who my Dad was, who is a part of me. She kept Dad available and ready at just the right time to meet Mom. Since Beth did not matter to me genetically, then the experiences, values, sense of commitment to marriage and family that my Dad had are examples for me and others to notice (or not notice), and to repeat (or not repeat). This is an example of some of our choices that we make consciously or unconsciously. Even cancer cells are part of the Soup of Life! Death, disease, and destruction are part of life! Got to turn over that compost pile to make nutrients and room for the next generation!

We found in my Dad's papers after he died that there were bills written for doctor's services for his first wife, Beth, in Honolulu, up until July 31, 1942. Then there were bills written for doctor's services for Beth beginning August 26, 1942 in California showing she was sent stateside within this time frame (all about August 1942). When the bombing of Pearl Harbor by the Japanese occurred on December 7, 1941, it was eight months before Beth was sent stateside, so while my Dad was mowing the lawn at home watching those "funny looking (Japanese) planes" fly overhead to bomb his ship (the USS Shaw and others of the Pacific Fleet of the U.S. Navy), I assume Beth was there also.

Dad told a story that the doctor in Hawaii gave them information about Beth's cancer diagnosis by getting out a book, opening it to a page about her disease, and then the doctor left the room for them to read. I wonder what the date was that they received the diagnosis? They were already dealing with questions of mortality while the Japanese killed 2,403 Americans that day, but what were they thinking and feeling?

Please be sure to read my Dad's story of his recollection of the bombing of Pearl Harbor (*Chapter 10 - John William Neel - My Dad*), if you haven't already.

There is a saying somewhere about when a butterfly flaps its wings in a South American jungle, that it affects distant galaxies in the universe. This is referred to as the Butterfly Effect. At the time of the printing of the 5th Edition of Family Hunger I think I had a pretty clear understanding of what this means: Even if we can't easily measure the impact on distant galaxies of what we think are minor events here, we do affect one another.

I have a picture in my mind of one of my sons throwing a rock into a mirror-smooth pond, and the concentric circles in the water that emanate out from it. One of these small waves splash a turtle sunning on a log, which startles it causing it to swim away, which produces more waves that shake up a water skipper bug on the other side of the log, which cause it to run from the little piece of food that was so small that I can't see it with my aging eyes (I don't have my glasses on, so this is all in soft-focus like a dream.) And my son next to me shouts with delight and throws another rock at the water skipper bug, causing more visible evidence of vibrations on the surface of the once still pond ... Maybe someday my son will remember this incident by the pond and me trying to tell him about butterflies in South America and how everything is connected. (He discounts it, claiming "That is a lesson from Star Wars," he says). He writes about it for a class project, which he saves and it eventually ends up in a book he writes ... or not ...

I thank you, one and all, large and small!

The germs. You see, I need to thank the germs of disease and germs of genius ideas.

-Todd William Neel
(This chapter was first drafted
on 12/7/2015, the 74th anniversary of the
bombing of Pearl Harbor,
and the final edit on 11/12/2018, Veterans Day)
Thank you, Veterans!
Always remember!

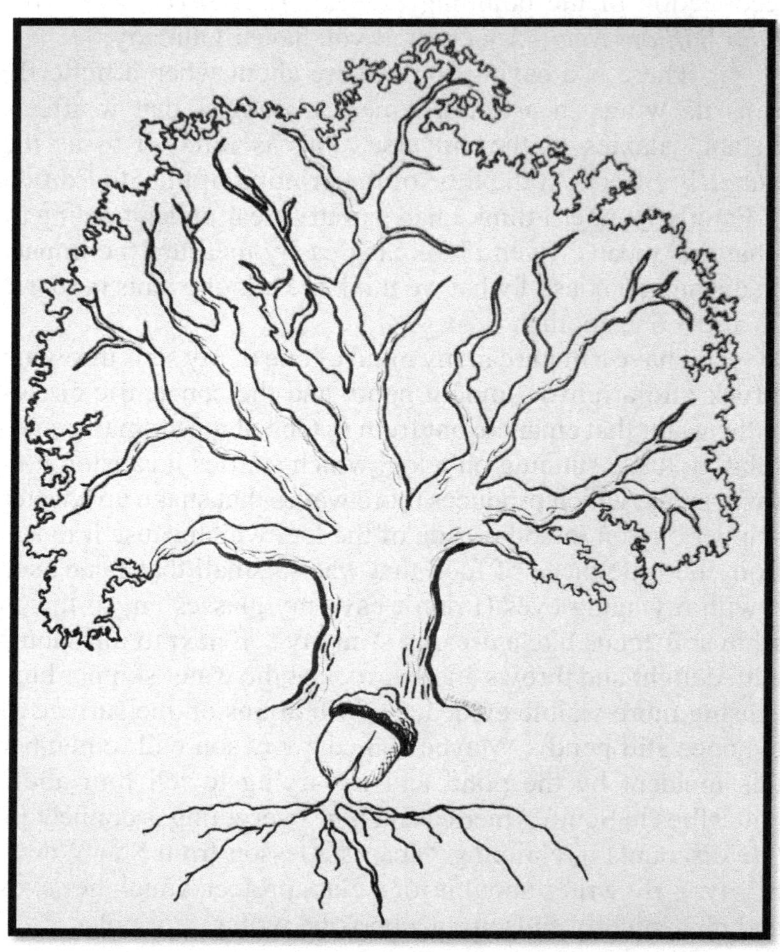

Acknowledgments

There is an infinite number of people responsible for the ripples in my consciousness that caused me to have these thoughts to move these fingers on this keyboard. (I can say infinite because this counts those not yet born – that reflects my faith and hope in humanity!) An incomplete list of people I want to thank are: my parents, grandparents, and "all my relations" as the Native Americans say; my wife, Mary, my sons, Nathan and Joshua; my siblings; my relatives found on the Internet who allowed me into their homes; the creators and staff of ancestry.com and the Family Tree Maker genealogy software programs; members of the Kootenai County Genealogical Society and Eastern Washington Genealogical Society; readers, listeners, and my friends who heard, read, and gave constructive feedback at various stages of these writings; etc.

I want to thank my friend, former neighbor and fellow band member, Jan Clizer, for the drawing of the oak tree and seed used throughout this book. (See more comments about Jan and her art below.) I also want to thank Jan for her help in providing me feedback on various stages of the production of this book, adding artistic taste where I lacked it, for her help with editing the title of this book, and her many other artistic supports. Jan and I are in a band called "The Nine Pint Coggies" where we explore our family and Celtic cultural heritage through music.

And, I especially want to thank Jeni St. Claire, my dear friend, and editor.

I told Jeni that she deserves more than just one short paragraph, more than only one sentence dedicated to her. I want to share how much I appreciate all the time that Jeni has graciously given to me. I have valued the hours and hours we have spent over coffee and desserts (healthy desserts, of course!). We shared our mutual love for books, how we love the texture and the smell of the paper, how we dog-ear the corners of the pages, and how we write our own thoughts in the margins, ruining the chances of ever re-selling it as a used book. I loved sharing with her Stephen King's book On

Writing (2000). The irony was not lost on how Jeni, a retired minister, began to love this gifted writer of creepy books. I shared with her the King books that I have read. I would love to shamelessly promote more advertising here for Stephen King, but because of copyrights, intellectual property, and his publishers I will stop here with only "fair use" of his book title, above, and recommend you grab a few of his books for your enjoyment.

We bartered an exchange of labor by calling Jeni my Editor, while I helped her with technical questions about her laptop, cell phone, etc. I know that I got the better end of the deal!

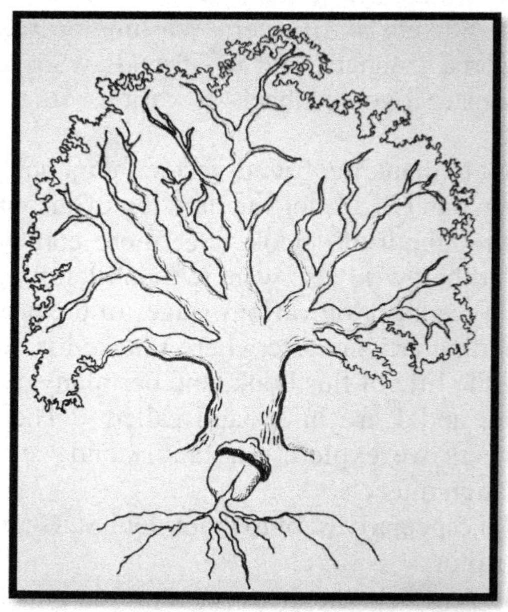

The original oak seed and tree drawing by Jan Clizer represent the fertile seeds of life, the vast potential of each individual living being, each of us different, yet each of us alike enough to call ourselves "kin," giving us a sense of attachment and belonging. It is perfect in its imperfection, like our own families, like our family of humanity, which make us what we are in this moment in time which is continuously ticking on, like whitewater over the lip of the falls. We can't stop it!

It also represents the interconnectedness of our roots, entwined and unseen under the soil, as well as the shade and comfort we can provide for one another from the harsh light from above. Not only does it represent the seeds of physical life, but also seeds of thoughts planted in another person if they are receptive to our sharing. It takes fertile ground and unique conditions for a seed to survive and thrive, ready to sprout anew, with creative ideas in one another. I didn't create the seed, it was a gift given to me. I'm just a gardener, trying to make the soil ready to receive and sprout the fertile seed.

Just like my own family tree, there are some broken and dead branches in it, some imperfections, but when you can step back, get perspective and can see the wholeness of it, you can see it has beautiful, vibrant and abundant foliage and much potential!

Please see Jan's web site www.janclizerpainting.com

Beginning in my last (5th Edition) of Family Hunger – A Neel Family History, I included a paper written by my nephew, Brandon Styles. Brandon wrote a very fine paper for a college class. I relate to this personal experience of being prodded by teachers to pursue our family's history because I began my career as a genealogist by writing a paper for college back in 1979 about my paternal grandmother who was living with us at the time and she has since passed away at age 97. My college professor at the University of Montana at that time was inspired by watching the TV series "Roots" by Alex Haley. So to my nephew, Brandon, maybe I have inspired you, and this will be the start of your long career as a genealogist, and you will be collecting and sharing our family's history long after I am gone. You are an inspiration! Keep the light shining!

Copyright Redux

I do have this family hunger, and sometimes it hurts. Disrespect can hurt more.

My intention is not to plagiarize (to take and use another person's ideas or writings as my own). My purpose is to pass on what was given to me, especially so it won't be lost forever. I didn't create anything; I just re-gift the favors that were given to me, mostly just rearranging the words and the letters. (Is there really such a thing as an original idea, anyway? There are only twenty-six letters in the English alphabet – how many different ways can we re-arrange them?)

I did not create these fingers on this keyboard, and I did not create this mind of mine, although I did make some conscious choices with my free will.

My demonstration is that life is a gift that was given to us and that it is a responsibility to pass it on with respect and honor. I hope that you are encouraged to not only record your own life story, but to interview and document the lives of others in your family before it is too late. They may be gone and/or mentally and/or physically unavailable through the aging process or other reasons way too soon.

Information on living and deceased persons should be respected and not exploited in any way. My intention is not to violate anyone's rights to privacy by publishing this book. My purpose is to connect with past, present, and future generations by sharing what was given to us. Any living person identified can take action against me if I publish any information on you without permission. Anyone can hire an attorney and file a lawsuit. I do not want that to happen. There are lions and tigers and bears out there, oh my. I do not want to be one of those that exploit others. I do not want to violate anyone's rights.

I have been as careful as possible to contact any living person in this book and to get your permission. If I have failed to do so, I apologize. If I could not find you, I either used an abbreviation for last names or used an alias. Please let me know if I stepped on your toes.

Todd William Neel, MSW, LCSW
twneel@gmail.com
familyhunger.com
Family Hunger, PLLC

ABOUT THE AUTHOR

Todd William Neel is the son of a sailor.

He is a social worker who retired in December 2017 after over 27 years working in a public agency serving the needs of child welfare for the state of Idaho.

He earned his Bachelor's degree in psychology, his Master's degree in social work, and is a Licensed Clinical Social Worker in the state of Idaho.

He has been married to Mary for over 29 years, and they have two sons, Nathan (age 26), and Joshua (age 24), at the time of this writing. (No, we're not expecting anymore.)

He has two surviving biological siblings and their families that he doesn't see often enough. And the family may have a surviving adopted brother, but the family has not had contact with this adopted brother for many years.

He "eats, breathes, and dreams" about families and relationships.

Made in the USA
Columbia, SC
29 March 2019